STEEPLECHASING

JOHN HISLOP

Steeplechasing

DRAWINGS BY

John Skeaping

J. A. ALLEN & CO. LTD · London

First published by
Hutchinson & Co. Ltd.
1951

Reprinted by
J. A. Allen & Co. Ltd.
1, Lower Grosvenor Place
London, SW1W 0EL
1970

New edition published by
J. A. Allen & Co. Ltd.
1982

© John Hislop

British Library Cataloguing in Publication Data

Hislop, John
Steeplechasing.—2nd ed.
I.   Title
798.4'5   SF359

ISBN 0-85131-375-2

Typeset by Colset Private Ltd.
Printed by Redwood Burn Ltd, Trowbridge, Wiltshire
Bound by WBC Bookbinders Ltd.

Contents

PHOTOGRAPHS of riders in action with explanatory notes and comment as necessary (i-viii) Between pages 160 and 161

Foreword

to the First Edition by

THE LATE LORD MILDMAY OF FLETE

I HAVE A voracious appetite for books written about any form of sport, and I rush to buy them directly they are published. This book, however, seems to me to stand head and shoulders above the many books on steeplechasing I have read. I am certain that all who read it, whether they be active participators in National Hunt Racing, or merely followers and lovers of this greatest of all sports, will derive immense pleasure from it.

It is not often that top-class performers at any game or sport are good coaches as well. More rarely still can they write on the subject. John Hislop, however, is an exception. Not only has he made a very close study of every aspect of racing, but he is, at the same time, a very talented jockey. He has ridden a great number of winners, both over fences and hurdles, and, as an amateur rider on the flat, he is in a class by himself. Moreover, he is a writer whose articles are always a delight to read.

This book is written, throughout, in a pleasantly light-hearted style which will appeal to all, as will the reality and vigour of John Skeaping's excellent drawings. Furthermore, when reading the chapters devoted to riding and jockeyship, one can rest assured that the author has practised everything that he preaches. Anyone whose ambition it is to become a successful steeplechase jockey cannot do better than to read and re-read these chapters. If he has the ability and perseverance to put into practice the advice given, he has every reason to hope that, eventually, he will find himself at the top of the tree.

A few days after this foreword was received, the tragic news of Anthony Mildmay's disappearance became known. One of the most eminent figures in the history of National Hunt racing, his loss is deeply felt, both by those who knew him personally and by the many who admired his courage and skill in the saddle, his cheerfulness in defeat and his modesty in victory. And it is to his memory that this book is humbly dedicated.

J.H.

Introduction

SO MANY CHANGES have taken place in National Hunt racing since **Steeplechasing** was first published in 1951 that the time has come for the work to be revised completely and brought up to date. Hence the appearance of the book in its new form, outlining the changes that have been made to rules, fences and courses, and their effects on the sport.

As in **From Start to Finish**, the flat-racing companion to this volume, a new feature consisting of photographs of jockeys in action, with detailed explanatory captions, has been included and the subject of riding styles investigated and evaluated. The photographs complement John Skeaping's drawings and illustrate various points discussed in the text.

The other new feature of this edition is a section of maps, with detailed descriptions, of every National Hunt racecourse in the country.

1
Origin and Development

THE ENGLISH CLIMATE lays itself open to much criticism: it is unreliable, damp and at times deplorably lacking in sunshine; mist and fog are only too common, and the cold and wet experienced during some of our more unfortunate summers would do more than justice to conditions that might be expected in winter. As a general rule the winter is not cold enough to permit winter sports, while the summer allows only sporadic indulgence in such diversions as sun-bathing and swimming, but there is one pastime to which our climate is eminently suited, namely, steeplechasing.

Although steeplechasing is an activity generally associated with winter, except for a few weeks between June and August, it takes place all the year round, a circumstance only made possible by the fact that the ground is seldom, for long, either sun-baked in summer or frost-bound in winter, so that steeplechasing can be carried on, unhindered, in a manner that is possible in no other country.

However, the climate alone cannot account for the popularity and prosperity of the sport in this country; its prominent place in English life is due to deeper reasons.

Apart from environment, the forces of inheritance and tradition do much to shape the ways and customs of any nation, and in the English, be they countrymen or townsmen, a love of every activity associated with the horse is strongly imbued. Of these activities, that of steeplechasing appeals most to the average man; hunting is a sport that is not easily enjoyed on foot and is too remote for the average townsman; polo has only a small circle of supporters in England; flat-racing is sometimes boring; but even the most unpretentious of steeplechase meetings is enjoyable.

Steeplechasing has about it rather more glamour and excitement than the flat, a trace of chivalry, a spice of danger and a certain refreshing vigour that the smooth urbanity of flat-racing lacks. The atmosphere is less restrained, more friendly, more intimate and more sympathetic. It gives the impression of being a sport and not primarily a business, for though it seems impossible to preserve any present-day pastime from the tarnishing influence of Mammon, the majority of those who patronize steeplechasing do so from a true love of its qualities, rather than for what it yields materially.

They comprise those who know and appreciate the points of a horse and the art of race-riding over fences, and to whom the spectacle of horses jumping at racing pace brings a thrill and enjoyment which they could never derive from the flat. To such as these a good 'chaser is a finer animal than his stablemate the flat racer, for he is possessed of the strength and power that would enable him to carry a man well to hounds, while his conformation is, of necessity, fairly true, or he would be unable to fulfil the task facing him. It is not uncommon to see a badly-built flat race-horse of considerable merit, but it is seldom that a good steeplechaser is not properly made.

Among the professional element there is more give and take; the life is hard and risky, and, on the whole, jockeys and trainers have a keener appreciation of each other's misfortunes and difficulties than is the case in the world of flat-racing, where the principle of 'every man for himself' seems more evident.

Before considering the various aspects of any subject in the light of the present, it is always as well to glance back upon its origin and history, in order that a true perspective may be obtained; thus, the birth and development of steeplechasing merit a few words in this book.

There is a couplet which runs:

> *These are the Britons, a barbarous race*
> *Chiefly employed in the Wars and the Chase*

from which it may be gathered that the two main occupations of our ancestors were fighting and hunting, and while the centuries follow-ing the obscure and uncivilized days, to which these lines refer, have wrought many changes in English life, they have neither devised a means of abolishing wars, nor obliterated a love of the chase, and it is in the chase that steeple-chasing found its origin.

While hunting on horseback and horse-racing on the flat had been flourishing in Britain a considerable time, the sport of steeplechasing had yet to be invented. Before the days of enclosures, it is probable that no hunting man was ever called upon to ride over any obstacle more formidable than a ditch or narrow stream; there were no hedges, no stake-and-binders, and post-and-rails were a pleasure—or downfall, as the case might be—which awaited later generations, so that jumping, as we know it now, did not come into the argument with regard to hunting. But times soon changed and, as the fencing of the countryside increased, it became necessary for the hunting-horse to be able to jump. It does not, of course, follow that the appearance of fences was accompanied by a universal desire to jump them, for the arts of equitation and venery do not always go together, and then, as now, there were probably a number of sportsmen to whom a sound knowledge of the countryside, particularly its gates and its gaps, was a more valuable possession than a good jumper, but, so far as the sport as a whole was concerned, jumping became one of the most important accomplishments necessary to its successful and enjoyable pursuit.

Added to this the craving for greater speed brought into the hunting-field faster hounds and better horses, with the result that many of the hunters belonging to followers of fashionable packs were as well-bred as a Derby winner.

The effect of these two influences, jumping and speed, was inevitable; it was that arguments arose as to the merits of one man's horse compared with another's, and that these arguments were settled by racing the respective horses against each other across a line of natural country. It was the running of these private matches that formed the first stage in the development of steeplechasing.

Appropriately enough, Ireland provides the earliest record of a match of this kind, the document referring to this event stating that, in 1752, a Mr. O'Callaghan and a Mr. Edmund Blake rode a match across country from Buttevant church to St. Leger church; it does not, however, give the result, so perhaps neither competitor finished the course. The choice of the two hallowed edifices mentioned as starting and finishing points is easily understood, for what could have been more conspicuous, in those days of no factory chimneys, pylons, or other such modern horrors with which the countryside is now desecrated, than a church steeple? and the common practice of competitors in the new sport using this form of guide soon acquired for it the name of 'steeplechasing'.

In the due course matches developed into races with three or more runners, the earliest contest of this description being held in 1792, when Mr. Charles Meynell beat Lord Forester and Mr. Gilbert in a race from Barkby Holt to Billesden Coplow and back, a distance of eight miles all told.

Hitherto all steeplechases had been run across a natural country, but in 1810 racing over made-up obstacles first became known. This was at Bedford, where the event was brought about through the stewards of the local race-meeting seeking a means of preventing flat racehorses, described as hunters, from taking part in races confined to horses who had been regularly and fairly hunted; their solution to the problem was to build eight fences in the three-mile course.

In order to make certain that the horses entered were genuine hunters, it was decided that the height of the fences should be four feet six inches, and that a 'strong bar' should be fixed along the top. But so effectively did the strong bar do its work that not only were any frauds scared away, but most of the hunters themselves; for, when the time came, only two riders were bold enough to bring their horses to the post. The enterprise had attracted interest throughout the neighbouring countryside, and the town of Bedford was packed to overflowing on the night before the race, but since the affair was a novelty, the spectators probably felt no great disappointment that there were only two starters, and they did, at least, see both of them complete the course without mishap.

By the middle of the 19th century steeplechasing had become firmly established. Most races were still run across country, as the lively and somewhat hair-raising pictures by Alken show, and the audience consisted chiefly of hunting men, many of whom galloped alongside the competitors, their interest in the race and consequent lack of attention to their own progress not infrequently resulting in a fall, which, as depicted by Alken, was invariably of a most alarming type. The other spectators comprised townsfolk, who came to the scene on foot and gathered at the more formidable obstacles, or climbed to strategic points of vantage in nearby trees, or rustics working nearby, who paused in their labours to view the fun.

In the early days, the jockeys were, almost without exception, gentlemen-riders; in one match, however, the respective horsemen were a valet and a whipper-in, a somewhat strange choice in the case of the former, but evidently not an unwise one as it turned out, for it was the valet who won the day. But as the popularity of the sport increased professional riders began to be employed more frequently, and when in 1839 the first Grand National Steeplechase was run at Aintree, it was won by Jem Mason, the leading professional of his day, on the no less famous Lottery.

From this date steeplechasing developed fast, and it was not long before it started to bear some resemblance to the form which it presents now. The practice of racing across a natural stretch of country died out; instead, courses proper came into being, with grandstands, weighing rooms, saddling paddocks and all the various other amenities that appeared, one by one, as time went by, and the stone walls, post-and-rails, open brooks and banks, which formed some of the obstacles in the first Grand National and other races of that period, were finally replaced by the standard birch fences of today.

Hurdle-racing was introduced and became part of almost every jumping programme, the National Hunt Steeplechase for Amateur riders took its place in the Calendar (1860), Cheltenham became the Ascot of jumping, and most of the important flat-racecourses made the changes necessary to hold jumping meetings as well.

Other influences, too, left their mark. An increase in stake-money brought better-class horses into the game, the introduction of the American seat on the flat resulted in a complete change in riding methods and in races being run at a much faster pace than before. From being an off-shoot of hunting, steeplechasing blossomed out into an entity of its own, having its own rules, characteristics and individuality, its particular supporters, and its special retainers, for whom it provides a source of livelihood, and it has taken its place in English life as one of the finest of our national sports.

To be in a position to appreciate or criticize the various points of any pastime or profession, it is necessary to understand the circumstances under which it is conducted, the rules governing it and the forces by which it is influenced. In this respect steeplechasing is not the most fortunate of sports, for whereas it is comparatively seldom that the boxer, footballer or cricketer is the victim of ignorant criticism, it is not infrequent that the steeplechase rider is the butt of the most vitriolic censure on the part of unqualified critics. For this reason the remaining pages of this chapter are devoted to an explanation and description of the machinery of steeplechasing, and the way in which it works, in order that the layman who may chance to read this book will have some idea what it is all about, and not be perplexed by such problems as, whether races are run over distances in the region of six furlongs or six miles, whether the weights carried approximate to eleven stone or seven, whether the obstacles are similar to those encountered at the International Horse Show, and whether any horse has won The Derby and the Grand National in the same year.

National Hunt racing, that is to say steeplechasing, hurdle-racing and point-to-points, is governed by the Jockey Club. Their headquarters are at 42 Portman Square London, W.1, Weatherby's being secretaries and stakeholders to the Jockey Club.

They have power to grant or withdraw licences, cancel or change dates of meetings, impose fines, warn any person off all courses where their rules are in force, and they are, in fact, the Government of the sport. They are assisted by stewards' secretaries, who are paid officials whose duty is, briefly, to observe, report and advise, only the stewards having any direct power.

At each meeting there must be four acting stewards, who control affairs and have powers to fine and admonish up to a point, but must refer any serious breach of the rules to the stewards of the Jockey Club itself; in general the ruling body is severe but just.

Every advertised National Hunt meeting must devote at least half its prize money to steeplechases (as opposed to hurdle races).

There must be at least two steeplechases in each day's racing, one of them three miles or over, and no race must be over a shorter distance than two miles. The longest race is the 4½ miles of the Grand National and there are a number run over 4 miles.

In all steeplechases there must be at least twelve fences in the first two miles, and at least six in each succeeding mile. Excepting Aintree, the course over which the Grand National is run, and a law unto itself—a subject to be dealt with on its own—all steeplechase fences are built more or less the same way and consist of birch, tightly packed into a wooden frame which is about three feet, probably rather less, from the ground. The birch itself slopes away as seen from the take-off side, is usually faced with gorse to within two feet or so from the top of the fence, which is four feet six inches from the ground, and is about two feet wide, its strength depending upon the tightness with which the birch is packed.

In the course of each mile there must be (to quote from Rules of Racing) 'at least one ditch six feet wide and two feet deep[2] on the taking-off side of a fence, guarded by a bank[1] and rail, not exceeding two feet in height, which fence must be at least four feet, six inches in height, and, if of dead brushwood or gorse, two feet in width'.

In every steeplechase there must also be 'a water-jump at least twelve feet wide and two feet deep, sloped gradually from the fence to ground level guarded by a fence not exceeding three feet in height'. Although fences vary in detail, consistency and size, with different courses, their chief characteristics are the same.

In the hurdle races the obstacles consist of three-foot six-inch hurdles made in the same way as a sheep-hurdle, but packed with gorse to show only the top bar and driven into the ground at an angle of some sixty degrees, the slope of course being away from the take-off; each flight comprises several hurdles, the height from the top bar to the ground being about three feet two inches. The top bar is padded.

The advantage of this type of obstacle is that it is mobile, convenient and simple; the disadvantage, that horses are liable to be staked if they hit one of the uprights. In France the hurdles are small brush fences—a preferable type of obstacle—but being permanent fixtures they can only be used on courses where the hurdle racetrack is separate from that upon which flat-racing takes place, which would be

[1]This sometimes takes the form of wooden boarding.   [2]or level

impossible on many English courses where the flat and hurdle racetrack is one and the same.

With regard to horses running under Rules all must be named and registered, either in the General Stud Book or at Messrs. Weatherby's, who own the *Racing Calendar*, the official publication for racing on the flat or jumping.

No horse can run in a steeplechase until he is four years old—racehorses count their age from January 1, regardless of the actual date of their birth—so that it would be impossible for a Derby winner to win the Grand National, or any other steeplechase, in the same year, though he could run over hurdles, and I believe that before Airborne's flat-racing merit was revealed by his victory in The Derby his owner had made up his mind to jump him that winter.

There is no restriction as to the sex of horses competing under National Hunt rules; they can be entires, geldings, or mares, but the majority are geldings.

The races over hurdles and fences fall into a number of different categories:

Maiden races: For horses which, either at starting or entry, according to the framing of the terms, have not won a steeplechase hurdle race other than a match or private sweepstakes, a National Hunt Flat Race, or a Steeple Chase at a Point-to-Point meeting, at any recognised meeting in any country. Unless otherwise stated a maiden means a maiden at the time of the start.

Handicaps: These being races in which an official handicapper allots different weights according to a horse's merit: unless a horse has won a steeplechase or hurdle race in Great Britain or Ireland he is automatically given top weight in any handicap, until he has run three times in any class of race. If the handicap is for horses of various ages, he may be given the weight-for-age allowance from top weight, if it is applicable in his case. The 'weight-for-age' scale is an official estimation of the amount of weight horses of different ages should carry so that each may have an equal chance in proportion to their years; it varies with the horse's age and the distance of the race, on the principle that a jumper is not in his prime until he is six, and that a young horse is at a greater disadvantage over a long distance than a short distance, compared to his seniors. The weight-for-age scale runs from 10 st. 13 lb. to 12 st. 3 lb., and in handicaps under 3½ miles the bottom weight cannot be less than 10 st., nor the top weight less than 12 st.

Weight-for-age races without penalties or allowances: These are sometimes known as Open races and constitute such events as the Cheltenham Gold Cup and the Champion Hurdle, in which each

Plain fence

horse carries, theoretically, the same weight, his actual weight being according to the official weight-for-age scale.

Weight-for-age races with penalties and allowances: In this kind of race the weight-for-age scale is modified, according to the framing of the terms, by penalties for previous victories and/or allowances for not having won a certain sum, a particular number of races, or for being a 'maiden'.

Restricted races: These may belong to any of the main headings mentioned here, except, of course, maiden races—but are restricted to horses that have not won a specified sum, a race of a specified value or a stated number of races; appropriately enough, the title of such races often incorporates the word 'moderate', such as 'The Moderate Handicap Hurdle'.

Selling races: In theory such races are devised to enable owners to get rid of bad horses, at the same time winning a race; in practice they tend to be used as mediums for gambling, fairly good horses often being run in them and bought back after winning, the sum expended to retain them having been covered by bets won.

At one time it was an unwritten law among owners and trainers that they did not bid for each other's selling-platers, it being the practice for the owner of the winner to guarantee the owner of the second a certain sum in return for his assurance not to bid—a highly irregular transaction by the Rules, which state that anyone acting thus or preventing a person from bidding for the winner shall be fined or reported to the stewards of the Jockey Club. Periodically notices of the punishment of perpetrators of this crime appear in the *Racing Calendar*, but the freemasonry which, before the war, was so strong in that particular stratum of racing and was usually left immune by the more ambitious factions of the jumping community, is now not what it was. The buying of platers which their owners want back, though likely to give rise to a measure of umbrage, does not result in the vendettas which used to be fought out for years over every racecourse in Britain from Perth to Totnes, while any outsider who had the temerity to poke his nose in and buy the winner of a 'seller' was regarded with misfavour. For full details of selling races see Rules 96–98.

There is a further aspect of selling races which has been similarly influenced by the passage of time, this being the claiming of horses out of 'sellers'. All horses who run in a selling race, excepting the winner, who comes up for auction, can be claimed for the published claiming price. If more than one claim is lodged, the claim is determined by lot by the Clerk of the Scales. To claim anyone else's horse is an action which was once considered the most dastardly that could be

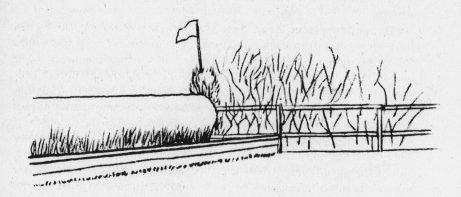

Open ditch

committed in the selling-plate world—a kind of stab in the back from which there was no opportunity to escape, since the deed could be done without the owner even being aware that a claim had been lodged.

It is not permissible for an owner to claim his own horse, but he can get a friend to put in a claim so that, even in the event of opposition claims being lodged, there is a chance of getting the horse back through a friendly claim. As in the case of buying the winners of selling races, the attitude of the racing community has changed somewhat with regard to claiming, and it is now not uncommon for horses to be claimed, whereas it was once a comparative rarity.

From the point of view of selling races being used for the purpose for which they were originally intended, the present-day attitude is, naturally, an advance upon the former state of affairs, but it has robbed racing of a certain colour and entertainment, which the old 'vendetta' days possessed. But the selling-plate world of today is by no means without its diversions and its guile, there being several subtleties to which owners and trainers may resort in order to retain an old favourite who can always be relied upon to 'get the wages' in a 'seller' when times are bad.

One is to run the horse in the name of the owner's wife, in which case a prospective buyer can sometimes be dissuaded by the owners tearful plea to 'let him have the old horse back for the little woman's sake', this thesis being, if necessary, enlarged upon by a detailed account of the latter's devotion, expressed in daily visits with tit-bits and a terrible anxiety as to losing him. If the truth were known, the 'little woman's' only interest in horses is probably the fact that they are the source of her husband's livelihood and a possible alternative to beef or mutton, her presence on a racecourse being due to a desire to get her spouse home sober and in possession of the greater part of his winnings, rather than to any enthusiasm for the alleged equine favourite. Be that as it may, it needs a hard heart and a strong will to ignore a skilfully presented appeal of this nature, which, as often as not, achieves its objective.

Another form of subterfuge is to feel the horse's legs while he is standing in the winner's enclosure, at the same time shaking the head doubtfully and maintaining a gloomy expression. This will not deceive the professional element, but it may well frighten away the gullible by intimating that the horse has broken down.

I have digressed somewhat in the matter of selling races and may have left myself open to criticism on the grounds of having strayed away from the main theme of this book, since all I have written concerning them could apply equally to flat-racing. But selling races play an important part in the life of the less-prosperous section of the jumping community, for expensive horses are beyond their purse and about their only chance of financial survival is to win an occasional bet, which can best be accomplished in races of this description, while the money obtained by running second in a series of 'sellers' can add up to an appreciable sum.

Besides the types of races already referred to, there are a number of steeplechases for horses who have been regularly and fairly hunted, a certificate to this effect being lodged with Messrs. Weatherby, which take place in the Spring and are only open to amateur riders. There is also an occasional N.H. flat race, the latter events being confined to 4, 5 and 6 years old which, at starting have not run under any recognised Rules of Flat Racing, Steeple Chasing or Hurdle Racing, except N.H. Flat Races in this country, ridden by Category 'B' amateur riders or conditional jockeys.

Having discussed the conditions under which horses can take part in N.H. racing, it would seem that the next step is to consider those governing the rider, the trainer and the owner, in order to clarify any future reference to them later in the book.

Riders under N.H. rules come under one of two main headings, professionals or amateurs.

A professional jockey must obtain an annual licence from the Jockey Club. Jockeys may be retained by a special agreement between one or more owners, such agreements being lodged with Messrs. Weatherby's, and the stewards have power to settle any dispute between owners and jockeys, or to cancel any private agreement between such parties, should they think fit.

Full details of the conditions under which jockeys' licences and permits for amateur riders are granted are to be found in Rules 60, 61 and 62 of the Rules of Racing. The conditions are liable to change from time to time and it is wise to watch for any such changes which are published in the Racing Calendar and, if important, in the sporting press.

There are two types of licence for professional jockeys: firstly, a conditional jockey's licence, to which a jockey is entitled if he is under the age of 25 and has not ridden 15 runners, and secondly a licence for jockeys who can no longer claim a riding allowance or are over 25.

There are two types of permit for amateur riders: Category A, whose holders may ride in any flat race, steeplechase or hurdle race confined to amateur riders, and Category B, holders of which may ride in flat races confined to amateur riders and in all steeplechases and hurdle races except those restricted to licensed jockeys. Below is

Rule 62 which affects amateurs:

'The following persons are not eligible to hold Amateur Rider Permits:

a) A person who has ever held a professional rider's licence from any recognised Turf Authority other than an Apprentice Jockey's Licence or a Conditional Jockey's Licence for a period of not more than twelve months from the date of issue of his first licence (subject to part (c) of this sub-rule).

b) A person who has otherwise ever been paid directly or indirectly for riding in a race, with the exception of expenses approved by the Stewards of the Jockey Club as set out in Appendix F to these Rules ((these refer to approved expenses for riding abroad)) and any trophy advertised in the conditions of the race to be given to a rider.

c) A person whose principal paid occupation is or at any time has been to ride or groom for a licensed or permitted trainer.

d) A person who is or who within the last twelve months has been paid as a groom in private, livery or horse dealer's stables or as a hunt servant.'

A professional jockey may not bet, nor be the owner or part-owner of a racehorse running under any recognised Rules, excepting horses taking part in Hunter Steeplechases only.

In the case of steeplechases and hurdle races, it is permissible to hold both a trainer's and a jockey's licence, which is not the case on the flat.

As regards owners, a man may not own a horse if he is a warned-off person or holds a jockey's licence. Any partnership, contingency or lease affecting owners must be registered at Weatherby's, and all entries made by owners or their authorized agents must be lodged there, either directly or through any licensed receiver of entries.

Owners must either register their racing colours at Weatherby's or declare them to the Clerk of the Course by the day before running. Failure to register or declare colours results in a fine, which is not infrequently incurred through the trainer or his travelling lad forgetting to bring them, or bringing the wrong ones.

So much for the general conditions under which N.H. racing is conducted. The rules themselves are published by Messrs. Weatherby and are reprinted in such publications as *Ruff's Guide to the Turf*, and it is no bad plan for every trainer to read them through before the start of the season, since they change in detail from time to time and such a perusal may save a later fine, caused by overlooking some new or altered clause. The inexperienced, in all branches of N.H. racing, are well advised to get to know the Rules thoroughly before they enter this realm of sport, since ignorance of the regulations is sure to lead to trouble sooner or later, in the shape of disqualifications or fines.

Point-to-Point meetings are the 'nurseries' of N.H. racing, so that the rules governing them are worthy of mention in this book.

These meetings come under Jockey Club rules and can take place on only one day in the year. The courses need not conform to those upon which N.H. racing takes place, but they must pass the inspection of the official Inspector of Courses; the fences are usually smaller than those on N.H. courses proper. Every race must be a steeplechase of three miles or over; all horses taking part must be registered as having been regularly and fairly hunted; no race can be worth more than a sum laid down by the Jockey Club to the winner; all riders must be amateurs. Races won, both from the aspect of horses and riders, do not, however, count as victories under N.H. rules.

Point-to-Point meetings are governed by 'Jockey Club Regulations for Point-to-Point Steeple Chases.'

Such, then, are the foundations and framework upon and around which N.H. racing of the present day has been built. The chapters that follow will endeavour to enlarge upon the detail.

It is advisable to acquire a copy of Rules of Racing, obtainable from Weatherby's, 42 Portman Square, London W.1. and, from the same source, a copy of Regulations Governing Point-to-Points, and to keep an eye on any changes of rules or instructions, which are published in the Racing Calendar, the official organ of the Jockey Club.

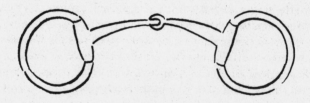

2

Riding over Fences

STEEPLECHASE RIDING IS a lodestone in which several powerful forces combine, the lure of speed, the excitement of jumping, the delight of bestriding a good horse, and that strange fascination that accompanies any form or degree of danger. There is about it a sensibility only experienced in activities concerned with the horse, and a lustre all of its own, so that it is not surprising that, for many, the life of a N.H. jockey is preferable to the drab and ordered security of the average profession, while as a pastime it is equally alluring.

But before contemplating this career, either professionally or as an amateur, there is a good deal to which the individual should give thought, since it is only too easy to be beguiled by the glamour, but fail to see the sterner side. It is better for the novice not to embark on the project at all, than to be dismayed by difficulties of which he had no inkling.

If a man is to succeed as a steeplechase-rider, his heart and soul must be in the game. It is not enough that he is possessed of a measure of talent and considers the life pleasanter than any other occupation he can think of at the time; he must feel that he cannot live without it, be prepared to sacrifice other interests, to renounce indulgences, to endure discomfort and pain, humiliation and disappointment, and to expect long runs of bad luck; joy in success must be tempered with the realization that he is, to a great extent, a puppet of fate—that the champion of today may have faded into obscurity in a season's time—and that the career of the average steeplechase rider is neither a long nor a lucrative one. He must have a fixed and undivided mind, free from influences likely to cause him to deviate from his purpose; sons and husbands who have to withstand repeated feminine entreaties to refrain from riding in steeplechases had better leave home, or dismiss the idea of becoming a jumping jockey from their minds altogether, while any woman who breeds, or marries, a man with jumping in his blood must accept the fact, or be prepared for indefinite domestic dissension; pleas such as 'I wish you'd give up, dear, for my sake' are liable to end in strife.

If anything of a sybarite, the prospective steeplechase-rider is choosing the wrong calling, for hardship will be his lot. He will have to endure the worst weather the English climate can offer—rain, sleet, occasionally snow and quite frequently bitter cold, the effect of these elements being, not improbably, aggravated by his having wasted in order to reduce weight. He will also have to get used to riding when stiff and sore from previous falls, to long drives to meetings through frost and fog, only to find on arrival that racing has been abandoned, and to early-morning journeys under similar conditions to ride work, or schooling at different training establishments, which, in the depths of winter, can be a cold and miserable business.

These, together with the risk of injury and the general nervous strain, are some of the exigencies that have to be encountered every jumping season.

Thus, there are a considerable number of people who are willing to accept the joys that steeplechasing can offer, and to continue riding, so long as everything goes well, but who start to think differently when the luck changes—when the safest jumpers fall with them for no explicable reason, when they are robbed of victory through sheer bad luck, when they have to face unjust criticism, are deserted by their patrons, and, having no sooner recovered from one fall are involved in another—they begin to wonder whether it is really worth while, and, as likely as not, fade out of the world of N.H. racing into a less exacting sphere of activity.

Those who are prepared to take the rough with the smooth and keep on riding until age or circumstances make retirement inevitable must, therefore, have a nature peculiar to itself.

To define such a nature is not easy, for no two personalities are similar; nevertheless, when individuals share the same experiences, dangers and joys, the dominant inspiration must be the same. It is, perhaps, an innate desire rather than the influence of environment, a craving of the spirit rather than of the flesh, a force to which such qualities as physical courage and talent, however desirable and necessary, are none of less secondary. It has, no doubt, some psychological foundation, perhaps a species of self-expression, a channel for the outlet of energy, or the working of whatever divine power shapes the paths of men's lives. But whatever its composition or origin, it is an influence without which few, if any, would bear the buffets of a steeplechase-rider's life for more than one or two seasons.

With it goes either a natural skill in the management of horses, or an inborn love of them; sometimes, but not necessarily, both. There is a sharp difference in these two qualities, for it is not unknown to find a first-class rider who is not a true lover of horses, one whose style is unimpeachable, whose control and power over his horse is complete, but in its execution ruthless and suggestive that, to the rider, the horse is a slave rather than a partner, with the result that his riding as a whole will lack that sense of sympathy which is always discernible in, the case of a true horse-lover. It is the difference between the hard glitter of the diamond and the soft sparkle of the dew-drop, between the power to lead and the power to drive, between the material and the spiritual.

The best example of these two aspects that comes to my mind is from the world of flat-racing—the riding of Fred Archer compared to that of Steve Donoghue. Both were the outstanding jockeys of their age, but whereas Archer's riding was pitiless in its severity, the horses he rode often coming in after a race bleeding from the effects of his spurs and whip, Donoghue could get the most out of a horse without touching him, a quality that was never better illustrated than when he rode Humorist to victory in The Derby.

And so, to my mind at any rate, the most important properties in the embryo steeplechase-rider are an unquenchable enthusiasm and a real love and appreciation of the horse—in particular, the racehorse.

That enthusiasm should be considered preferable to inherent talent is because the enthusiast, even though he may lack natural skill, usually has the humility to learn—and go on learning, regardless of any success he may have achieved—whereas the man to whom things come too easily is often tempted to think himself better than he is and that he knows it all, and though he may reach a fairly high standard in a comparatively short time, it is not improbable that this very fact will prevent him from going much farther, with the result that the slower but humbler pupil may surpass him in the long run, because he has had to battle every foot of the way.

Technical ability, however brilliant, can never overcome fear, the dislike of discomfort, or the effect of falls—enemies that are burnt up in the flame of enthusiasm—and many first-class riders 'hand in their cap and jacket' because they find, after tasting the rougher side of the game, that their heart is not really in it, in the same way that a good peace-time soldier is often useless in a battle.

That sympathy without natural skill is put before the opposite state is because skill can be acquired and sympathy cannot. The true horse-lover may take longer than the less considerate expert to achieve the same result, but his work will endure—as will the horses he rides.

It is often said that riders are born, not made, that hands and seat are an inherited, not a manufactured, product, and as a result, that no one who is not a rider by birth will ever make one through teaching. This is a precept which must have deterred many an unfortunate novice whose pedigree extended no hope of his deriving the benefits of ancestral ability, and one of which any others down whose throat it is rammed need not take too much notice.

As I have endeavoured to point out, ability is nothing without enthusiasm, nor skill without sympathy, and the inheritor of all these qualities in equal and powerful degree is as fortunate as he is rare, so that there is no need for the beginner to lose heart because he is not born an equestrian prodigy. If he is reasonably intelligent, there is no reason why he should not acquire good hands and a good seat—when all's said and done, his anatomy is controlled by his brain—provided he is possessed of the two qualities named above, and he has the luck to fall into the hands of good teachers.

After the somewhat gloomy picture I have painted, it may seem strange that so many consider the game worth the candle, but to the enthusiast it will always be so.

He will be undeterred by adversity, by the disappointment of losing a race through bad judgement or through falling off, the cold misery of waiting for the ambulance after a bad fall, listening to the first-aid men whispering among themselves as to the nature and extent of his injuries and how they should deal with them, the loss of a favourite horse; the humiliation of being 'jockeyed off' by dissatisfied owners, and the many other blows of fate that can beset him.

For a dozen such set-backs one good ride will atone. As he swings into the saddle, his worries slip from his mind as a soldier's pack slides from his back at the end of a long march, leaving in both mind and body a strange feeling of unnatural lightness.

As he canters down to the post, he will experience the comforting sense of confidence and well-being that a good horse in fine fettle inspires, will seem to gain strength from the symmetrical bulge and sweep of the shoulder and neck-muscles before him, and draw courage from the bold heart that beats beneath him.

At the start, he will know that sharp tingle of anticipation in the pit of the stomach that precedes every race, which, once the gate has gone up, is replaced by a glow of exhilaration at the strong, piston-like beat and rhythm of his horse's stride, the leading foot shooting out almost beyond the nose, the stroke of the hind legs wrenching the ground from under them. Every fence is a fresh thrill as it draws nearer and he picks the place at which to jump it, sighting the spot through the resolute, unmoving ears pricked eagerly towards the obstacle and assuring a measured approach made with the confidence of a skilled tradesman, which is justified a second later as the horse leaves the ground, picking up (it may seem) outside the wings but landing safely as far the other side and galloping on without a check.

In this way fence after fence flicks by, the stands are passed, and groups of spectators out in the country, but these are sensed rather than perceived, as if their world lay on the other side of a thick glass through which form and sounds penetrates but dimly, the only reality being the race itself, which acquires an atmosphere and consciousness peculiar to itself: one in which senses are sharper, but only towards the task on hand, and from which fear and fatigue have unaccountably departed, to be replaced by a glorious exaltation.

When the race is over there remains a joy mixed with the relief of relaxed muscles and nerves, the pleasant tiredness that follows physical exertion and the knowledge of a task well done.

As opposed to material treasures, it is something that can never be lost, which neither wars nor sickness can take away, a memory to bring gladness to the times when riding days are over.

Good steeplechase jockeys have made their way by many different roads: some have graduated from the hunting-field, some from the flat-racing world, others from the show-ring, but as a rule if a man is to make a top-class steeplechase-rider he must be a horseman as well as a jockey, whatever his background.

Since this is not a treatise on general riding, the elements of which art are adequately expounded elsewhere, the requirements of a good practical horseman (the soundest basis from which to build a steeplechase jockey) will be considered rather than the principles of equitation.

So far as racing is concerned the only matters of real importance are practical. It is results that count, and a jockey's success depends upon his ability to ride winners—not upon his conformity to any particular theory of riding—and so far as horsemanship bears upon steeplechase riding, style is of secondary moment to effectiveness.

The first aspect to be considered is the question of what constitutes a good practical horseman.

A good horseman should in the first place, know something about the horse as an animal. He should know what he ought to look like and the names of the various parts of his anatomy; how to feed and care for him, and something of his common ailments; his mental and physical capabilities in order that he may not be led to expect the impossible; how to saddle and bridle him properly, and the purpose and working of the different pieces of saddlery.

All this should come before he learns to ride, for without the elements of this knowledge the novice is liable to make avoidable mistakes and the horse to suffer unnecessary discomfort as a result of ignorance. In the days before the labour shortage in racing stables, and when lads could leave school earlier, an apprentice often worked a year or more without being allowed near anything in the shape of a racehorse, in fact, he was probably not even allowed to ride a pony for the first few months, his first duty being to learn how to be a stableman.

With regard to riding itself, a good horseman should be secure, in control, adaptable, independent and versatile. He should be able to look after himself, get on and off and adjust his equipment, without requiring other people to run about holding his horse's head or giving him a leg up. He must be able to accommodate himself to any build of saddle, and should be capable of coping with such situations as having to ride schooling in a saddle without forward flaps, riding with uneven stirrup-leathers, with one stirrup-leather only, or without any at all, and he should bear in mind the precept that incompetence can seldom, if ever, be attributed to equipment.

He should, in any reasonable instance, be able to make his horse go where he wants, and know when and how to administer chastisement.

He should be able to remain in the saddle in the case of the average horse jumping and kicking, bucking, or whipping round, and he should be able to cope equally with a light-mouthed horse or a 'puller', a 'free goer' or a 'slug'. He should be able to give a passable performance in the hunting-field, over a show-jumping course, and in a point-to-point on different types of horses—there are many who can ride the horses they know adequately but are hopeless as soon as they have to get on anything strange—and he should be able to ride a 'green' one.

When a man can do all these things proficiently he can be considered a good practical horseman, and is ready to think about learning to be a steeplechase jockey. There is a danger, to anyone who specializes too much in a particular branch of equitation, that he will not be able to adapt himself to the peculiarities of another, so that before taking up any one it is not a bad plan to acquire a measure of experience in all, which will avoid that undesirable quality in any field, extremism.

Becoming a good practical horseman depends upon two things: experience and teaching. An intelligent and gifted individual could achieve the object through experience alone—aided by keen observation of experts—but this is almost an impossibility for the ordinary man whose standard of riding will largely depend upon the instructor under whom he happens to learn.

So far as elementary riding goes it would be difficult to improve upon the methods that used to be employed in the army, or those of any reputable riding school, and the opportunity for early instruction is probably better now than it ever was in England before, but once past that stage the next step is not so easy. As was said above, it is not of the slightest use sticking to one horse, but unless anyone is in the fortunate position of being able to own three or four at a time—and even then it is necessary to keep changing them—it is not easy to find the opportunity of riding a large number of different horses.

The best way is to make friends with a horse-dealer and persuade him to let you help his nagsman to exercise, school, break and generally cope with the ever-changing stream of horses that passes through his yard. In this way it is possible to gain more experience in a week than could otherwise be acquired in a year, for to an apt pupil and willing worker will probably come, in due course, some hunting and an odd ride in a hunter trial, show-jumping competition and a point-to-point, and all the time there will be opportunities of riding new horses, each with different peculiarities, and of learning from practical experience and expert advice.

It is, I think, preferable to have some such grounding before entering the racing world at all, but there is no reason why the two stages, learning to be a horseman and a jockey—should not overlap, and that, for example, the novice rider, if he is lucky enough to be able to do so, should not spend his mornings riding out with a racing stable and his afternoons with a dealer. When he becomes established as a N.H. rider he will have little time for anything else.

That such an education—experience of different branches of riding—is a sound preparation for a steeplechase-rider is evident in the brilliance of so many great N.H. jockeys down the years, of whom Fred Rees, Bryan Marshall and John Francombe are shining examples who were all horsemen before they were jockeys.

To say that it is impossible for a rider to succeed unless he has followed such a programme is obviously ridiculous; Billy Speck, and David Mould as good steeplechase jockeys as you could have wished to see, took to jumping when they became too heavy for the flat, and the equitation of the racing world was probably the only form of riding they ever knew, but were born horsemen, and for those in a less fortunate position experience of practical and varied horsemanship is invaluable.

When the beginner to steeplechasing enters the racing world the benefits of his early experience, as described above, may not be as obvious as expected, for everything will be new and strange. But if they are not particularly noticeable they are, nevertheless, a strong and present force which the possessor uses more by instinct than consciously. It is evident in the way a jockey rides a horse into a fence, in the way horses jump with him, in his ability to adapt himself to the horse he is riding and the type of fence he is jumping, and to the fact that, in the case of a good horseman, the percentage of horses that fall, refuse or run out is small, while he will invariably be a better schooling rider than one who, though possibly a capable jockey, is not a good horseman.

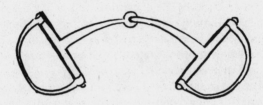

3

Rider's Seat over Fences

I GENERAL INTRODUCTION

THERE ARE FEW more controversial subjects than that of the way in which a rider should sit when negotiating a fence in a steeplechase.

Every winter when there is a spell of frost and the lack of racing deprives the sporting papers of subject-matter, and frequently on other occasions, too, this theme creeps into the correspondence columns. The most eager for the fray are by no means always those with most practical experience of steeplechasing; in fact, it is seldom that a name known to the steeplechasing world is seen at the foot of any of these letters, whose authors range from such as the gentleman who professed his willingness to demonstrate his theories over a bench in Hyde Park—the suggestion that a steeplechase would be a more appropriate trial successfully sheathed his pen—to eminent theorists and lady riders; in almost every case the most important factors are not brought into the argument, these being the characteristics of our fences, the prevailing going, the pace and the peculiarities of the horse in question.

Apart from Aintree, which merits a chapter of its own, the chief characteristics of English steeplechase fences are that they are fairly big, and that they are fairly stiff, though generally softer than before the war. This means that, while the average horse who tries to treat them with disdain will fall, it is possible for a powerful, resolute and well-made horse to hit a fence hard without coming down. Another aspect being that, as several of our courses are undulating—Plumpton and Cheltenham, for example—the obstacles may be met going uphill, downhill and on the level, and sometimes on the turn, such tracks as Windsor and Fontwell being in the form of a figure of eight.

Owing to the amount of rain encountered during the season, the going is often heavy or greasy with the result that horses tend to make mistakes, which they would not in good going, through fatigue or through loss of footing brought about by such conditions.

Pace is important in relation to the strength of the fences and the tiredness of the horse.

Every horse has its own peculiarities of conformation, temperament, and style and standard of jumping; many are, to all intents and
purposes, the same, but to take the view that they all are, and to ride
accordingly, is to court disaster.

Consequently, the way in which a rider sits over any particular
fence will depend on circumstances, or a combination of circumstances; that is why good riders are often seen in different positions,
and it is difficult to say exactly what the English style of riding really
is, as opposed to the Italian, which is consistent to all types of
jumping, and the Continental, which is consistent within the different
branches of show-jumping and steeplechasing, but is not exactly the
same in each.

One of the most frequently used terms in discussing the rider's seat
over fences is the Forward Seat, but what exactly is meant by this is
not always clear. In the racing world it is a loose description of what is
sometimes known as 'sitting up their necks', that is to say leaning
forward throughout the parabola of the leap, regardless of the position
of the leg below the knee, but in the world of equitation it is taken to
refer specifically to the Italian method of riding.

As regards jumping, the Italian school requires that the lower part
of the rider's leg from the knee downward should be drawn slightly
backwards and the heel pressed well down, so that a perpendicular
line running down from the knee would pass through the point of the
toe; that the body should be inclined forward from take-off to landing,
with the back hollowed and the shoulders square (not rounded) and
the seat clear of the saddle, the angle between the thigh and the lower
part of the leg being approximately 90 degrees, the length of rein short
and unchanged during the whole movement. This seat, its pro-
tagonists maintain, should be adopted under all circumstances,
hunting, show-jumping and steeplechasing.

It is quite common to see French and, sometimes, English jockeys
leaning forward, but with the lower part of the leg thrust forward in
varying degrees, but this is *not* a true example of what is understood by
the Forward Seat, in which the lower part of the leg must at no time be
thrust forward.

So much for the principle of the Forward Seat; its application to
steeplechasing will be dealt with later.

It has been pointed out that one of the chief characteristics of
English fences is that a horse can often hit them fairly hard without
falling, and that because of the going and the fact that he is called upon
to ride all sorts and conditions of horses, including a number of
indifferent jumpers and horses which, owing to their conformation,
are badly balanced, the steeplechase rider will have to be prepared for

The Italian seat

the not infrequent occurrence of a horse making a bad mistake, in which case his first objective is not to fall off.

When a 'chaser hits a fence hard, his speed is suddenly and violently reduced from about 30 m.p.h.—to anything down to about 5 m.p.h. The inclination of the rider is to continue at the pace at which he was originally travelling, and if he is to avoid falling off he must find some way to absorb the very considerable shock caused by the sudden drop in the speed of his horse.

By the principle of the Forward Seat this shock is taken up by the muscles of the thighs, knees, calves and ankles, which, using the stirrup as a fulcrum, press the knees into the saddle and prevent the rider from falling off. At hunting pace, or in the case of an insubstantial obstacle, this is possible, but when racing over English fences the adoption of this type of seat will, if a horse hits a fence hard, almost certainly end in disaster, for the shock is so great that this means of counteracting it is not powerful enough, with the result that horse and rider part company.

Critics of English riders appear to think that not only have the latter never heard of the Forward Seat, but they have never tried it. This may have been the case years ago, but times have changed, and not only have many modern riders given the matter considerable thought, but they have tried it out, and, like myself, have found that when riding a well-balanced horse which jumps perfectly it can be used with success, but that on the whole it is not practicable, and has no advantage over a properly executed 'via media' seat which, so far as there is such a thing, is the English school. It is not uncommon for critics to pick out photographs of English jockeys riding in bad and exaggerated positions and hold them up as typical of the English seat. This is neither a sound nor justifiable argument, for they are nothing more than examples of bad or obsolete forms of riding which good jockeys do not practice, except when, as will sometimes happen to the best of us, they are caught unawares by the horse taking-off unexpectedly—or not at all.

The first duty of a steeplechase-rider is to get round, which he will not succeed in doing if he falls off. This can easily happen if he is not on his guard when his horse makes a mistake, an eventuality that can come about through no fault of the horse or rider, so that in the ordinary course of events he cannot risk employing methods that do not allow for this happening.

When riding exceptional jumpers, jockeys can afford to take a chance, so that the better a horse jumps, the more likely is the style of the rider to approximate to the principles of the Forward Seat—I have a picture in my scrap-book of the late Bob Everett on Easter Hero at which no 'Forward Seater' could quibble—but the keynote of a good English rider is not that he is a slave to any particular school, but that he can adapt himself to circumstances, so that his seat at any one fence will depend upon the ability and consistency of his horse's jumping, the state of the going, and whether the horse has made, or seemed likely to make, a mistake.

An interesting light is thrown upon the question in a letter to *Horse and Hound* from the great Italian rider, Piero Santini, an extract from which reads; 'I . . . would not in any case dream of riding any English or Irish steeplechaser for the excellent reason that, according to my lights, all your horses are defectively balanced from the habit they acquire of leaning on the hand with their mouths half open, that they would, for an Italian, be impossible rides.'

The English steeplechase-jockey is not in this happy position. He has to get up on any horse that is produced for him, regardless of the fact that it is badly balanced through faulty conformation, or bad handling on the part of someone else, and he must therefore employ whatever methods are most efficacious to the case on hand. I have ridden horses which, for some reason or other, would 'bury' a forward-seater, but were guaranteed to get round when ridden in the

English way, i.e. with a long rein and a slightly backward inclination of the body on landing, others on which the forward seat method could be safely used round any course in England, including Aintree.

As a point of interest I once made an experiment in the matter. I used to ride a selling-'chaser whose form was as accurate as Greenwich time, and since he invariably ran with the same horses he provided excellent material for investigation. On one occasion I rode him, using the Italian style, on the next, using the 'via media' of the unexaggerated English seat. In each case he was beaten by the same horse, the form working out exactly right. From this I deduced and I have had no reason to change my views that as far as steeplechasing is concerned there is nothing to be gained by the Italian seat, but possibly a good deal to be lost if a horse makes a mistake.

It is a view in which I do not think I am alone, for that good amateur, Lt.-Col. H. M. Llewellyn, who finished second in the 'National' on Ego and has ridden a considerable number of steeplechase winners, and is even better known in the show-jumping world, adapted his style of riding according to the particular branch of equitation he was pursuing at the moment. Another example is that fine all-rounder, the late Tim Hyde, rider of the 'National winner, Workman, and of Prince Regent on whom he won the Champion 'Chase and finished third in the 'National at Aintree, who was also a good show-jumping rider and changed his style in the same fashion.

From a jockey's point of view steeplechasing is a highly competitive profession, and although the English are conservative by nature, any jockey who could discover a better way of riding than his neighbour would not be slow in adopting it, and had the Italian seat proved as effective over fences as has the American seat on the flat, there would surely be no rider using any other. I for one would gladly have cultivated it, since I felt sure when I began riding under N.H. rules that it was the correct method, but having put it to a practical test and discovered that there was no advantage in it I gave it up, and can only suppose that the reason why it is not generally employed in this country is that others have experimented in the same way and have arrived at a similar conclusion.

Having considered the pros and cons of the Forward Seat proper (the Italian method) let us turn to what, for want of a better definition, might be termed the Continental school. That is to say the style in which the rider's body is inclined forward throughout the leap and a short length of rein is maintained, but which allows for the lower part of the leg being thrust forward to an extent governed by individual taste. This school is followed by almost all French jockeys, by most

English jockeys when riding over hurdles, and sometimes by English jockeys over fences.

With regard to the theory of this style, it is necessary to return for a moment to the circumstance of a horse hitting a fence, in which case it will be remembered that an instantaneous drop in the horse's speed resulted, producing a force which had to be counteracted if the jockey was to avoid falling off. Having discovered that the Italian method was by no means always effective in this respect, jockeys instinctively sought some other way of achieving the necessary object, hitting on the somewhat obvious solution of advancing the lower part of the leg so that the shock was taken jointly on the stirrup-leathers and the muscles of the legs, knees and ankles.

According to the theory of the Italian school this is incorrect, as it means that, instead of the shock being absorbed by the muscles of the rider's legs and the spring-like action of the knee and ankle joints, a great deal of it is taken by the stirrup-leathers, which in turn pass it on to the horse. If the rider is sitting forward the horse will, therefore, have to bear, not only the rider's weight on his forehand, but the additional shock which, whether he has hit a fence or not, is conveyed to his frame through the stirrup-leathers and has the effect of, as it were, driving him into the ground. The steeper the angle of descent, and the farther forward the legs are thrust, the more accentuated will this action be, particularly if the rider's weight is forward as well, and in the case of a horse with bad shoulders the effect will be intensified.

In France the fences are usually smaller and more resilient than on English steeplechase courses, with the result that, in general, the effect on the horse under the circumstances described is negligible, and jockeys find that, while they can counteract the consequences of a horse making a mistake by the action of slightly thrusting the leg forward, they can still lean forward through the leap without prejudicing the equilibrium of the horse.

In England, however, the fences are both bigger and stiffer, though since the war they have become softer on most courses, so that the angle of descent is steeper and the strain on the horse is greater. Owing to the strength of the fences, not only is there a very fair chance of the horse getting rid of his jockey if he makes a mistake and the latter is leaning forward (even if he is taking some of the shock on his stirrup-leathers as well), but, particularly if possessed of bad shoulders, he will sometimes fall simply because he cannot cope with the combination of the rider's weight on the forehand and the shock translated from the stirrup-leathers, this being more evident at down-hill, or 'drop', fences.

In the case of horses with good shoulders who jump with a flat, rather than a steeply-curved trajectory, this aspect is less marked, and on suitable horses it is quite common to see English jockeys riding over a fence in almost exactly the same way as would a Frenchman.

Thus the situation facing the steeplechase-rider in England is somewhat complex. He will have to ride a great many different horses, some of which he has never ridden before, many of them novices; he will often have to race in going that may cause the best of jumpers to make an unexpected mistake, and he will always have to bear in mind the possibility of a similar occurrence resulting from such exigencies as interference from loose horses, his horse being unsighted or misjudging his take-off under the stress of being ridden all out into the last fence, his horse not having been properly schooled, or having conformation unsuited to the task.

He knows that he cannot pin his faith with any confidence in the Italian interpretation of the Forward Seat, however correct its principles may appear in theory, nor can he place full reliance upon Continental methods. He must, therefore, fashion a general-purpose method which will give him the best possible chance of staying in the saddle when the unforeseen occurs, at the same time avoiding interference with his horse, and he must also be versatile enough to vary the execution of his methods according to individual horses and circumstances.

If he were destined to go through his career riding nothing but good, consistent jumpers he could possibly begin and end with the Forward Seat, but such will not be the case, and even the best and most reliable of jumpers will blot their copybook sometimes, so that he must always be prepared for the unforeseen which, in all branches of the racing world, is the predominating factor, and his guiding principles must be Preparedness and Adaptability.

In the last few pages I have endeavoured to expound the principles of the two foreign methods which, as mentioned earlier on, are generally considered as one in the English steeplechasing world, and for all practical purposes they can henceforth be referred to under the single title of 'the Forward Seat', as it is so rare to find the Italian method executed in its pure form, even by French riders, almost all jockeys who lean forward from take-off to landing being in the habit of advancing the lower part of their legs to some degree or other, however slight.

The next task is to consider the methods most suitable to English conditions.

II THE SEAT

Books on general equitation are usually very dogmatic as to how a rider should sit in the saddle at all paces from the walk upwards, but as far as the practical side of steeplechasing is concerned it does not matter in the least what a jockey looks like when he leaves the paddock. His horse knows that he is going out for a race and his attention is therefore fixed on the task on hand, and it is unlikely that his rider will have to compete with any such situation as his horse trying to get rid of him by jumping and kicking or bucking. At the most he need only be prepared for him whipping round as he goes out on to the course to canter down to the starting-post, which is most liable to occur if he is the first out, or a light-hearted fly-jump during the preliminary canter.

It is therefore quite common to see good riders going out in positions that would reduce a theorist to tears: toes down, knees perceptibly away from the saddle and backs slouched. They have probably already ridden in the last four or five races and are instinctively keeping every muscle relaxed and rested till the last possible moment, the benefit derived being more important to them than their appearance to the onlooker.

This is all very well for jockeys who have made their mark, but for riders, professional or amateur, who have not established themselves it is as well to create as good an impression as possible at all times, and whether they feel like it or not, it is more probable that they will get on in their career if they present a neat and business-like figure when they ride out of the paddock, than if they are completely careless as to their style.

Everyone has their own ideas regarding the correct seat on a horse, at rest or at any other time, and in presenting a personal view I in no way suggest that it is one which anyone else should adopt, unless they feel so inclined.

It is, I think, as well to sit as far forward in the saddle as is comfortable: the farther back the rider sits, the more likely is he to give the horse a sore back, especially in such cases as riding at exercise when he is on the horse for an hour so on end. At the same time he is as well to keep his back straight, his head up and his shoulders square, his knees into the saddle and his heels pressed well down, the lower part of the leg falling slightly behind the perpendicular. The theory of this seat is that in the event of a horse jumping and kicking or bucking, the rider will have a reasonable chance of remaining 'in the plate'. The farther back he sits in the saddle, the more will he feel the force of the hindquarters when the horse kicks, while the action of straightening his back, squaring his shoulders and keeping his heels down will help to prevent him from going over his horse's head, the lowering of his heels at the same time bringing his knees close into the saddle.

I have a preference for riding with my feet on the *inside* of the stirrups, a habit which would probably be looked upon with the gravest displeasure in other spheres of equitation, but from the racing point of view I think it has a good deal to commend it. It brings the maximum area of leg into contact with the saddle, thus affording as good a grip as can be obtained, and it helps to prevent the unsightly spectacle of the toes being turned out, an occurrence which is particularly evident when the lower part of the leg is thrust forward in jumping. At rest, it is liable to cause the toes to turn in too far, so that they touch the horse, but this will not happen if the heels are kept well down and a little care is taken.

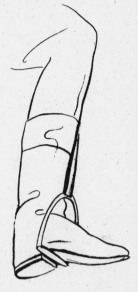

Foot on inside of iron

The general appearance will be neater if the elbows are held into the sides, as opposed to being allowed to flap about at will, and the lower the hands are kept the better.

The over-all look of a good seat can be spoilt by a rider looking down, and if he wishes to avoid this he should look straight ahead of him at approximately the level of his own eyes. Those who have undergone any form of military instruction in equitation will doubtless remember being told, with picturesque and robust force, that as there were no sixpences on the riding-school floor, it was unnecessary to look down for them.

So much for the general pattern of what might fairly be described as a rationally designed seat with which to begin operations.

In passing from the general pattern of the seat to a consideration in detail the first matter that should be dealt with is, I think, the length of the stirrup-leathers.

The fundamental reason for riding with shorter leathers when racing than at other times is that, when a horse is galloping, a rider with long leathers is not as well balanced as one who is riding short. The reason is, I believe, that the faster a horse is going the greater is the period of suspension (the moment when all four legs are off the ground); in practice what happens is that, while a rider with his leathers long feels comfortable and well balanced at slow paces, when

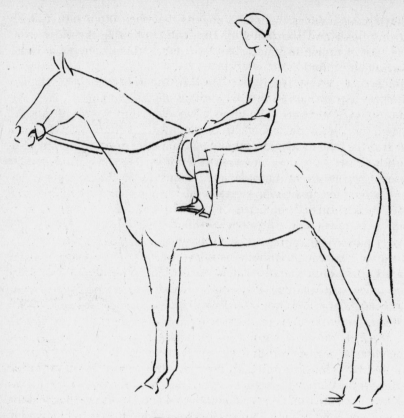

Typical 'chasing seat

his horse is extended his stirrups seem to become suddenly lower, so that he has a slight difficulty in keeping his feet in the irons. Riders such as cowboys, who have ridden with very long leathers all their lives, accommodate themselves to this style and are quite at home at any pace, but the phenomenon described is particularly noticeable to anyone who is accustomed to ride fairly short when galloping, and suddenly, for some reason or other, finds himself riding long.

While galloping it is hardly necessary to remark that the rider's seat is out of the saddle, thus placing the rider's weight where it can most easily be borne.

The other main reason for riding with shortened leathers is that it is considerably easier to control a racehorse this way. The bit used is almost invariably a snaffle, this being the most suitable for the task, since it is comfortable for the horse and convenient for the rider. It is a very mild one in its action, which, together with the natural keenness that racing induces in horses, means that they often take a fairly strong hold, and shortened stirrup-leathers enable the rider to sit 'against' his horse and control him to a degree that would not be possible to one riding long.

Flat race jockeys often carry this measure to extremes, but as they have no fences to jump it does not make such difference to their efficiency. A steeplechase jockey's seat, however, is more severely tested, and if he tries to ride too short his departure from the saddle is not likely to be long delayed. A great deal is a matter of practice and habit.

The actual length is a matter of individual taste and must depend to a certain amount on the rider's build and the particular style he has cultivated. Amateurs who ride too short when they are not used to it tend either to get cramp in the thighs, or to stand almost straight up in the stirrup-irons, the angle between thigh and shin being nearer 180 degrees than the approximate of 90, which is correct.

Continual practice and experiment is the only way to determine the particular length suitable to the individual. The best plan for the novice in such matters is to study the style of a first-class rider of approximately the same build as himself and model his style on the expert's, adjusting his leathers accordingly.

Muscles do not assume unaccustomed positions easily, and because the beginner finds it is more comfortable to ride the length he is used to out hunting and hacking, it does not follow that it is the most efficient on the racecourse, and in giving way to comfort he will be sacrificing control, and will certainly look awkward, particularly when it comes to riding a finish. In order to get used to riding short it is not a bad plan to ride a hole or two shorter at exercise than is intended on a racecourse.

I have asked a number of good professionals whether they ride a different length according to circumstances, and have found that tastes vary. As a matter of interest, I used to alter my length according to individual horses and the task on hand, riding about the same length on the flat and over hurdles, a couple of holes longer over fences if the horse is in the habit of taking a fairly strong hold, three holes longer if he is not, or if the race is three miles or over.

As a general guide, it is easier to ride short if the horse pulls and the pace is fast, i.e. the race is not a long one, or when riding on the flat and over hurdles, and more satisfactory to ride rather longer when the pace is not so strong, i.e. in long-distance races, and at Aintree. I sometimes rode a further hole shorter on the flat, if the race was a short one and the horse a particularly free goer.

It is also, I think, advisable to ride fairly long on a horse who is a bad jumper, one which has not been well schooled, or one which is very light in the mouth, as, in the first case it gives a better chance of staying on, in the second, greater ability to drive him with the legs, while in the last it is easier not to interfere with his mouth, since he will probably have to be ridden, as it were, on a thread.

In the mid-1960s, Lester Piggott pulled his leathers up to such a degree that when he stood up in his irons his knees came well above the top of his saddle. Slaves to fashion, and, doubtless, believing optimistically that by doing so they could almost become Piggott, most flat race jockeys copied him. All that happened was that Piggott retained his status not because of his change of style, but through his superior understanding of tactics and strategy, his judgment of pace, coolness, sense of balance, strength and resourcefulness, all of which he possessed to a greater degree than his rivals. Piggott's opposite number in the world of jumping was Andy Turnell of whom the same can be said, simply that he has succeeded despite his style and not because of it.

In choosing the way in which he sits, a jockey's object should be to dispose himself on the horse so that his weight can be carried most easily, his body offers the minimum wind resistance, he is able to exercise control of his horse, is secure in his saddle and effective in a finish either with or without the use of the whip.

Having found the length of stirrup leathers that enables him to fulfil all of these demands, there is nothing to be gained by riding any shorter. By riding with exaggeratedly short leathers, a jockey deprives himself of the use of his legs as a means of guidance, propulsion and security. Provided he is riding a free-going horse who runs straight, a jockey is under no disadvantage on the flat with ultra short leathers: all he has to do is to sit still and ride the horse out with his hands. On a lazy horse, having deprived himself of the use of his legs, he is entirely dependent on the whip. If the horse will not go for the whip, the jockey's role is reduced to the level of luggage. He is unable to use his legs without sitting down in the saddle thus throwing his weight right back on the horse and, incidentally, reversing the evolution of the racing seat by about a hundred years. Those jockeys who attempt to use their legs when riding too short find themselves in grotesque positions, often with their weight further back on the horse than if they were riding longer.

American jockeys do not use their legs at all and are almost entirely dependent on the whip. As a result, they look more stylish than English riders who are trying to use their legs despite the extreme shortness of their leathers.

In the case of a jump jockey riding with excessively short leathers, not only do the same factors apply as in flat racing, but the jockey is in danger of injuring a horse's back on landing and of falling off.

In race riding, as in all activities, extremism is to be deprecated.

On the way to the post, and between fences, assuming that he has cultivated a suitable length of stirrup-leather, the rider's seat should be such that the angle between thigh and shin is somewhere about 90 degrees, with his bottom clear of the saddle, but not stuck up in the air, and above all *still*. It is the first sign of an inexperienced and unstylish rider if his bottom bumps up and down in the saddle, which will occur of his knee-joint is not rigid.

The lower part of the leg should be kept still unless it is being used to kick the horse; if it is swinging about for no reason it will only confuse and irritate him, since he will have no idea what message it is trying to convey to him, and such an action continued throughout a race may even end in chafing his sides.

If the horse is pulling hard it is a help to advance the lower part of the leg slightly, whether the heel is sunk or not is a matter of individual taste. If a rider is a natural stylist he will look well whatever way he rides, and it would be hard to say whether such as Danny Morgan and Jack Molony, who favoured a slightly pointed toe looked better than Frenchie Nicholson or Gerry Wilson, whose heels were always sunk hard down, or than the 'via media' style of Bryan Marshall and others. The more the heel is sunk, the less need the lower part of the leg be advanced, but there is no difference in the practical result with either method, and each man must make his own choice. When a horse is not pulling, the lower part of the legs need not go beyond the perpendicular.

Whatever style he does adopt must, however, conform to the fundamental principles of keeping his knees and legs close in to the saddle, his seat just clear of it and, as far as is humanly possible, motionless.

A jockey should be able to adjust his leathers himself almost by instinct. He should be able to pull them up or let them down without looking, and whether he is walking, trotting, or (in reason) cantering, and one of the first signs of an unskilled or inexperienced tradesman is that he requires his horse to be held by an attendant while he fumbles about counting the holes in his leathers. The chances are he has counted them wrong, and in any case the only way to tell whether you are riding the right length or not is by the feel, and some people, owing to habit or deformity, ride longer on one side than the other.

Every jockey at some time or other has probably ridden out of the paddock in a dither as to whether he is riding the right length or not, but under such circumstances there is no need to become unduly worried as the canter down to the post will soon show whether the

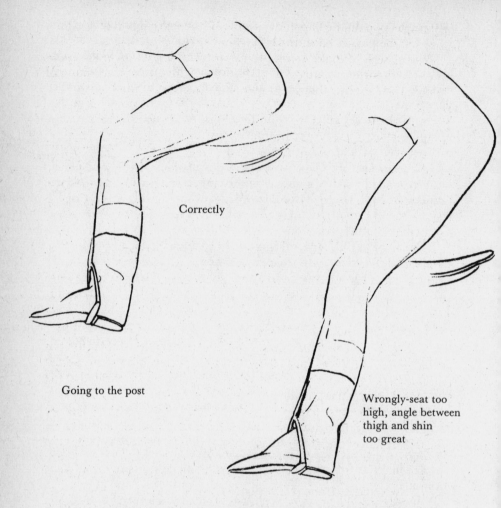

Correctly

Going to the post

Wrongly-seat too
high, angle between
thigh and shin
too great

length of his leathers is right or not, and they can be adjusted at the
starting-gate. If, as sometimes happens, there are not enough holes in
the stirrup-leather, undo the buckle, wrap the leather a couple of
times round the stirrup itself and do the buckle up again.

A point of detail worth considering is the way of dealing with the
ends of the leathers. Riding-school instructors, so far as I remember,
like them tucked under the leathers themselves (on which the stirrups
hang), so that the ends lie behind the calf of the leg. This, I find, sometimes results in the fold being slightly prominent and a cause of discomfort, as it comes just behind the knees. Instead, it is quite a good
idea not to tuck them round the part of the leathers that support the
stirrups, but to pass them straight back and tuck them into the

surcingle loop on the flap of the saddle. If the ends are much too long they can be passed back under the loop again.

It is as well to make some provision for them, as there are quite enough important matters to think about, without the distraction of odd straps flapping about and getting in the way.

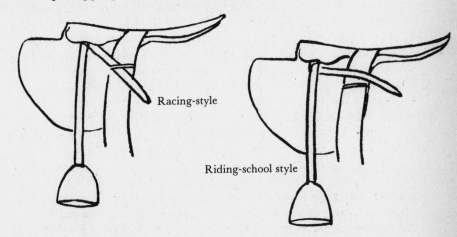

Racing-style

Riding-school style

A detail of considerable importance is to see that the leathers are not twisted when the foot is placed in the iron, as this will cause the added discomfort of the edges rubbing against the shin-bone, instead of the latter resting against the flat surface.

If this only occurs on the way to the post it is of no great moment, as it can be put right before the 'off', but to set out to ride some three miles over fences under these conditions is liable to result in a mild but not ineffective form of self-torture.

As regards the stirrup-irons themselves, they should be big enough for the foot to slip in and out easily, but not so big that the heel can go through as well; there are quite enough unavoidable ways of getting hurt in steeplechasing without adding to them by using irons that are either too big or too small (the worse evil) and taking the chance of being caught up by the foot and dragged.

There are two shapes of iron in general use: one being more or less the same pattern as that used for ordinary riding, the other with the sides rounded, but which kind is used is purely a matter of taste. My own preference is for the former, as the position of the foot in them is more definite, but I have often used both sorts, and, in fact, for all practical purposes one is as good as the other.

The next point to deal with should be, I think, the angle of the body as far as the general aspect is concerned, that of jumping being left to a separate chapter.

I used to think that wind-resistance was a very important factor in race-riding, but in practice I do not believe it is. I came across what appeared to be an authoritative article on the subject and, as far as I remember, it stated that below about a hundred miles an hour wind resistance was negligible, but that above that speed its effect increased in a very much greater proportion to the pace. Concerning this it is worthy of note that two of the most successful riders on the flat of their day, Harry Wragg and Gordon Richards, both rode with their bodies fairly upright. It must, however, be borne in mind that the average rider under N.H. rules is very much bigger of frame than a flat race jockey and, therefore, presents a greater area to wind-resistance, in which case this factor may be worthy of some consideration, and provided he does not adopt a position so exaggerated that he cannot see where he is going it will be just as well if the jockey tucks himself away when galloping; certainly his appearance will be neater.

As a rough guide the body should be leant forward so that the rider's line of vision runs through his horse's ears, that is to say if his horse carries his head at an ordinary angle. If he carries it 'on the floor' the only guide is to lean as far forward as is compatible with looking where he is going. A jockey's appearance benefits if he keeps his back fairly straight and does not hunch his shoulders, and if he presses his elbows into his sides. Exaggeration in all forms is to be deprecated and I have a rather shaming recollection of remarking to a friend before the first 'National in which I rode that though I did not expect to get very far (and I did not do so!) at least I intended to go down to the post looking like a jockey, the only repercussion of this operation being that the said friend overheard one spectator ask another who the idiot looking like a monkey up a stick was, as I cantered to the post with a crouch so extreme that, in comparison, Tod Sloan would have seemed a Life Guardsman.

It looks even worse, particularly when riding among professionals, to assume a position similar to that of a mounted policeman clearing the course, a fault that will be magnified in direct proportion to the rider's height.

So far as galloping on the flat is concerned there is no need to change position at all, in fact the quieter and stiller a rider sits, the easier it is for the horse to keep on an even keel. When it is necessary to jump, or ride a finish, other factors arise, but that is a matter for later consideration.

III HANDS

One of the most difficult departments of riding to write about is that of hands. To say that hands are born and not made is a comfortable way of dismissing the subject, but it is no great help to the beginner, and as has been said earlier in this book, hands are the servants of the brain, and a rider with a certain amount of intelligence and imagination should be able to cultivate reasonably good hands, even if he is not bred to be a horseman.

Before attacking the question of the best way to hold the reins when race-riding, it is, I think, profitable to consider the horse's point of view. Because a racehorse usually takes a fairly strong hold of the bit when his blood is up, it does not follow that he will react favourably to a permanent 'half-Nelson' on his mouth from the time he leaves the paddock to the finish of the race, and although he may give the impression of having an insensitive mouth because he takes a strong, steady hold while he is galloping, this is not necessarily so.

When he is racing he is keen to go, sometimes faster than would be advisable with regard to the conservation of his energy for the end of the race, and to steady him his jockey will sit against him with a fairly strong, even hold. When he settles down his jockey will ease this hold and let him bowl along 'in his hands', his pressure on the horse's mouth being just sufficient to keep him balanced and under control. This state of affairs will be maintained until the rider 'picks his horse up', that is to say take a fresh and firmer hold to collect him and let him know that he is going to be asked for his finishing effort. As a result of all this the message conveyed to the horse's brain by the jockey shortening the reins and taking a firm hold of his head is that he is going to be asked to gallop fast. If, then, a jockey gets a short and firm hold of his horse as soon as he is in the saddle, the chances are that the latter will become excited and start pulling at his bit, in which respect it should never be forgotten that the shorter hold a rider takes of a horse, the tighter does he hold him instinctively, and that the longer his rein (the further his hands from the horse's mouth) the lighter will the pressure on the horse's mouth tend to be.

This is very noticeable in the case of foreign jockeys, with whom English horses seldom seem happy in their slow paces, because they are not accustomed to being held short and hard by the head from the moment the jockey gets on their back. A horse that will not turn a hair when ridden with a long rein will often leave the paddock as if he was treading on hot bricks, when carrying a jockey who is exerting a vice-like pressure on his back teeth.

The first aspect to bear in mind is, therefore, that a horse's mouth conveys an immediate message to his brain, and that upon the handling of the reins depends the coherency with which that message is received.

The horse is not a particularly intelligent animal; moreover, he is easily bewildered and upset, and he should therefore be made aware of his rider's desires, quietly, calmly and simply. So that the movement of the rider's hands must be neither violent, rough nor sudden. The instrument they have to operate is easily thrown out of gear. For its successful manipulation it may often be required to use strength, but never violence, and guile will go far farther than force.

The guiding principle that should be kept in mind is that the two predominating factors in the case are the mind of the horse and that of the rider—not the horse's mouth and the rider's hands, which are only the particular parts of machinery by which these two controls are connected. It is not a case of the rider's hands *versus* the horse's mouth—no jockey on earth can hold a horse by sheer strength, if the horse really means going—it is the human brain against the equine, and the latter will react according to the tactics and strategy, with which the powers at the command of the former are employed.

Since the bit almost invariably employed in racing is a snaffle, or a variation of the same, the way of the jockey is considerably simplified by the fact that he will be using a single-rein bridle, but even so simple a contraption as this offers a number of variations as to the way in which it can be held.

Some jockeys hold the reins outside the little finger, others between the third and little finger, and I have even heard of them being held between the second and third finger—it is largely a matter of taste. When I began race-riding I used to hold them outside the little finger, but later I changed, and for a long time now have held them between the third and little finger. This style, I think, tends to give more sensitivity than the other way and is less inclined to make the rider look 'mutton-fisted', though it is what is done with the reins rather than the way in which they are held that matters in practice.

There are good jockeys using both methods. Needless to say, whichever of the two styles is adopted it is necessary to ride with the little finger on the outside in the whip hand, in order to hold the whip.

Unless the reins are on the short side it is advisable to tie a knot at the extreme ends, the object of this being as a precaution against the buckle coming undone and in order that the surplus length does not get in the way—it sometimes has an irritating habit of getting between the knees and the saddle.

In the case of a horse with a long neck, or at Aintree where it will often be necessary to give a horse the full length of the rein, it is not wise to knot them (unless the buckle is so insecure that a shorter rein seems the lesser of two evils), but riding over hurdles and on the flat it is the usual procedure.

The operation sounds a simple one and is, if done the right way, but it is not uncommon to see riders fumbling about, with their whip getting in the way, and not making much progress.

The correct drill is to put the whip under the left arm (if the rider is right-handed, under the right if he is left-handed), take the reins in the left hand, using that for steering purposes, and tie the knot with the right.

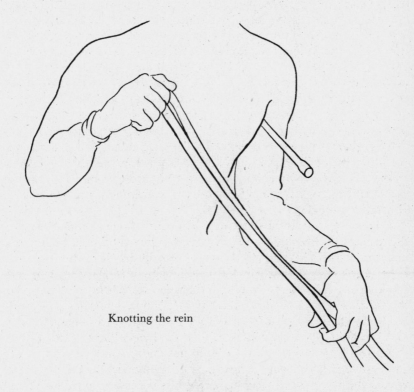

Knotting the rein

While racing, it is good plan to hold the reins in the form of a bridge, that is to say (for a right-handed man) to hold the slack of the left rein between the thumb and forefinger of the right hand. This ensures an even pull on the horse's mouth, as it helps to strengthen the weaker pull of the left arm. It can also be a considerable help in remaining in the saddle if the rider should, in an awkward situation, be thrown forward. The practice is apt to be frowned upon in riding-school circles, but is to be recommended so far as race-riding is concerned.

The lower the hands are held, the less probability of interfering with the horse's mouth.

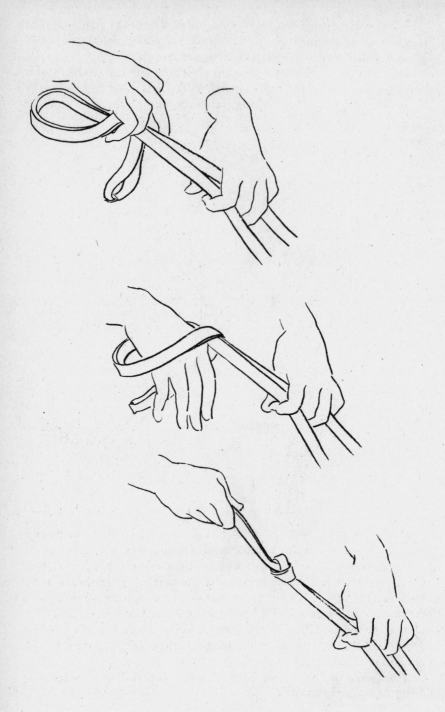

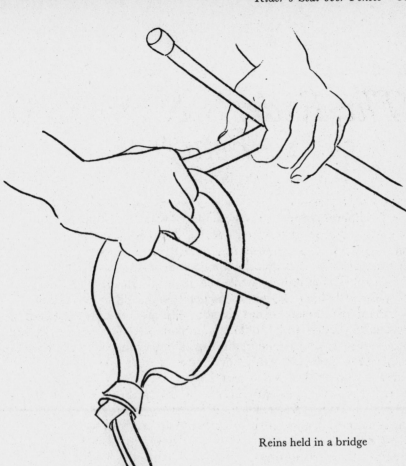

Reins held in a bridge

4

The Rider's Seat over a Fence

I INTRODUCTION

THE FAULT OF most theorists in equitation is that they try to govern different branches of the activity by the same rules. In the past one was adjured to 'sit well back', whether the occasion was the hunting-field, a show-jumping course or a steeplechase. Later instructors laid down that the Forward Seat was the correct method for all types of jumping, while the Army used to teach a general-purpose seat which was something between the old style and the new. On the perfect horse, as has already been pointed out, the Forward Seat as laid down by the Italians would answer all requirements, but perfection is seldom found in this world, and even when it is as nearly achieved as makes no difference, other factors crop up to raise a barrier between theory and practice.

This barrier is probably greater in England than in any other country, and there is a reason for it. We are both an enterprising and a casual nation, and we like a quick return for our money. The effect of these traits with regard to our methods of riding are clearly discernible: the keen hunting man will set out to follow hounds on a horse which he has never ridden before, knows nothing about and of whose jumping ability he is completely ignorant. He will, when hounds find and get away, face it at whatever jumpable obstacle happens to appear between himself and the direction in which hounds are running, and hope for the best.

If he falls off, or his horse comes down, he will find himself at the tail of the hunt, or perhaps out of it altogether, and since his horse may be an indifferent, unwilling or erratic jumper—it is even possible that, for all the rider knows, he has never been hunting before—he will indeed be a fool-hardy horseman if he takes it for granted that he is on the finished article, and sits up his neck according to the precepts of the forward seat. Thus, most practical horsemen have had to form for themselves a general-purpose seat that is best calculated to keep the horse between them and the ground, under different and unforeseen circumstances which—and if you do not believe it, try riding a bad horse across country—is not the forward seat.

The schooling of our horses is often equally as casual. A horse will be taken out cubbing a few times, be given a couple of easy days hunting, and then have to take his place in the forefront of the battle. If he is owned by a rich man who can afford to have him carefully and gradually schooled over a period of two or three seasons, that is a different matter, but it is far more likely that he is his owner's one hunter, and that his master, if he rides to hunt and does not hunt to ride, will not want to miss a good hunt through messing about teaching his horse by easy stages. If he is owned by a dealer the sooner he is sold at a profit the better, and it is therefore the nagsman's job to waste no time in teaching him to cross a country.

The steeplechasing world offers a similar parallel. Many owners cannot afford to keep horses in training at ever rising costs for fun: they must get out and earn their living. If they are novice hurdlers they are put over two or three flights of hurdles at home and then sent to run in a race; if novice 'chasers, their *debut* over fences is, as likely as not, preceded by no more than a few runs over hurdles and a school or two over practice fences on the training-ground, and it is by no means uncommon to find a flat race horse, who has not even seen a hurdle before November, running in a steeplechase early in the New Year.

Occasionally one finds that a horse is a born jumper and is as good a ride in his first race as he is at any other stage of his career, but, as can well be imagined, this happy state of affairs is the exception rather than the rule, and a considerable proportion of the horses a steeplechase jockey is called upon to ride are far from being proficient and reliable jumpers.

All this has influenced the style of riding in England, both in the hunting-field and on the racecourse, and is the reason why it is impossible to lay down any hard and fast rule as to a steeplechasing seat.

Abroad, the situation is somewhat different. The fences are neither as big nor as substantial, and horses are more carefully schooled, over a longer period of time—it is quite common for trainers in France to school two-year-olds—with the result that a more or less similar style of riding is in use with regard to all horses and all obstacles.

Since no set formula can be offered to cover steeplechase-riding as a whole, the subject is, I think, best approached from the different aspects of some of the most common situations by which the rider is likely to find himself faced. Before this, however, it is well to give some thought to the first objectives which the rider must achieve, these being to keep the horse on his legs and himself on top of the horse: 'you won't win if you don't get round; you won't get round if you fall off' is a far more valuable precept upon which to base one's method of riding than any theoretical principle. It is no consolation to owners and trainers that, in spite of riding exactly as Col. McTaggart or Captain Santini—or whoever his pet guide happens to be—the jockey fell off: they are only interested in results.

II RIDING A GOOD JUMPER

There is a good deal to be said for 'leaving the best to the last' in all aspects of life, but in the world of steeplechasing this by no means follows. It is true that, at the start of his career, a jockey will, indeed, be fortunate if he does not have to ride some extremely indifferent jumpers, but if such rides are not interspersed by a few pleasanter experiences he may never reach the stage when good horses come his way.

It is with the desire, therefore, to present the best first that the viewpoint of riding a good jumper is now approached.

A horse that is entitled to be described as a really good ride in a steeplechase must be possessed of a number of qualities. First, he must be a fluent jumper, that is to say he must negotiate his fences smoothly, carefully and quickly; he must approach them neither too hastily nor over-deliberately, and must be prepared to adjust himself to sudden changes of circumstance such as having his view of the obstacle obscured by another horse swerving across him, being obliged to accelerate quickly in order to keep a position, or checking his speed to avoid a collision, he must be resolute and impervious to the general rough-and-tumble of the game, be easy to manoeuvre, well balanced and nimble enough to recover from any reasonable error in jumping that misfortune may cause him to commit. He may not be a particularly good racehorse—perhaps he will be no more than a selling-plater—but his rider will have the knowledge that he can place complete confidence in him, his only requirement being not to interfere with him unduly.

Such horses are always a pleasure to ride and a great help to the beginner in the matter of gaining confidence. But although he is riding what amounts to a 'patent-safety' the rider is well advised to bear in mind that his horse may make an unexpected mistake through no fault of his own: through slipping on taking-off, or as a result of interference from another horse, and while he is justified in riding confidently there is no excuse for carelessness. Falling off a horse of this description is a humiliating experience, and one which is not likely to be well received, either by the owner and trainer, or those members of the public who have backed the horse.

Generally speaking there are two schools of thought with regard to riding a horse over a steeplechase fence: the one is to apply the legs during the last few strides, the other to sit perfectly still and leave everything to the horse. Mr. Harry Brown, the outstanding amateur rider of his day, in an excellent article on the subject in Colonel Lyon's delightful book, *In My Opinion* published in the 1920's, express the view that the best results are obtained by riding a horse into a fence with one's legs rather than by sitting still.

In principle I am in complete agreement with him, but, as he himself points out, it is as well to take into consideration the peculiarities of the horse in question: only a few weeks ago I rode a hurdler who is as perfect a ride as possible provided he is left completely alone, but who, when ridden into his hurdles, invariably gets too close to them and hits them hard, a circumstance which, over fences, might well prove disastrous.

Riding a horse into a fence with the legs does not necessarily mean trying, as it were, to kick his ribs in, which may be necessary in the case of a sluggish or unwilling jumper: it refers to squeezing the horse with the legs, in rhythm with the last few strides before taking off. The object of this is, first, to overcome any hesistancy in the mind of the horse, conveying to him the fact that the rider is determined to get to the other side; second, to get him going well into his bridle, so that he will jump off his hocks; third, to ensure a crescendo approach, which will enable the horse to jump quickly, and, if he hits a fence, will furnish him with the impetus to carry him through it without losing too much ground.

When about fifty yards away the rider should start to pay attention to the matter of negotiating the jump that lies ahead of him. This distance it may be thought, is unnecessarily great, but at racing speed it is soon eaten up and any changes of position should be made in good time, so that the horse's attention shall not be distracted from jumping by being pulled about a few strides before he has to take off.

On a good horse, the rider will not have to think about such eventualities as getting the horse balanced, or preparing to stop him trying to run out or refuse; his only concern will be not to interfere with the horse and not to fall off. He should, therefore, concentrate on his own position in the saddle, maintaining a light but firm contact with his horse's mouth: too tight a hold on a horse's head takes his mind off his task, while a loose rein is synonymous with lack of control.

It is then advisable to decide at what place the fence is to be jumped. Having done this it is essential to keep a straight line, to change one's mind at the last moment, unless circumstances allow for no alternative, is fatal: it confuses the horse and may cause the downfall of one's own and other horses. One must always give a horse a clear view of a

fence, either by pulling a couple of lengths behind the horse immediately in front, or taking a position just to one side or the other.

In the case of a faint-hearted or unwilling jumper a policy of not
letting him see the fence until the last possible second is sometimes
preferable, as he will then have little or no time to think about anything but jumping, and there are some horses, usually very free goers,
to whom the sight of 'daylight' is too rich for their blood, and who, as
soon as they are pulled out from behind another horse and given an
uninterrupted view of the course, are uncontrollable. But for the
moment such problems can be shelved, for an honest, sober horse
who is a good jumper will always jump quicker and better if he can see
what he is about and has time to measure his take-off.

As he approaches the fence the rider will be in the position described earlier on, namely, leaning as far forward as is compatible with
seeing where he is going, his seat slightly clear of the saddle, his hands
in the immediate region of the withers (on either side of them or just
above them), his back straight rather than rounded, his knees and the
inside of his legs pressed close into the saddle, his toes turned neither
out nor in, his heels slightly sunk (according to individual taste), and
his elbows close to his sides.

About twenty yards from the fence it is as well to bring the body to a
slightly more upright position: on good jumpers who are going well
there is a strong temptation to remain in exactly the same position the
whole time, and it can often be done, but the day is sure to come when
the unforeseen occurs and the horse hits the fence hard, an occurrence
which may be of no particular moment in the case of a Continental
obstacle, but in that of the average English fence is liable to spell
departure from the saddle. In a less crouching position the rider will
be able to see exactly what he is about, and will be better placed to
guard against the unexpected.

By this time he should have a pretty good idea as to where the horse
is going to take off, or in how many more strides, so that when the
horse leaves the ground the rider will neither have anticipated him,
nor have been 'left behind'. With the type of horse under discussion,
such a unity will present no particular difficulty, for the horse himself
will have begun to measure his take-off with a smooth movement
which the rider will have been able to foresee and which will give no
cause to endanger the security of his seat.

I have found it quite a good plan—and a number of other riders
think likewise—to slip the reins to the greatest length at which
complete control can be maintained just before coming into the
wings. This gives one a better chance of not interfering with the
horse's mouth, or being pulled over his head, if he takes off sooner

than expected. The alternative of slipping them after the horse has taken off tends to result in them being slipped too far, with a consequent loss of control, since the operation must, perforce, be undertaken hurriedly and, not improbably, clumsily.

Some riders—Fred Rimell was one—cultivate the art of going into a fence with a very short hold of the reins and slipping them to exactly the right length as the horse takes off, but this method requires a good deal of skill and practice, and in the case of the beginner is liable to end in him slipping them too late (resulting in the horse getting a violent jerk in the mouth, or the rider being pulled over his head, if he has in any way got 'left behind'), or too much, so that his elbows are somewhere round his ears and he is left with yards of rein to 'wind up'.

It is often possible to ride with the same length of rein throughout a race, but sometimes, as when riding a hard puller, it is necessary to have a shorter hold of the reins between fences than is desirable when actually jumping, and it is then advisable to lengthen them as described, before taking off.

At the take-off the rider should never have his arms stretched out with no bend at the elbow, for such a position will afford no elasticity between his hands and the horse's mouth and makes it difficult for the rider not to interfere with him.

Except when using the whip, the rider's hands should always be on the reins from the moment of taking off to that of landing. Not infrequently one sees a jockey with one arm raised, in varying degrees, or a hand taken off the reins, which is known as 'calling a cab' and is one of the most glaring faults of horsemanship. By taking a hand off the reins and raising an arm the rider interferes with his own balance and also with that of the horse, and the more exaggerated the action, the more marked the reaction, since the tendency is for the body to twist as the arm is raised.

Cab-calling may merely be a bad habit unwittingly acquired and resorted to, but it may also be due to a desperate effort to avoid interfering with the horse's mouth after he has jumped sooner or quicker than the rider expected, an eventuality that should have been met by slipping the reins, or it is a sign that the rider is losing his nerve—if he has not lost it already.

It was suggested that the rider's body should assume a position something between the pronounced crouch adopted on the flat between fences and an upright stance, in other words, that it should be leant slightly forward, in which position it can remain as the horse becomes 'airborne'. As the horse describes the parabola of the leap and lands, the body will, without any effort on the part of the rider, tend to return to being approximately perpendicular to the ground.

The exact angle will depend upon the steepness at which the horse himself lands, so that while it may be forward of the perpendicular in one case, it may be more upright in another. As, or just before, the horse's hind legs touch the ground the body can be brought forward to the flat-racing position, so that the horse can gallop on without delay.

During the whole manœuvre the rider's weight is taken through his knees and feet, as opposed to his seat; he does, in fact, stand rather than sit, though the bend of his knee will bring his seat so close to the saddle on landing that he may seem to be actually sitting in the saddle. Photographs are very deceptive and often give the impression that a rider is balanced solely through his feet and his hold on the horse's mouth via the reins; if the horse's mouth is wide open and the rider's position exaggerated, this is probably so; if not, such is not likely to be the case, since his position will then have been maintained by the grip of his knees and legs, the tautness of the reins being no more than the contact necessary to control. A loose rein, except in moments of stress, is technically a fault.

So far as his legs are concerned (since he is riding a willing horse), the rider will have no need to apply them with any violence, but from his own point of view it will do no harm if he presses them into the horse, in rhythm with his stride, as he comes into the fence: it will give both the horse and himself confidence and will ensure that he is gripping with his legs and knees. As the horse takes off he can bring them slightly forward to guard against the possibility of him hitting the fence.

On landing the rider can, if he wishes, shorten his reins to a flat-racing length. Since he will not have slipped them to an uncontrollable degree this manoeuvre will present no problems, nor will it interfere in the slightest with the horse's progress. Forward-seat extremists frequently bring up the theory that 'winding up' after having slipped the reins results in a horse getting slowly away after landing and loss of control. In the case of a rider who has slipped his reins too far, or who, when his horse has made some appalling blunder, has had to 'give him the lot', this may be so, but it certainly is not, when the length of rein throughout has been such that control has never been lost.

The method set out above is offered as being one which is soundly practical: it does not interfere with the horse's speed and efficiency in jumping, and it gives the rider a fair chance of retaining his seat in the event of the horse hitting a fence unexpectedly, and as far as it is possible to put a name to it may be described as the English method.

It can be modified, if so desired, to approximate to the Continental style and, where necessary (as will be discussed later) to the 'back-

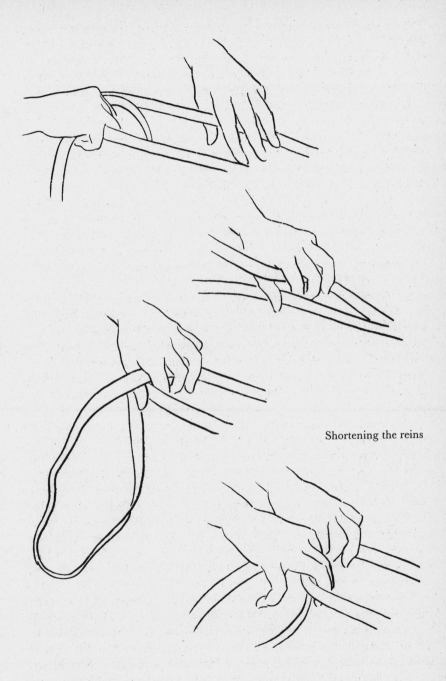

Shortening the reins

ward' school, and a good jockey will vary its execution according to circumstances, as a skilled bowler varies the length and speed of his deliveries. But such artistry can be developed only by experience and practice, and the beginner is advised to hold to the 'middle way' until he has become sufficiently proficient to recognize the appropriate moments for a particular modification—and even then he is sure to be caught out one day.

I have purposely avoided going into too great detail over a rider's actual style, for that is of secondary importance to the essentials, namely: control, remaining on the horse, and enabling the latter to jump quickly, efficiently and without interference.

In almost all books on equitation far too much stress is placed upon adherence to some particular method, too little to the practical aspect which, in racing, is the only one that really counts. I have a personal theory that a rider is better balanced if he keeps his back as straight as is reasonably possible, whether he is leaning forward or not, but I have seen many first-class riders who rode with their backs rather rounded—Ted Leader, who won the 'National on Sprig, was one—and I prefer a slightly sunk heel to the 'toe-pointing' style. But this does not mean that these theories are any sounder than those of anyone else, and the beginner cannot do better (as was suggested earlier in the book) than copy a first-class jockey with a similar build to himself.

III RIDING BAD JUMPERS

As will have been gathered from the last few pages, the riding of a good horse over steeplechase fences presents no particular problem. The performance of the horse himself can, to all intents and purposes, be taken for granted, and the rider's objectives of not falling off or interfering with his mount will be achieved without difficulty, and the whole experience will leave an impression of simplicity and delight, together with a wish to repeat the operation as soon as possible.

But even if it were possible to ride nothing but perfect horses, such bliss can only be truly appreciated by the contrast of riding bad ones as well, and it is only from experience with all types that a good steeplechase-rider can be evolved. Broadly speaking there are two departments into which bad horses can be divided: those who have no desire to jump, and those who are too anxious to get to the other side of the fence to bother about the way in which they do so. Each trait is unpleasant, but the former is the worse of the two and is, therefore, I think best considered first.

There are, I would say, few less pleasant sensations in steeple-

Approach

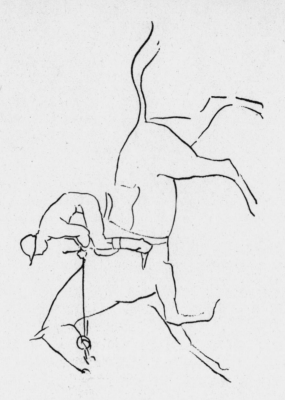

About to take off

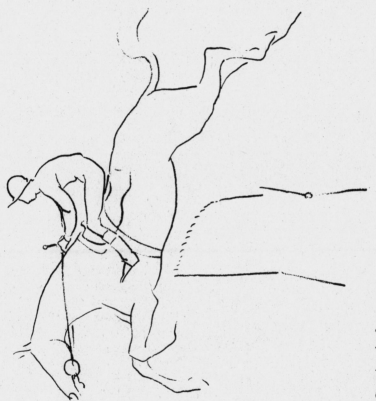

Crossing the fence

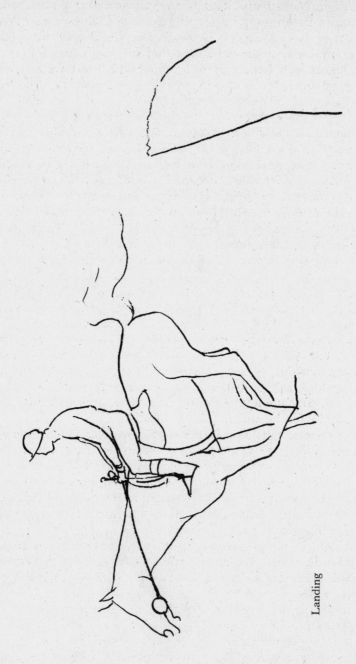

Landing

chase-riding than that of approaching a fence upon a horse who is determined not to jump it; one who, in spite of the strongest application of every known aid to propulsion, responds only with a sullen and inexorable decrease in pace, so that the rider knows that, at the most, he can only hope that his horse will lurch awkwardly over to land on all fours, but is more likely to flop on top of the obstacle, or come to a standstill on the take-off side.

Horses of this type are usually those who are completely soured with racing, a condition resulting, perhaps, from some physical infirmity such as a strained heart, unsound limbs, too much galloping on hard ground, unpleasant memories of previous falls, or a natural lack of courage. If they are confirmed exhibitors of the trait, they are almost certainly past curing; if young and inexperienced it may still be possible to reform them by careful and patient schooling, but as far as the rider is concerned he must take every horse as he finds him and do his best to get him round.

Before he goes out for the race a jockey receives from the trainer, owner, or whoever is in charge of the proceedings, instructions as to how the horse in question should be ridden, and an account of any peculiarities he may possess. It does not always follow that the latter information will be entirely accurate or comprehensive: some owners and trainers will lie shamelessly to jockeys in this respect, perhaps on the principle that too revealing a knowledge of a horse's characteristics and behaviour will shake the rider's confidence to such an extent that his chief, and probably only, concern will be his own safety, rather than any attempt to win the race which, in many cases, would undoubtedly (and justifiably) be the case.

Nevertheless, it is a moral crime to give the rider no hint as to what his horse is likely to do: to be launched, without any warning but instead some such exhortation as 'good luck, he'll give you a grand ride', on a brute who has gone through the wing, turned a somersault or stuck his toes in, when last schooled at home, is an experience which is extremely disillusioning, but by no means uncommon in a steeplechase-rider's life.

But I am in danger of wandering from the immediate issue, to which I must return, presuming that the rider is in full possession of all information that the trainer can truthfully impart concerning the horse he is about to ride.

In the riding of every kind of horse there is one golden rule to bear in mind:

'Never go into a fence with a loose rein.'

There is a common idea, arising possibly from a too-zealous perusal of the principles of equitations expounded in *How we brought the good news from Ghent to Aix,* that in order to make a horse go fast he must be ridden on a completely loose rein. This theory may be admirable so far as the field of poetry is concerned, but in everyday life the rider must think, not merely of how fast he can go but where he is going, and to the practical horseman it is somewhat surprising that the hero of the stirring piece of verse referred to ever reached Aix at all.

To jump well a horse must be both balanced and under control: his balance will depend a great deal upon his conformation, but it will also be governed by the smoothness, or otherwise, of his progress and the concord or discord between him and his rider; the control which the rider exercises over his horse is reflected in his ability to regulate his pace and steer him.

A well-balanced and controlled horse should jump off his hocks; the speed of his approach towards the obstacle should be a crescendo rather than a diminuendo, and he should answer the applications of the aids, to the extent of his rider being able to check or increase his pace in order that he should not get too close to a fence or stand too far back, when he takes off.

When a horse is ridden on a loose rein it is the horse and not the rider who is in control. The latter can, of course, take hold of his head if he feels the horse is going to try and deviate from a straight path, but in that fractional space of time before direct contact with the horse's mouth has been established, a great deal can happen: the horse can swerve, or even run out, eventualities which could probably be overcome when no such hiatus exists. The situation might be compared to that of a man driving a car in which the steering has too much play, resulting in a measurable time-lag between the turning of the steering-wheel and the moving of the wheels of the car itself.

The first precept, therefore, is 'always have the horse going well into his bridle'; that is to say, taking a perceptible hold of his bit. If he is a light-mouthed horse the answer to the problem is not to ride him on a loose rein, but to put an easier bit on his mouth, a rubber bit, for example.

In the case of a horse that has taken a real dislike to jumping there is little or nothing the jockey can do. It will be no use hitting or kicking him, as he will have become inured to such measures, and about his only hope is to jam him between two other horses, with a horse immediately in front of him, and hope that he will jump for the simple reason that he will not have time to think of stopping, or be in the position to run out. The best answer is not to ride him at all!

Proceeding to the less formidable cases of 'sticky' jumpers, there are three further sub-divisions: the horse who is merely indolent, the one slightly lacking in confidence, and the one who, though he does not dislike jumping, derives more pleasure from thwarting his rider than obeying him.

Indolent horses are often very good rides when ridden by resolute jockeys. They will respond to the recognized aids vigorously applied and can, if well and properly ridden, be made to jump quickly and accurately, and the only matter the rider has to worry about is acceleration—he has no need to be frightened of going into a fence too fast.

Such horses will stand a reasonable amount of encouragement from the whip, without becoming sour, and any amount of kicking. On them it is advisable not to ride too short. The shorter the stirrup-leather, the more difficult it is to use the lower part of the leg as an aid to propulsion, and before the start it is as well to let down the leathers one, perhaps two, holes if in the habit of riding on the short side in the ordinary course of events.

In extreme cases of indolence it is sometimes a sound move to give the horse a couple of good cracks with the whip at the start. In nine cases out of ten a horse should be hit with the left hand, since most horses always tend to go to the left rather than the right, an inclination accentuated by the fact that the average rider is right-handed and, therefore, hits a horse with this hand, so that the application of chastisement with the left hand comes as something of a surprise, and is consequently more effective. An alternative or additional measure is to get the starter's assistant to administer the same treatment with his hunting-crop, round the horse's hocks. By these attentions the horse will be aroused from his lethargy and put on his toes, and will jump off with more alacrity than he would otherwise be disposed to exhibit.

Whether or not this plan is resorted to must depend upon circumstances, and be left to the discretion of the rider.

As he approaches the first fence the rider should drive the horse up into his bridle by kicking him hard with his heels and keeping a firm, even hold of the reins. If he has succeeded he will find that the horse is taking a stronger hold of his bit, and he should continue the procedure until he has actually taken off.

Should the horse show no signs of going into his bridle it is still essential to keep a firm contact with his mouth, but the vigour of the application of the heels must be increased to the maximum. If he begins slowing down with the intent to stop, severer measures must be brought to bear in the form of a couple of good cracks with the whip. When using the whip under such circumstances it is more important than ever that contact with the horse's mouth is not lost, since the rider will be attempting to steer with one hand only, and while the reins should not be held too short they must on no account be loosed until the horse has taken off. Then they can, if necessary, be slipped or eased, to enable the horse to stretch himself out as he lands.

As noted above, the most effective use of the whip is almost always to be made with the left hand: this is best done by carrying the whip in the right hand and pulling it through with the left, letting it fall right round the horse's quarter, as far back as possible. A horse should never be hit in the flank or ribs, as this will make him curl up rather than extend himself, and when hitting him it is as well either to have another horse on the right or to wait until one is just coming into the wings, so that the horse cannot run out.

The average horse will swerve if hit with the right hand, but is more likely to keep straight when the left is used. If a horse shows a tendency to veer to the right when he has been hit, the next application of the whip should be delivered with the right hand, and *vice versa*. One of the first accomplishments necessary to a competent steeplechase-rider is to be able to use the whip equally well with each hand, and until a jockey has mastered the art there will always be a chink in his armour; if he is left-handed by nature he is lucky.

Horses such as the type under discussion usually jump best when there is a horse leading them and when they are bunched up with other runners, but there is little or no need for the rider to worry that he will find himself in front, as his horse will not run freely enough to take him there. Occasionally he will find himself in the bewildering situation of riding a horse who is free on the flat but a sticky jumper, in which case he will have to take pains to restrain him between the fences, so that he always has a horse in front of him when he is jumping, at the same time riding him into his fences in the manner described previously, so that he jumps quickly.

The second category referred to is that of the horse who jumps slowly through lack of confidence. Such a one may be anything but indolent, so that it is more than likely that his confidence will be reduced rather than increased if he is hit. Improvement in his jumping can best be effected by experience in public in the hands of a good rider, who will handle him firmly but gently.

He should be ridden into his fences with the heels, but not, as a rule, with the whip, as the chances are that if he is hit he will be confused and left with unpleasant memories. He should be given every encouragement, in the shape of a clear sight of his fences, no interference from other horses, or from his rider, so that he learns to regard racing as a pleasant experience and to have no fear of the obstacles, then he may eventually jump with boldness, accuracy and alacrity, but if he is hit without knowing what it is all about it is far more likely to discourage him with regard to the future than make him jump well or quickly, and it is quite possible that it will cause him to lose his head completely and fling himself haphazard at the obstacle, with disastrous results to himself and his rider.

In many ways the horse who shows a disinclination to jump for no other reason than that it is contrary to the rider's wishes, is the worst type of the lot. He is usually one of those who refuse to leave the string out at exercise, will either not go on the gallop at all or tears up it twice as fast as the rider wishes, and generally behaves like a spoilt child. Such horses are usually strong-willed by nature, and once they have been allowed to have their own way do not like giving in to their riders' wishes, should these be contrary to their own. They resent any form of corrective chastisement by making every endeavour to get rid of any rider who is bold enough to attempt to administer it, and since they usually succeed, their last state is always worse than the first.

On a racecourse their character is usually expressed by attempts to run out at the slightest opportunity; they seldom try to refuse, but more probably lock the bit in one corner of their mouth so that they are more or less uncontrollable and run out or go through the wing. After the manoeuvre has been successfully exploited they make their way calmly back towards the paddock with what, to the victim, feels like an air of devilish satisfaction. If they do not get the chance to 'do it' on the jockey they often jump well, being too cunning to fall and too bold to refuse.

The curing of such horses can only be effected by a tough, skilled and experienced horseman, of whom there are few, and who will prove to him forcefully and effectively that he cannot have his own way whenever he wants it. As far as the jockey is concerned he can only do his best to see that the horse never has a chance to go wrong; he must always endeavour to have a horse between himself and the wing, never get into the position of being left in front, and never relax his vigilance for an instant.

Even when they have been reformed, such horses can never be trusted. If a rider becomes careless or tries to take a liberty, he may lure the horse back, for the moment at any rate, into his old ways, and I have a very galling recollection of being taken through the wing by one such individual, whom I had been riding for over a year without him ever showing a sign of doing anything wrong, but who dived out in a flash the first time I tried to come up on the inside when there was not much room.

With such horses it is always better to sacrifice going the shortest way to making certain of getting over every fence, and to approach each one under the assumption that one's horse is going to try and run out.

To refer to a horse that gets himself and his rider into trouble because he is too keen as 'bad', is not altogether fair, but the jockey who has taken a crashing fall through his horse's impetuosity is not likely to speak of him in particularly favourable terms, so he must be classed as an undesirable as far as riding him goes.

Horses of this nature are usually honest and straightforward: they have no desire to run out or to refuse, their fault lying in the fact that they are over-bold, with the result that they are undeterred by falls, have no objection to hitting fences, and learn nothing by their mistakes. They usually pull very hard, and in a number of cases their falls are due to the fact that their rider can neither restrain nor control them, so that they are approaching the fence too fast, uncollected and not in control.

In the hands of one experienced in the schooling of show-jumpers and hunters, they could, perhaps, be made to view the obstacles with a measure of respect, but the average trainer has neither the apparatus, time, nor experience to effect this type of cure, and it is left to the jockey to do what he can to keep the horse on his legs and himself on the horse's back, and a strong and skilled rider will often succeed in doing this, but one weaker and less experienced will be certainly doomed.

I speak with a measure of feeling on this subject, since I began—and very nearly ended—my steeplechasing career with a ride on a horse of this description. He was a big, strong chestnut horse, who in the hands of his usual jockey (to whom I do not think he ever gave a fall) won a number of races. When presented with a fence he could not get to it quick enough in his eagerness to reach the other side, and he would hurl himself at it regardless of whether he was meeting it right or wrong. His regular rider was strong enough to prevent him from going too fast and to keep him fairly collected, with the result that he jumped well, and if he did hit a fence was sufficiently well balanced not to fall. However, under my weak and inexperienced handling he was quite out of control, and it was not long before we were both on the ground.

With such horses it is always better to ride a hole or two shorter than usual, as there is then more chance of holding them. They should be kept as calm as possible before the start, in which respect it is advisable to hack-canter down to the post, going down early or well after the others in order not to excite them by working up speed or having horses galloping round them. They should never be jumped out of the gate when the race starts—it is sometimes worth losing ground to the extent of starting in the second rank—and if possible they should be kept in behind the leaders for the greater part of the race.

There will be no question of kicking them into their fences, it will be a matter of holding them, which will depend upon strength, fitness, skill and knowing the individual. A steady pressure is probably better than moving the bit about in his mouth, as that may only throw them off their balance, and the stiller the rider remains, the happier the outcome is likely to be. If he keeps going too fast, one can only lean back, sit tight and hope for the best.

When riding bad jumpers one of the chief problems is to remain on the horse's back when he hits a fence but does not fall himself. As has been said earlier in the book, even good jumpers make mistakes sometimes, but since bad ones naturally are guilty of them much more often I think that this is the place to face the problem in question.

Broadly speaking a horse hits a fence for three reasons: he gets too close to it, he stands too far back or simply does not rise high enough. The first-mentioned type of error is the most likely to end in disaster: it causes a more acute drop in the horse's speed and therefore tests the security of the rider's seat more highly. It is more disastrous in the case of a horse who is going too fast than in that of one who is going to slow, and it takes more out of the horse.

As a general rule, particularly if he knows his horse, a jockey can tell a stride or two away from the fence whether the latter is going to get too close to it or not. If he thinks the worst is going to happen he must prepare to cope with the situation. I think that his best procedure is to straighten his back, sit up, brace his shoulders and take a strong, even pull on his horse's mouth in an endeavour to steady him and in order to try and make him stand back a trifle farther than would otherwise be the case, decreasing his speed slightly, so that the shock of hitting the fence (as far as the rider is concerned) may be lessened. He should slip his reins to as long a length as is reasonable, bring his legs forward and grip as tightly as he can with his legs and knees. Once in the air there is nothing to be gained by hanging on to his head, but the more he can 'fetch him back' before he takes off, the more likely are the pair to survive.

It is not easy to go from the extreme of 'pulling his head off' to giving a horse freedom to land and recover from the shock of hitting a fence, which is the reason why jockeys are so often depicted in the unhappy position of having executed the first half of the operation but not the second. However, they are sometimes rather harshly judged by the camera for though one phase of a jump may show a jockey 'standing on his horse's mouth', in the next he might be seen easing the hold on the reins and starting to bring his body forward, before the horse has landed, so that when they actually touch down the horse has the freedom of his head and his rider is in a position which will offer no hindrance to recovery.

However much it may horrify the theorist, in view of the strength of the average English steeplechase fence, a jockey will have a better chance of staying on the horse in circumstances such as these, if he follows out the method just described, than if he rides according to the text-book. There is no need for him to lean back so that his shoulders are somewhere in the region of the horse's tail, he will do just as well if he sits up straight and squares his shoulders. If he resorts to extremes of leaning back he will find he sacrifices balance and control, but, at the same time, it is worth bearing in mind that when a jockey falls off, in nine cases out of ten it is over a horse's forehand that he goes and not backwards.

To attempt to apply one method to all horses, irrespective of individual traits, is obviously ridiculous, and there are some horses who, when meeting a fence wrong, will put themselves right if left completely alone, but when any effort is made by the rider to 'fetch them back' will become confused and make a mistake. With horses such as these the only measure a jockey can adopt is to sit and suffer, and hope that the horse will put himself right; the less he moves, the better, and while he will be well advised to sit very tight he should neither increase nor slacken his hold on the horse's head while approaching a fence.

If a horse blunders on the landing side he needs complete freedom of his head to regain his balance, and it is better to 'give him the lot' as far as the reins are concerned, at the expense of a temporary loss of control, than to risk 'throwing him down' by interfering with his balance by holding on to his head.

There are several reasons why a mistake made by a horse standing back too far is preferable to that of a horse getting too close to a fence. To start with, horses who stand back at their fences are nearly always bold, keen jumpers. Besides, there is not the same shock to the equilibrium of the rider, since the action of the horse will be more in the nature of sliding over the fence than meeting it head-on—except, of course, in the case of a horse who stands so far back that he dives into it, when he will be very lucky if he does not come down—and save for losing some ground and taking a certain amount of energy out of the horse, it is a predicament from which it is usually not too difficult for the horse and rider to recover.

When a horse stands too far back it is a disadvantage to him if the rider's weight is on his loins, as it will hamper him while he is dragging his hind legs through the fence. This, perhaps, is not the best

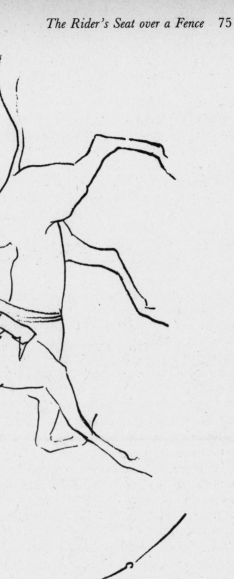

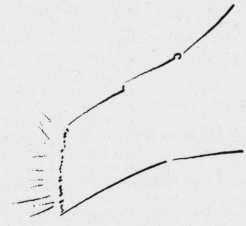

(b) Hitting a fence; the correct way to cope

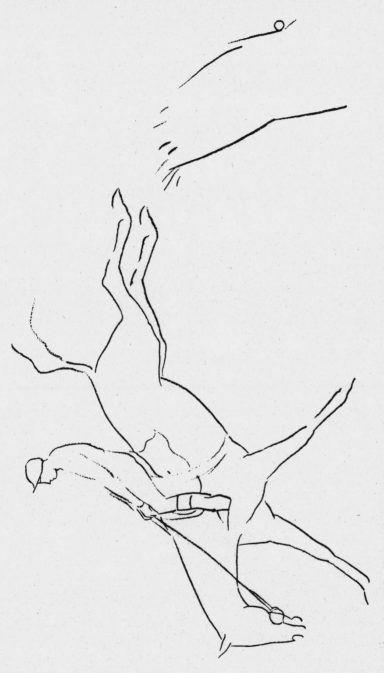

(c) Hitting a fence; the correct way to cope

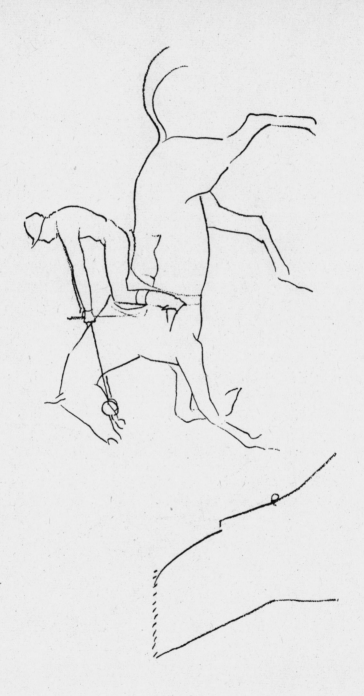

(a) Hitting a fence; the wrong way to cope

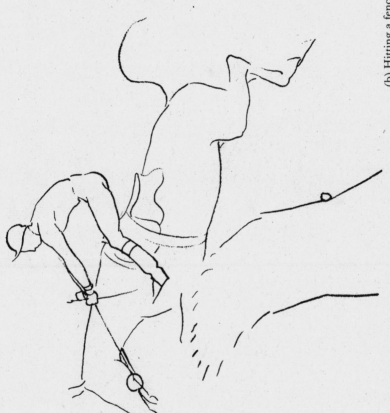

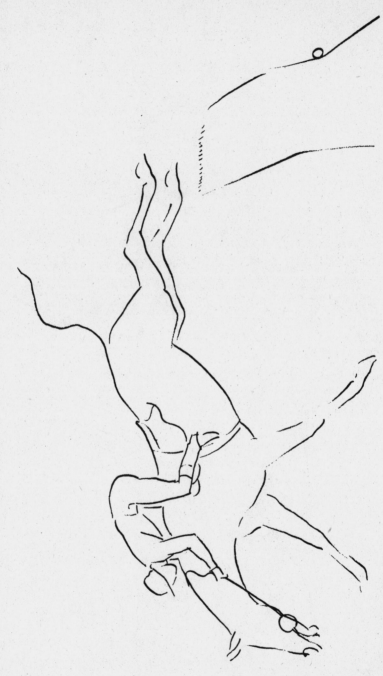

(c) Hitting a fence; the wrong way to cope

(d) Hitting a fence; the wrong way to cope

way of expressing the manoeuvre, since it all happens so quickly, but it is at least indicative of what occurs in, as it were, slow-motion. The rider will, therefore, be best placed if he does not move from the position he took up when he left the ground, which, provided it was not one of exaggeration, should see him through.

So far most of the aspects of a horse making a mistake at a fence have been concerned with the take-off side, but a horse can clear a fence without touching it and still fall on landing. This may happen if he is inclined to land at too steep an angle, perhaps through his particular style of jumping, because of faulty conformation, or as a result of him pecking or stumbling. When riding horses who are inclined to nose-dive on landing, it is advisable not to use any form of forward seat, but instead to keep the body behind, or at least not in front of, the perpendicular to the ground as the horse's fore-feet touch down. As he lands the rider will instinctively feel if all is well or not, and if the former is the case he can swing his body forward again as the hind feet replace the fore-feet, and the horse gallops on. An upright or slightly backward position on the part of the rider does, I think, tend to make the horse land at a less steep angle, and in the case of a horse going on to his nose gives the rider a shade better chance of remaining 'on board' than if he were sitting 'up his neck'.

It is more than probable that he will be shot up the horse's neck in any case, but the fraction of a second taken in being precipitated from the upright or backward position to that on the horse's neck may represent the difference between remaining with the horse and going straight over his head.

When a horse pecks or stumbles after he has landed—as opposed to doing so as he lands—it seems easier to keep with him, even though one is sitting forward, possibly because he is by then horizontal to the ground, and one tends to go down with him rather than in front of him. In this case the rider will be able to afford the horse every opportunity to recover by keeping his weight off the horse's loins, without endangering his own security.

Staying on a horse when he makes a mistake is dependent upon three factors: balance, grip and luck. It is sometimes possible to recover from the most impossible-looking situations, if the horse's body neither twists nor changes direction as a result of its impact with the fence. If, however, this does happen, it is only too easy to be catapulted into the blue, as a result of what seems, from the stands, a comparatively insignificant occurrence.

'You're never off until you're on the floor' is a precept worthy of remembrance, and a jockey who has no more than a grasp of the mane and one heel on the pommel of the saddle has still a chance of getting back into the 'plate'.

IV THE OPEN-DITCH AND WATER-JUMP

In the course of this chapter I have referred to the fences as if each one were exactly similar. This, of course, is not the case, for, apart from Aintree, they fall into three categories: plain fences, open ditches and the water-jump.

While all I have written can, in general, be applied to these three types, such a treatise as this would not be complete without some reference to their individual characteristics and the manner in which they affect the rider's behaviour.

To the plain fence I need not refer, since it is completely covered by all I have ventured to expound already, and it is the open-ditch and water-jump which must now come under consideration.

The open-ditch is an alarming-looking object from the ground, consisting of a fairly substantial ditch, about four feet broad by three deep, guarded by a rail about two feet high, which is boarded or banked so that there is no space between it and the ground, the whole lying in front of a fence some four feet six inches high and two to three feet wide.

It is, therefore, an obstacle spread over quite a considerable area of ground, so that a horse must jump both up and out to clear it successfully. Mercifully it does not look so formidable from a horse's back, since the ditch is not visible, and in the case of those courses at which all fences, except the water jump, are faced with a low board, it is often difficult to distinguish the open ditch from a plain fence, until one is right on top of it.

In view of the wide spread of the obstacle a horse should be going faster rather than slower as he approaches it, in order to have the impetus to carry him over; this does not necessarily mean that he should be tearing into it at a break-neck speed, but that he should be increasing his pace, as opposed to slowing down, in the last few strides.

The fact that the fence itself is preceded by a ditch and a low guard rail means that it is virtually impossible for a horse to take off too near the fence, since the ditch and guard rail force him to stand back, whether he wants to or not, unless he is pig-headed enough to prefer galloping straight into the ditch. Thus there is very little danger of the horse taking off too late, the chief possibility of disaster arising from the likelihood of him taking off too soon and landing on top of the fence.

To avoid these pitfalls the rider's best plan is to make sure that the horse is going well up into his bridle, ride him into the fence with the legs, and not loose his head until he is actually taking off. The more he is ridden into the fence 'on the bridle', the less likely is he to take off too soon, but if his head is loosed a stride too soon he may easily take it as a hint to leave the ground. Horses usually jump this fence better than any other on the course, the reason being, I am sure, that they have to stand back at it. Since it is important that the horse's pace should be increasing rather than decreasing as he comes into the wings, it is essential that he should meet with no interference during the last few strides, and he should, therefore, be given a clear path and time to see the fence—unless he is one of those who will try and shirk the issue if given time to think about it.

A great deal of what has been written about jumping the open-ditch can be applied to the water-jump. The fence is so low in front of it that a horse comes to little or no harm even if he takes off literally underneath it, and the most important factor is that the horse should be going faster—not slower—during the last few strides.

Another aspect of the water-jump is that a horse jumps it at a very flat angle, and that the chief cause of grief at this obstacle is horses tending to land short on the far side; the fence on the take-off can be disregarded as a source of trouble.

From these facts it will be understood that when jumping water it is even more important that a horse should approach at a growing speed, and that he should not take off too soon, and a similar emphasis must be placed upon the necessity of pushing the horse well into his bridle about fifty yards away from the fence, riding him strongly with the legs, up till the last moment, not loosing his head until he is taking off, and giving him a clear view of the fence. Since the angle of descent is very slight there is no need to lean back at all; in fact provided that the horse is going right, the water can be negotiated in the flat race position, but that does not mean that all a rider has to do is to 'set the horse alight' about fifty yards away and sit up his neck—the vital seconds are the last two or three before the horse takes off, and it is not the slightest use starting off at a furious speed and then allowing the horse to slow down as he approaches the wings. The mere fact that the rider is sitting forward will not make the horse spread himself sufficiently to clear the water, in fact, a horse going into the fence properly—at a crescendo—is far more likely to clear the water, even if the rider adopts the backward seat, than is one whose rider is leaning forward, but whose speed is dying.

In jumping the water the situation will sooner or later arise when it will become unpleasantly obvious to the rider that the horse is not

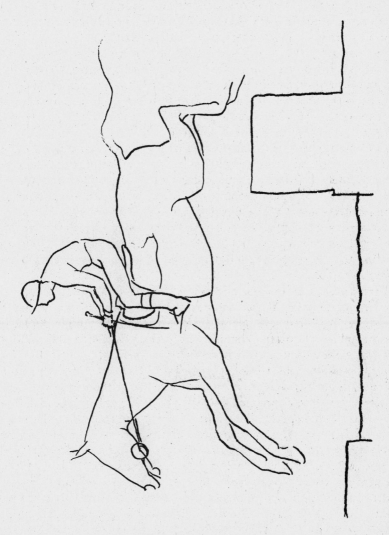

Water-jump; in mid-air

Water-jump; landing

responding sufficiently to the aids applied with the legs to ensure his developing the momentum necessary to carrying him over safely. He will then have to have recourse to the whip. In using this he should take care not to apply it in such a way that it will cause the horse to take off too soon—a lesson brought sharply home to the writer by a Bank Holiday immersion in the water at Wolverhampton. If hit suddenly when within two or three strides off a fence, a horse may take off as soon as the blow falls, which does not matter very much in the case of an ordinary fence, but which, when jumping the water, may easily cause him to land in the middle of it.

I think that the best way to avoid this is to start hitting him well outside the wings, and to 'pepper' him with a series of sharp, quick slaps right up to the moment he takes off, at the same time keeping a firm, even hold of his head.

It is sometimes enough to give the horse a couple of good cracks about fifty yards away, which may answer the purpose by putting him well into his bridle and making him quicken his pace at the rider's wish, because he is wondering when he is going to receive another dose of the treatment, but the choice of measures must be made according to the characteristics of the horse in question and the manner in which he is going.

In this chapter I have endeavoured to present the purely practical aspect of the rider's task, suggesting the means by which, from my own experience of the subject tempered with that of others, he is most likely to remain with his horse from start to finish, under some of the various circumstances with which he may be confronted, and on some of the types of horses he may be called upon to ride.

That practice should walk hand in hand with theory is, I realize, eminently desirable, and it is only by careful study of, and experimenting with, different theoretical ideas, that the best practical answer can be arrived at. But at no time should the theoretical be allowed to take precedence over the practical, for a steeplechase-rider is judged, not by his style, but by the results he produces, and rather than attempt to mould himself to the pattern of any particular school, he should concentrate upon the best practical means of remaining in the saddle, keeping the horse on his feet and getting from the starting-gate to the winning-post before his rivals.

He must learn to recognize and cope with the various predicaments in which he may find himself; he must be able to adapt himself to the different types of horses he will have to ride, and his aim should be the perfect execution of the various methods best suited to all the situations in which he may find himself.

Since his first objective is not to fall off he must give thought to the best means of remaining in the saddle, not only when his horse is jumping well—which is not a very difficult matter—but when he is riding a bad jumper, and he must always be alive to the possibility of a horse making an unexpected mistake.

His next aim being to keep his horse on his feet he must concentrate upon how he is going to ride into every fence, determining his actions according to the characteristics and behaviour of his horse, keeping him clear of trouble and giving him a fair chance to jump.

Steeplechasing in England is a very specialized branch of equitation, to which the rider will often have to sacrifice precepts by which other branches are bounded. As he approaches each fence he should ask himself: How are we meeting it—are we likely to hit it? What is my best way of getting this particular horse over quickly and safely? In what position am I least likely to fall off?' Not, 'Am I doing as the so-and-so school says I should?'

Good style is the artistic application of effective measures and marks the difference between the purely practical and the polished horseman. It is a pleasing adjunct of any activity, but is not an essential quality. Gordon Richards did not have a good style, but no one could say he was not a good jockey, and while the beginner should be encouraged to develop a good style as he learns, it is more important that he should pay attention to his actions than to his appearance.

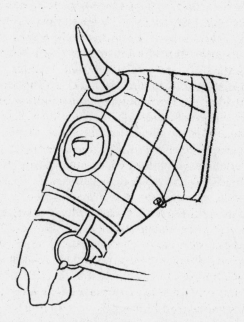

5
Keeping Fit

NO MATTER HOW good a jockey a man may be he cannot do either
his horse or himself justice if he is unfit. Fitness for any particular task
might be described as the state of mind and body in which that task
can best be carried out, so that though a man may be thoroughly fit for
one activity does not by any means ensure that he will be in a condition to produce his best performance in another, and badly-planned
training can be as ill-effective as none at all.

One of the reasons I am devoting a chapter to this subject is that
nowadays even the keenest of amateur riders do not always have the
opportunity of keeping themselves fit by riding work every day of
their lives, which is the best way of achieving the objective, and it
therefore becomes necessary to find some alternative method of
preparing the various muscles and the breathing apparatus to withstand the strain that will be placed upon them when riding in a race.

To arrive on a course in an unfit state to ride a horse is as good as
swindling the owner and the public, as it will amount to placing anything up to a 14-lb. penalty on the horse's back, and so far as the rider
is concerned is likely to terminate his association with the stable in
question, discourage anyone else from putting him up, and not
improbably cause him to have a bad fall.

Success cannot be bought. Rich young men (if there are any
nowadays) may imagine that all they have to do is to buy a good-class
'chaser to sweep the board in races for soldiers and amateurs, in which
their more impecunious opponents are nothing like so well mounted,
but such meetings as the Grand Military at Sandown prove, time and
again, that a good horse is useless unless his rider can sit on him, is fit
enough to control him and offer him no interference, while a moderate horse ridden by a capable rider in good condition will always beat
a good horse, whose jockey is unfit and unskilled.

It is a popular misconception among laymen that hacking and
hunting can keep a rider fit for racing. This might have been so in the
days when the same length of stirrup-leather was adopted for all types

of equitation, but today, when the more effective results of using shortened leathers when race-riding have made the practice necessary to good performances over fences, this is not so. The two methods require the use of different muscles—or the use of the same muscles in a different way: a long hack or a day's hunting with one's leathers at racing length, though it might answer the purpose as regards getting the rider's race-riding muscles in trim, would in all probability end in giving the horse a sore back, while riding in a steeplechase at hunting length results in a faulty distribution of weight and difficulty in holding a puller.

Hunting is a very good foundation to steeplechasing, and it is a great help in keeping the muscles of the arms and back in good order, but it will not answer the whole question of the steeplechase-rider's fitness problem, for, except for the wind, the most vital part of the anatomy with regard to race-riding is the muscle that runs along the top of the thigh, which, particularly in the case of those who are long from knee to hip, is liable to cramp when the rider has been sitting for some time in the racing position. This is accentuated on the flat and over hurdles, where, as opposed to riding over fences, almost no change of position takes place throughout the race, so that it is most important to ensure that this muscle is in good order, which cannot be done by ordinary hunting or hacking.

Provided a rider has laid a good foundation of fitness by past experience and practice, it is quite possible for him to keep perfectly fit without even seeing a horse. I tested this theory out during the war with some effect. Admittedly I was a hundred per cent fit when I rode an exercise gallop for the last time before being sent abroad in September, but from the end of September until towards the end of the following May, when I had a ride at Newton Abbot when on leave, I never went near a horse beyond two half-hour rides on ponies borrowed from the Indian R.A.S.C., during which sessions it was not possible to go out of a trot.

I kept fit by doing exercises (for my thigh muscles), running (for my wind) and digging (for my arms and shoulders)—the gun-pits upon which my energies were directed in the last-named operation, proved more valuable as a means of preparing me for Newton Abbot than as any deterrent to the foe—and I finished fifth in the race, a two-mile steeplechase—without feeling any more distressed than if I had been riding a dozen races every week.

I do not say that this would have been possible in the case of anyone whose frame had not been moulded and hardened by several years of riding—I had been a pupil in a racing stable for the previous nine years and had ridden hunting, racing, exercise gallops and schooling during that time—but I do know that I would have been quite unfit to do justice to the horse had I not taken somewhat drastic measures to preserve the condition I had achieved. I am sure that it is of the greatest help for any rider, not only to employ some of the means which I shall suggest, when riding exercise gallops and schooling is impossible, but to use them as an addition to the latter activities, until he is getting enough regular riding in public to preclude any further necessity for their practice.

To keep one's wind clear is a simple business and can be done by any such means as running, playing squash, or boxing. I do not smoke myself so cannot say to what extent this habit affects a jockey. At one time, something like four out of the six leading N.H. jockeys were, I believe, non-smokers, but I think that this was probably coincidence, and I doubt if smoking makes much difference, provided that a jockey is riding regularly and often in public. If he is not doing so it might mean that he has to take more trouble in keeping his wind clear than in the case of a non-smoker, and I think smoking is probably a help to restraining the pangs of hunger among those unfortunate riders who have to waste to keep their weight down.

The question of wasting is a serious one in the life of a great number of jockeys and will be discussed later, but for the moment the subject is the general fitness of the body, and of the thigh muscles in particular. There are several ways of keeping these trained: one is to ride a motor-bicycle, adopting the same position as when riding on the flat in a race, with the seat just clear of the saddle. This is still more effective if done on a bumpy road (cobbled roads as found in France provide excellent going for this purpose, as the vibration exercises the arm muscles as well). Another is riding a bicycle with the seat much too low by ordinary standards, standing on the pedals without sitting down in the saddle. Though not particularly enjoyable it is better to ride uphill, as this makes harder work and provides the dual purpose of exercising the lungs as well.

The third is the simplest and, in many ways, the most useful, as it is also a great help in maintaining rhythm in riding a finish. It consists of two stages: the first merely in squatting down in the exact position adopted when riding on the flat, and holding it. It sounds extremely simple—and is, if one stops when one's muscles begin to tire—but its value lies in holding the position as long as possible, and it is as well to start rather unambitiously with a minute, working up to five or more—I once got as far as nine. Besides training the thigh muscles to stand up to the strain of remaining in one position for some time on end, this exercise helps a rider to cultivate the habit of sitting still and not bumping up and down in the saddle.

It is quite a good plan to check one's position in the mirror, in order to avoid getting into the habit of hunching the shoulders and rounding the back; if desired the boredom can be relieved by reading a book, though the discomfort of the situation is liable to distract one's attention from the interest of the text.

The second phase consists of going from the position already described to one in which the buttocks are just clear of the heels, at the same time moving the arms forward in the position generally adopted in riding a finish, and then returning to the original stance, drawing the arms back. If this is repeated about a hundred to two hundred times (the number can be worked up gradually) in approximately the same tempo as employed in riding a finish on a horse, it not only exercises all the muscles used in the operation on a racecourse, but it helps one to co-ordinate the action of hands and heels—when he rides a finish on a horse the rider's hands should go forward as his heels go back—and avoid the embarrassing situation of getting out of time with the horse, which not only looks bad but is detrimental to the horse's progress.

If examined carefully it will be seen that the movement of legs and arms in this exercise are exactly the same as in the real thing. A further modification is to swing the left or right arm as one would when using the whip, that is to say forward when the buttocks go down towards the heels and back when they come up again. It is a good way to become accustomed to using the whip in whichever hand one finds it most difficult; after hitting a horse once in the eye, once on the ear and at the third attempt missing it altogether, I came to the conclusion that it was preferable to become comparatively proficient with my left hand in private, before experimenting in public, and I have found the method described a considerable help to improvement in this respect.

Another way of doing these exercises is to fix a saddle on an ordinary saddle-room horse and go through the motions of both holding the flat-racing position and riding a finish. It has the advantage of offering scope for bringing in to play the additional factor of the reins, which can be fixed to the wall opposite, and of the whip for the swinging of which there is ample room, so that one can practise changing the whip from one hand to the other without dropping the reins or getting them tangled into a sort of 'cat's cradle'.

The whip is a subject which deserves a section on its own, so details of its use—and abuse—will not be attempted here.

Clenching and unclenching one's hand helps to strengthen the wrist and hand muscles. The exercise can be varied from opening and shutting one's hands continuously and hard, to keeping them tightly clenched for a minute or two on end. It is possible to buy spring grips for this purpose, and various other apparatuses, but it is a nuisance having to carry such things about, and equally good results can be reached by the simple means I have described, and by manual work—turning the handle of a clipping-machine or chaff-cutter, using an axe and so on.

Other ways of strengthening these muscles of the arms used in riding are by doing 'pull-ups' on a bar, or any convenient place—a stair-landing sometimes presents a possibility—by clasping the hands behind the head and pulling against each other, and any other similar exercise: 'press-ups' are not of much value, as it is the pulling muscles that are the important ones in race-riding.

The best exercise of all is, of course, to ride horses that pull and bore, the worse the better, and, in fact, in all aspects of riding, bad horses, so long as they do not finish him off altogether—do more towards making a competent rider than good ones, though an occasional good ride is, of course, essential in imbuing—or restoring—confidence, and preventing complete despair.

Wasting is one of the worst aspects of a jockey's life. It is harder on a jumping jockey than on one who rides only on the flat, since it has to be done during the coldest part of the year. While the prospect of riding an indifferent jumper in a novices 'chase in a freezing wind tempered with sleet is bad enough at the best of times, it is even less attractive on a diet of dry toast and sauna baths.

Unless a great deal of weight must be removed I think it is less enervating to reduce one's weight by exercise than by a sauna bath, but the latter means is much simpler. I am not well qualified to write on this particular subject, since I have only had to take off weight about three times in my life, but I think it is preferable to put up a couple of pounds over-weight and be strong, rather than waste to the extent of being too weak, and anyone likely to have to keep his weight down over any long period of time is well advised to do so under medical supervision with regard to diet and procedure in general.

Apart from wasting, the question of eating before riding is, I think worth mentioning. It is not advisable to ride on a full stomach, for besides tending to make one sick after a fall, and possibly to complicate any internal injury, the brain is not so clear, the perceptions so quick, nor the breathing so easy, as on an empty one. It is my personal habit, when I have a ride, to eat nothing from after breakfast until after the race, but there are probably a number of different views on the subject.

It is also as well to wait half an hour or so before eating much after the race is over, otherwise the penalty may be indigestion. To make hard and fast rules for different individuals is impossible, and I have seen jockeys cramming the most formidable-looking slabs of race-course cake into their mouths between races with no apparent ill-effects, but I would not advise it on principle, suggesting instead a stimulant in the shape of glucose barley-sugar, which is a source of energy without bulk.

I have often been asked about partaking of 'jumping-powder' in the form of alcohol before a race. This, again, is a matter for personal taste and must depend upon the effect of alcohol on the individual, which can be extensive and startling in its divergence in different people. I have only resorted to the experiment once, that was to have a glass of port between races at a point-to-point, because I was feeling ill, but, excellent though it was, I do not attribute the fact that I rode the next winner to the glass of port, since the horse in question had about three stone in hand.

It has not been unknown for jockeys to ride good races when drunk, but such cases have been in respect of good jockeys who have succumbed either to dissipation or the necessity of a panacea for lost nerve; in the former case it seems reasonable to expect that they would probably have ridden a rather better race sober, in the latter it is a sign that the end of their career is at hand. Without claiming to be any authority on the subject I think that the effect of alcohol on a jockey is to make him think that he is riding better than he is, and that when he feels the need to avail himself of 'Dutch Courage' he should retire, before an over-generous dose brings about an interview with the stewards and the loss of his licence or permit.

A jockey who is really fit is not so liable to hurt himself as one who is not. To start with, he is less liable to fall off, has better control over his horse, and as a result is more likely to keep his horse on his legs, besides which he stands a better chance of not hurting himself if he hits the ground.

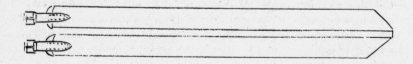

6
Riding Work

ON THE PRINCIPLE that a jockey should be physically fit to ride before he engages himself to do so, I have attacked the chapter devoted to this subject before approaching that of riding exercise work or schooling gallops, which he will most probably be asked to do on the horse he is to ride in a race.

In the case of an experienced rider there may not be much to be gained by riding a horse at home before partnering him in public, unless he has some particular trait that wants knowing. An old hand will size a horse up as he canters down to the post, and it will be sufficient for the trainer to mention any peculiarity which the horse may possess: perhaps a tendency to jump to the left or right, the fact that he does or does not want kicking into his fences, or some other such detail, for him to be able to decide upon and put into practice the actions he will take in order to overcome it. It may even be better not to ride the horse at home at all: some horses are bad rides on the training-ground but do nothing wrong on a racecourse—I believe the great Golden Miller pulled very hard at home but was a perfect ride in a race—in which case it will probably only upset the horse and fray the jockey's confidence, if the latter rides him in a pre-race gallop at home, but on the whole I think it is a great help to be able to get to know a horse before riding him in a race.

When riding out at any racing stable the first rule is to arrive on time. If a stable is to be run on efficient lines punctuality is essential: a trainer's plans may be completely thrown out if he is delayed in his morning's work, so that any jockey or amateur who turns up half an hour late is neither likely to be well received nor asked to ride out again, particularly if his presence is due to the trainer's indulgence rather than to any particular ability of his own.

Although we live in an informal age impression counts for a good deal, and while some trainers are not in the least interested in the appearance or turn-out of their jockeys or employees, it is never particularly advisable—in fact it is a breach of manners—to arrive unshaven and 'dirty on parade'. The most suitable wear is jodhpurs and some form of golf jacket, the former are light, neat and easily packed, the latter allow for free movement round the shoulders and the wearing of several layers of sweaters underneath. Boots are more comfortable than shoes, but they should not be too heavy or clumsy: the average stirrup-iron provided is small compared to a hunting-stirrup, and a big boot or shoe might get stuck in it with regrettable results in the case of a fall. A regulation safety helmet is essential.

Most trainers are not at their best at about 7.30 a.m., and they react better to silence than to chatty accounts of their guest's riding ability or triumphs in the local point-to-point, and unless he happens to be a prospective, wealthy owner—in which case his conversation will be endured for diplomatic reasons—the guest will create a far better impression by keeping his mouth shut and doing what he is told. The trainer is probably thinking about his morning's plans, a subject quite complicated enough in itself without interruptions, and any form of distraction will only serve to annoy him. The course to follow, therefore, is to listen attentively to any instructions concerning the horse one is told to ride, and then go and get on it. The horse will be led into the yard from his box by the stable lad who 'does' him and who will give the jockey a leg up.

When this has been done his task is over. From then on the horse is, in theory if not always in practice, under the command of the man on his back, and the latter cannot expect the lad to hang about holding the horse's head while he adjusts his stirrup-leathers: the lad is probably riding out himself, if not he will be required to help in getting the other horses out and his time is precious.

Before leaving the precincts of the yard for the gallops the string usually walks round until every horse is out. This gives an opportunity to try the girths, take a quick look at the bridle, martingale and any other piece of equipment the horse may be wearing, and to adjust one's stirrup-leathers to a suitable length. If the opportunity arises it is better to slip into the box beforehand and have a look round the horse's tack: stable-boys, particularly these days, are by no means infallible and are quite capable of sending a horse out with the bit too low or too high in the horse's mouth, the saddle pressing on his withers, the nose-band chafing him, or the martingale improperly adjusted, and though the responsibility does not rest with the visiting rider, he will have to put up with any effects that the consequent discomfort may produce in the horse. It will be to his advantage if he can see anything wrong and make the necessary adjustments to prevent any undesirable occurrence taking place.

When riding in the string the first point to bear in mind is not to get too close to the horse in front; he may kick, and a direct hit on one's own horse will not be popular with anyone.

Some trainers have no objection to their boys smoking out at exercise, others take the gravest exception to the practice, and it is therefore a more tactful policy to find out his idiosyncrasies by observation than by the trial-and-error system.

The routine in various stables varies, but probably because of the cold most jumping trainers give their horses a trot before they work. At all times the rider's attention should be on his horse. If he goes to sleep he may find himself in the most obscure of predicaments, from the horse going over backwards through playing with his martingale and getting the ring over his tooth, to finding him making amorous or bellicose advances on one of his stable mates, according to sex and circumstance. When riding a colt it is advisable to keep him clear of other horses, when on a filly it is tempting providence to parade her under the nose of a colt. When the string is trotting one should keep one's eyes and ears open for the word to walk again, in order to avoid running into the horse in front, when he returns, sometimes very suddenly, to the walk.

In an early chapter the various aspects of the rider's seat were considered in some detail, so that it will not be necessary to refer to them again. The length he rides depends upon his individual taste, but if he has been warned that he is riding a horse who is liable to 'put one in', he will be advised not to try and show off by riding shorter than the average flat race jockey; it is always possible to pull one's leathers up before working, and one is more likely to stay on the horse's back by riding reasonably as opposed to exaggeratedly short.

With practice it is possible to remain on the horse, in spite of short leathers, in some surprising circumstances, but it is very difficult to do so if he bucks. However, as a rule horses in training do not do anything much worse than whip round, jump and kick, or occasionally stand on their hind legs. Many of them, particularly when they are in strong work, are as quiet as an old hunter. As horses nearly always whip round to the left rather than the right, it is, therefore, as well, when riding at exercise, to carry one's whip in the left hand.

Nearly all horses go best when ridden on a long rein, and when walking in the string, provided a perceptible contact is maintained with his mouth, a horse is best ridden in this way, and not irritated with a short and vice-like grip of the reins.

Before doing strong work the team usually do a steady canter in single file. Horses get to know the routine and they will often take only a light hold of their bit in the preliminary canter, but pull hard when they work the second time, knowing that they are expected to go a degree or two faster. Unless he has 'had his card marked' the stranger will have to find this out for himself, but he is almost certain to have been given some form of warning of what he must expect in the way of his horse's behaviour, so that he can mentally prepare his plan of riding him.

The two chief crimes to avoid when cantering in the string are: first, getting too close to the horse in front, and second, passing the horse in front. It is bad enough getting too close to a horse when walking or trotting, but it is a hundred times worse when cantering, since there is a very good chance of one's horse striking into the horse in front and cutting through his tendon, or otherwise injuring him.

When riding horses that pull hard there is a strong temptation to get on the leading horse's tail, in order to try to induce one's own horse to drop his bit and stop pulling, but apart from the risk involved, the move is more than likely to upset the horse in front and cause him to pull, to the resultant natural anger of his rider.

The same thing happens when one horse passes another in the string, and if the unfortunte rider in question is sufficiently out of control he is liable to go dashing past one horse after the other, until he has reached the head of the string, having given his horse a good gallop instead of the prescribed steady loosener-up, and caused all the horses he has passed to catch hold of their bits and try to follow him.

In riding all horses that pull, half the battle is in how they set off at the beginning of the canter. If a horse jumps straight into his stride and gets, as it were, first run on the rider, the latter has little or no chance of steadying him. If he begins quietly and sedately he will be well up the canter before he starts really to take hold and pull, and with luck he may not pull at all.

To see a good horseman set a horse off up the canter is both an education and a delight. The pair walk on without any fuss or flurry, the horse's pricked ears showing that he is keen but at peace with his rider, the latter sitting down in the saddle, still and quiet, with a long rein, his hands giving and taking to the pull on the reins, playing the horse's mouth as a good fisherman plays a salmon. Finally, the horse breaks into a canter with the smooth, liquid movement of a wave gently breaking and sliding up the beach, the rider leans forward, bringing his seat just clear of the saddle, and the pair get under way with the rhythm and precision of a faultless machine. From such an example more can be learnt than from anything that it is possible to put on paper, nevertheless, there are several principles which, if carefully observed, help to produce a happy result.

One should never start clawing at the horse's mouth about a hundred yards from the canter's end; it will remind him that he is going to work and will make him start thinking about it before he need, with the result that, if he is keen or excitable by nature, he will be bouncing and pirouetting about like a ballet dancer by the time he has to set off. Instead of going quietly on to the canter and setting off slowly, he will probably begin to sweat and will dash away with a Nijinsky-like bound, continuing, either at much too fast a pace, or with his rider pulling him all over the place in an attempt to restrain him.

Whenever a horse feels a change of grip on the reins he knows that something is up, so that the longer he is left without being given any such warning the quieter is he likely to remain. It is therefore best either to go on to the canter with the same length of rein as in use when approaching it—that is to say a long rein—shortening it as he breaks into a canter but before he has been able to get up speed, or to shorten the reins with so light a touch that the horse does not know what is happening, before he reaches the point of departure.

As a general rule the first-named method is the most satisfactory, but it is important to acquire the desired length of rein for the cantering pace itself, before the horse has got going, since a change of grip when once he is under way is sure to make him want to go faster. The success of the manœuvre depends upon the psychological moment at which the reins are shortened from the walking length to the cantering length, which is largely a matter of practice, experience and observation. Until he has actually broken into a canter the rider will help to preserve the horse's calmness if he sits down in his saddle, only assuming the racing position when he has got going.

There are some horses who go best when ridden on a very short rein, with one's hands held low down on either side of the neck. Such horses usually carry their heads rather high, and tend to swing them about as soon as the rider's hands come up at all, and, except for being told beforehand, the way to ride them must be discovered by trial and error.

A great many racehorses have one-sided mouths, brought about by various causes, such as being ridden by boys who cannot quite hold them except by pulling their heads round to one side or the other; they have little or no feeling on one side, but throw their heads about when touched on the other. With them one can only feel one's way and try to find the key that produces comparative comfort to the horse and a measure of control for the rider.

If a horse hangs to one side or the other, I think it is usually best to ride him on the rein of the side to which he hangs: if he hangs to the right, ride him on the right rein, and *vice versa*, otherwise he will tend only to bring his head round more, but make no change of inclination.

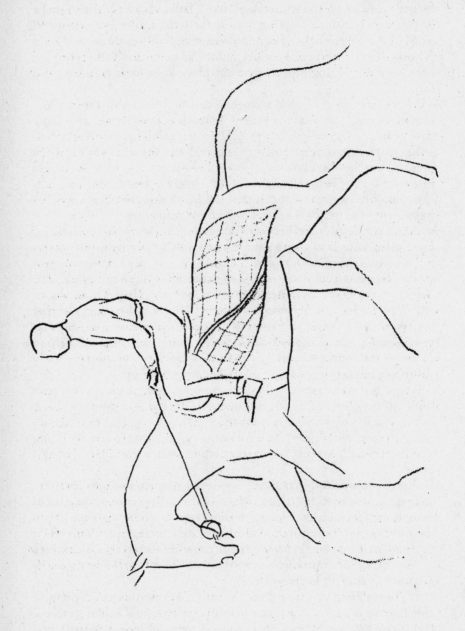

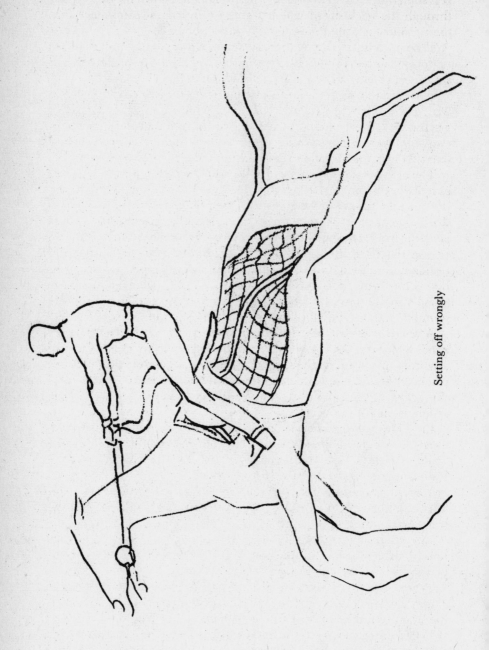

Setting off wrongly

It is sometimes a help to ride bad-mouthed horses with the little finger through the neck-strap, which seems to give them confidence that their mouths are not going to be mauled about.

The way a horse goes is directly dependent upon the ability of the man who has been riding him regularly, and a good or bad horseman can make or mar a horse if he rides him long enough.

When pulling up at the end of the canter it is again necessary to look where one is going, in order to avoid running into other horses, getting kicked, or having to pull up so sharply that the horse is in danger of jarring or straining a muscle or tendon. Having pulled up one should return to one's place in the string.

The next procedure will be to walk round for a few minutes, before either working on the flat or schooling over fences or hurdles. During this time the trainer will begin sorting out the horses that are going to work together and changing over the riders to apportion the weights according to his liking. This is no time to day-dream about the stylish way in which (in one's own mind at any rate) the last manœuvre has been accomplished, but to pay attention to what is going on, in order not to miss any order that may concern oneself, such as taking the horse's rug or sheet off, changing on to another horse, or joining a group or stable companion preparatory to going off to work.

At this stage it is extremely important to try the girths, to see if they need tightening. At a slow exercise-canter there is no great danger of anything untoward happening in the way of the saddle slipping, but when galloping or jumping a much greater strain is placed on everything, and it is essential to take every precaution in seeing that the saddle is reasonably secure.

In riding gallops and schooling there are several principles that must be observed, if it is hoped to repeat the procedure with the same trainer. Always make quite sure you understand exactly what the trainer wants you to do. If not, ask.

Never go faster than you have been told to: going too slow never hurt any horse, but going too fast may mean leaving a race on the training-ground.

Keep a straight course, avoiding crossing or interfering with other horses; the gallop has been arranged for the benefit of all the participants, and is not a race.

When riding schooling on a good jumper do not show off at the expense of the less experienced jumpers in the school. Your horse is there to teach them, not to discourage them.

When the work is over, the horse's girths should be loosened immediately, about three holes, so that they are slack enough to give him the full benefit, but not so loose that the saddle can move about.

Some trainers have their horses led home, allowing them to stop and graze for a few minutes on the way in. At such times one should be careful to see that the horse does not get his leg over the rein, as it is likely to scare him, resulting in him, and possibly some of his companions, getting loose and perhaps slipping up on the road, running into a wire fence, or light-heartedly kicking other members of the string. Before dismounting it is essential to put up the stirrup-irons by sliding them up the leathers as far as they will go and threading the leathers through; if they are allowed to hang loose the horse may take a grab at one and get it caught in his mouth.

Occasion may arise when the trainer requires the visiting jockey to come out on a hack instead of on a racehorse, and to accompany him until the time comes for him to get on the horse he is going to ride schooling or work. Under these circumstances it is worth remembering that if there is one action calculated to infuriate a trainer, it is for his guest to ride between him and his horses. He will be scrutinizing them for any sign of lameness, excitability or indisposition, and he cannot do this with someone on a horse between him and his string, and anyone riding with him should always keep on his other side.

As with huntsmen, trainers do not appreciate having someone riding 'in their pockets'; they may wish to canter off to give a fresh order to lads who are trotting away towards the start of the gallop, or they may wish to jump in during the last furlong or so of a gallop: if there are other riders immediately beside or behind them it is not difficult for a collision to take place, so that trainers should always be given room to manœuvre and not be too closely shadowed.

To be able to ride out regularly in a racing stable is the best training a prospective steeplechase-rider can have, once he has learnt to ride—unless he is a moderately competent horseman already his presence will not be very welcome—and to have the opportunity to do so is a privilege which should be both recognized and appreciated.

Some people appear to think that they are doing the trainer a good turn by placing their services at his disposal, which in respect of top class riders may certainly be the case. But inexperienced amateurs—or professionals—do not belong to this category and should, therefore, take pains to cause the trainer no displeasure, since there are only too many rivals anxious to obtain this type of practice, and one who is either a nuisance or is incompetent is easily replaced.

From the time a rider leaves the yard to the time he returns he is under the trainer's orders, and must do as he is told. If he wishes to remain in favour he should avoid asking whether he may ride another horse instead of the one appointed to him, and should raise no objection regarding riding a school or a gallop, even if he feels extremely disinclined to undertake the task.

Anyone foolhardy enough to take up steeplechase-riding must be prepared to take the rough with the smooth, and no trainer is going to be bothered trying to teach an embryo jockey if he is not enthusiastic enough to do what he is told, regardless of the possible consequences.

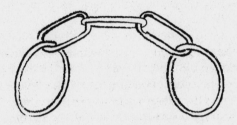

7

Equipment

THE TWO MOST important factors with regard to equipment is that it must be comfortable, and it must be reliable. There is nothing worse than riding in a pair of boots that are too tight, and faulty girths or stirrup-leathers may mean losing a race: it is therefore essential to be properly set up both sartorially and with regard to saddlery.

Anyone who is riding regularly and often should be possessed of two pairs of racing breeches and a pair of macintosh breeches, which are a great boon in wet weather, a pair of racing boots, which should on no account be made to fit too tightly, a crash-helmet, a pair of leg-guards (elastic stockings without a foot, which stretch from below the knee to the ankle bone and are sold at any chemist for the use of those with varicose veins) to prevent one's shins being chafed, a white scarf to go round the neck, pants (long and short), vest, sweater and women's stockings.

He will also need two saddles of weights proportionate to his own—I had a 14-lb. saddle and another about 6 lb.—so that he can do light weights conveniently and big weights without undue bulk of weight-cloths; the last named are provided by the valet.

A rider who is just starting on his career need not be alarmed at this long list, for he can arrive on the course without a single article of equipment and be fitted out with everything he requires by the valet appointed to look after him, but he cannot expect this to be done indefinitely if he is going to ride regularly, in which case he must set about getting these things for himself.

In the matter of breeches, boots and saddles it is advisable to go to firms who specialize in making these articles for racing purposes. The expert in making hunting-breeches is not guaranteed to prove as skilled in the cutting of racing breeches, and a firm which specializes in hunting saddles does not necessarily produce as good racing saddles.

In all matters of equipment it·is advisable to consult the particular racecourse valet into whose charge one is given, by whoever brings about the introduction to the dressing-room. He will obtain all such garments as vests, pants, leg-guards, skull-cap, sweater and scarf, and will probably be able to help in the matter of finding second-hand boots and saddles, if one wishes to save the expense of buying new ones.

He will also, if necessary, produce a whip, but I think it is more satisfactory to buy one, as the matter of length varies greatly with individual taste, short-armed riders tending to prefer long whips, and *vice versa*. In the matter of whips, too, it is better to go to a saddler who specialises in racing equipment rather than to a fashionable London shop, whose whips look exceedingly smart but in comparison with those of a saddler who specializes in racing tack, are apt to lack balance. All whips should have a leather tab on the end, to prevent them from cutting a horse, but it is better to have the tab cut fairly narrow in order that it can be pulled through the hand easily, when the whip is brought into action by the hand other than that in which it is carried. If the tab is too wide it necessitates opening one's hand to let it through, which may cause the rein to be dropped.

There are two main designs in whips, one having the shaft of the whip quite plain, the other bound with leather for about six inches down the shaft, the binding finishing with a ring made of the material with which the shaft of the whip is covered, which is usually cat-gut, but sometimes kangaroo hide. I prefer the latter design, since the ring affords a pivot upon which to twist the whip between the fingers when producing it for use in the hand in which it is carried, as opposed to pulling it through and using it with the other hand, and prevents it from slipping through one's fingers when carried at rest.

Most jockeys who use the plain-shafted type wind an elastic band round the shaft at a convenient pivoting point, and in this case there is the advantage of being able to put the ring so formed in any desired place. I have used both types and there is not really anything to choose between them, except that the elastic can wear through and break and needs watching and periodical replacing, whereas the handle type is a permanency.

On no account should a whip with a wrist loop be used. This gadget may be admirable in the case of cowboys, who have to use a lassoo as well and therefore have to drop their whip when doing so, and is excusable in polo players who have the additional complication of a polo stick to cope with, but in racing it means that the whip can only be used in one hand, and a jockey who is so uncertain of his ability to carry a whip without dropping it as to need a wrist loop would be better occupied learning how to hold and use one in the Row, than in appearing in an operational capacity on a racecourse.

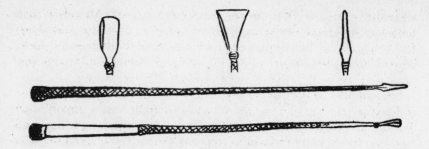

The layman finds interest in details which, through familiarity with them, the professional would not even think of mentioning, and the case of the amateur rider who appeared at his first point-to-point in the unusual guise of having his racing jacket outside his breeches and when questioned about it answered, 'but what does one do with one's braces?' prompts me to deal with the sartorial question from the most elementary of aspects.

Every garment a jockey wears has its particular use and meaning, and though details differ according to individual tastes, the general plan is the same.

Riding in winter is a cold business, and it is therefore advisable to wear enough to keep reasonably warm without hindering the freedom of arms and shoulders, so that most jockeys, unless they are having difficulty in doing the weight, put on a vest and a woollen sweater with long sleeves under the racing colours. I have, on occasion, worn two sweaters—when the colours provided were silk and not in the form of a woollen sweater—but I am inclined to think that this is too much of an encumbrance, particularly on a horse that is likely to need a good deal of hand-riding at the finish, and that it is a case of sacrificing efficiency for comfort.

With ordinary racing breeches, as opposed to macintosh breeches, I think it is better to wear short pants as (if cut well) breeches must fit fairly tight round the knee, so that the additional thickness of a pair of pants tends to hamper the action of the knee joint and stop the circulation. With macintosh breeches, which fit much more loosely, long pants are better; some jockeys even wear macintosh breeches over their ordinary ones, but this, I would say, is not a good plan, as it is far too cumbersome an arrangement.

On one's legs long women's stockings are best. They are not too thick, so do not interfere either with the action of the knee or with the circulation, and they prevent the inside of the knee from being chafed, while they are warm but light.

If one's breeches are on the loose side round the legs it is neater to wear the leg-guards over the stockings and under the breeches, than between breeches and boots, since in the latter case they show above the boots, but if the former method means that one is going to be uncomfortable it is wiser to wear them over the breeches in spite of appearances. With one pair of my breeches I adopted the first style, with the other the second.

Having put on my breeches I twisted them round so that the buttons lie on the outside of the shin and cannot therefore press into the shin during the race, but nowadays, modern stretch-material enables breeches to be worn without buttons at all.

Tailors who cater mostly for flat race jockeys are very inclined not to allow enough room round the waist of their breeches, since they forget that the rider will, in all probability, be wearing a vest and two thicknesses of wool, instead of a single vest or sweater and a silk jacket only, which is the usual under garb of flat race riders, and it is, therefore, as well to remind them about this when ordering breeches.

As mentioned before, it is essential to have one's boots made so that they do not fit tightly round the calf, which is brought home with some force by a walk back from some far corner of the course after a fall. It is advisable to have fairly substantial heels on one's boots, unless, of course, the wearer has difficulty with his weight, as it reduces the chance of a foot slipping through the stirrup-iron, with the consequent danger of being dragged. It is incorrect, and indeed unnecessary, to have tabs or garters on racing boots: the former belong to the hunting world and the latter are replaced by a small loop designed to fit over one of the breeches buttons, and in any case the breeches should be made to continue well down the leg, to about the bottom of the calf, so that there is no danger of a hiatus between boot and breeches.

There may at first seem to be no particular object in wearing a handkerchief or scarf round one's neck, but this garment has, in fact, a very definite use: it helps to keep one warm, and it offers that slight extra support which, in case of a fall on the head, may mean the difference between a broken neck and a ricked one.

One of the most valuable articles of a jockey's equipment is the crash-helmet or skull-cap, the wearing of which is compulsory. It is most important to replace it by a new one should it have become damaged as a result of a fall.

The silk racing-cap fits over the skull-cap and should be tied securely on with the ribbon attached to the cap for that purpose, so that the cap comes outside and not inside the ears. Should the ribbon be broken, or not long enough, the cap can be secured by an elastic band, of which each valet keeps a supply.

Every jockey worthy of the name should be capable of tying up his own cap, and should see to it, or if in difficulty should get his valet to do so, before he leaves the weighing-room. Society papers are very fond of depicting competitors in races having the ribbon of their caps tied by their wives or feminine admirers, but whatever the pictorial value of such an incident, so far as the racing world is concerned it merely suggests that the hero of the scene either cannot do his cap up because his hands are trembling too much from apprehension, or is too slovenly to get it seen to before he comes into the parade ring. Whether tied in a bow or a knot, the ends of the ribbon should be tucked away and not be left hanging down or emulating the bow on a chocolate-box.

If he is wearing a silk jacket the rider will be provided with a safety-pin by the valet to hold the collar together, and with a pair of elastic bands to put round the wrists in order to keep the sleeves from flapping about. These are usually also worn round the wrists if the colours are in the form of a woollen sweater, but in the latter case are not so necessary.

Spurs should only be worn if the trainer of the horse one is riding gives directions to this effect; the valet will provide them, and they should on no account be sharp, in case they lacerate a horse, which may easily happen in the course of a fall or during moments of stress.

In wet weather gloves are a help; they also are provided by the valet, the best kind being thin cotton or string ones.

One should always get ready for a race about three-quarters of an hour before it is due to be run, in order to give the valet, who may have to cope with some dozen other riders, a chance to see that everything is as it should be, and the trainer time to saddle the horse. This means changing before the race in front of the one in which one is going to ride, or, if riding in the first race, thirty to forty-five minutes before its advertised time.

On arriving at the racecourse it is usual to go straight to the dressing-room and tell one's valet the races in which one is riding, the weight to be carried and any peculiarities in the shape of spurs, martingale, breast-girth or blinkers, that the trainer may have ordered. When the time comes the valet will weigh out his jockeys on the trial scales and do up the saddle with its number and weight-cloths, and any additions, ready for the jockeys to pass the Clerk of the Scales in the presence of the trainer.

The Clerk of the Scales is always amenable to passing a jockey early, say, during the running of the previous race, but a jockey should never pass the scales by himself unless with the sanction of the trainer, and even if he has been told to do so he should take great care that his saddle is kept in a safe place until it is handed over to the trainer, since the jockey will be responsible for carrying the correct weight: if he has left the saddle about carelessly he may find someone else borrowing some lead from his weight-cloth, which will throw his weight out and may produce very serious results, in the shape of having to explain the matter before the Stewards. Should he be in the slightest doubt about his weight, a jockey should always verify it with the Clerk of the Scales, in order to be on the safe side.

A jockey's racecourse valet is so integral a part of his riding career that some words upon the part he plays are essential to a book of this kind.

Valets hold a licence from the Jockey Club and look after some twelve jockeys each. They take care of their riding gear, including saddles, see to the washing, mending and repairing of it, and cart it round from meeting to meeting. Each valet has one, perhaps two, assistants, who attend the meeting at which the valet himself is not present when two take place on the same day, and there are a separate set of valets for the North and the South. Each member of the two factions has a valet in the other with whom he is affiliated to the extent of sharing each other's clients when they ride out of their usual

Everything wrong

district. In this case a valet sends his jockey's tack to the representative in question, by post or some other means, or, if the time element makes this impossible, packs it up for the jockey to take it himself.

For all this service (except the repair of saddles, boots and those repairs to breeches which necessitate them being sent back to the tailor) the jockey pays a set fee for each individual ride. If he rides a winner he should give the valet a bonus according to what he can afford.

The valet service on a racecourse is one of the most remarkable institutions in existence, and after nearly twenty years of riding it is still a mystery to me how one's clothes appear clean and in order after having been wet and covered in mud the day before. A number of riders are inclined to take all the valet's work for granted, and to offer little consideration in return, but it is only fair, in order to enable the system to maintain its high standard, to give one's valet as much warning as possible as to where and when one is likely to be riding and what saddle one is likely to be using, and to inform him of any changes of plan.

It is extremely irritating for a valet to have to transport all a jockey's tack, including perhaps a 14-lb. saddle, to some obscure meeting, when the rider in question had no intention of going, but had not taken the trouble to let his valet know.

One of the reasons for the efficiency of the racecourse valeting system is that jockeys are, on the whole, most unselfish about the use of their tack, allowing valets to lend it to other riders at their discretion, with the result that a jockey who, through a sudden change of plan, finds himself at a meeting with no equipment can be fitted out from that belonging to other jockeys, or from the spare tack which the valets gradually accumulate from odd articles bequeathed to them by retiring riders. If, therefore, as may be the case, a rider sees another jockey using his saddle, he should not grudge him its use as he may one day find himself in the predicament of wanting to borrow one himself, and he can rest assured that his valet will not lend it to anyone irresponsible. The same applies to such articles as boots and breeches. A valet will always avoid lending a jockey's best tack, unless he has obtained the owner's permission, and will fit out an unequipped rider with second-best articles.

Racing colours are the responsibility of the trainer and are not kept by the valet, but are handed to him by the trainer or his representative on the course.

In this chapter I have dealt only with those articles of equipment for which the rider is directly responsible; those which come under the trainer's supervision will be considered in the chapter on training.

8
In the Paddock

CONTINUING THE CHRONOLOGICAL progress of events, having weighed out, the rider's next stage will be to leave the dressing-room for the paddock, when the participants in his race are called out by the official responsible for summoning them.

The more empty a rider's bowels and bladder, the less likely is he to develop complications to any internal injuries he may receive as a result of a fall, and while this state will probably be brought about by the combined forces of nerves and nature, it is an aspect worthy of attention.

When the weather is cold it is always advisable to put on an overcoat when leaving the dressing-room for the paddock. Apprehension increases with cold, while hands and muscles stiffen under the same influence, and the warmer one can keep until the moment of mounting, the better. It is not, however, altogether wise to appear in one's best blue coat for the occasion, as it is quite possible that, having been momentarily laid on the ground while the trainer or his representative adjusts the girths, it will be trodden on by the horse, particularly if he is restive by disposition.

The remarks I have ventured to make on behaviour, in various parts of this book, may seem both pompous and pedantic, but they are made with a view to letting the ambitious but inexperienced rider see in what light his employers are likely to view him and in order that his path to success may be no harder than it need be. As I have said before, the general impression a rider creates counts for a great deal, and he will have to be possessed of a very much superior riding ability to his contemporaries if he is to succeed in the face of rudeness, unpunctuality and other breaches of conduct likely to annoy his patrons.

It is in this vein that I would, therefore, suggest that when a rider comes into the paddock, he should be sober, properly dressed, smoking neither a cigar nor a cigarette, and if possible that he should refrain from chewing gum, unless he is forced to resort to this rather unattractive habit in order to stop his teeth from chattering from fear. He should seek out the owner and trainer for whom he is riding and go straight up to them to receive his orders, touching his cap or not according to the age, sex, or circumstance of his patron. He should avoid carrying on conversations with friends among the spectators, or fellow-riders in the ring, while his patron or trainer is waiting to deliver instructions; these he should follow carefully, making quite sure that he understands them fully and asking questions concerning any point about which he has a doubt.

When the horse is brought up for him to mount the rider should throw a quick glance over the saddle, bridle and any other piece of equipment he may be wearing, in case an adjustment may be necessary. This, strictly speaking, is the responsibility of the trainer, but there are trainers and trainers, and while a horse coming from a reputable stable is almost certain to be turned out with his tack adjusted correctly—but it should be remembered that, in all walks of life, no one is infallible—there are some trainers who give the impression of having received their licence in error, instead of one for a TV set or a dog: any jockey being unfortunate or unwise enough to engage himself to ride for one of these will, unless he carefully checks the horse's equipment, find himself paying the penalty of ignorance and incompetence.

It is a wise precaution to see that the lad in charge of the horse unbuckles the leading rein and slips it through the ring of the bit, before one gets into the saddle, the reason being that if the horse should plunge and pull the rein out of the lad's hand it will increase the confusion by swinging round his legs and possibly, if he treads on it, make him turn a somersault.

Having mounted the horse the first thing to do is to adjust the stirrup-leathers to the correct length—this may have to be altered after further experience of the horse gained while cantering down to the post—at the same time seeing that the leathers themselves are flat against the shin bone and not twisted so that the sharp edge presses into the shin. This can be done while the stable-boy leads the horse round the parade ring and out on to the course.

These being correctly adjusted, the next move is to tie a knot in the end of the reins, if they are long enough to merit such a measure; both the shortening of the stirrup-leathers and knotting of the reins were explained in some detail in an earlier chapter.

Once out on the course—possibly before—the lad will slip off the leading rein and the horse will be, as they say, 'all yours'.

9
Going to the Post

THE RIDER'S SEAT when cantering down to the post has already been discussed, and I will now attempt to deal with, not the manner in which he sits, but the different ways of taking various types of horses down to the post.

In the case of horses having no particular characteristic there is little to write about that is not governed by the rules of common sense. They should be taken down at an even, steady canter; the rider should avoid following too close behind another horse, should look where he is going in order that he does not get in anyone else's way, and should pull up gradually and not suddenly. He should try to ride stylishly, but naturally and not affectedly, and he should endeavour to pick out the best going he can find, keeping clear of bare patches (in dry weather) and boggy places when there has been a lot of rain.

Idle or sluggish horses sometimes benefit by being taken to the post at a fairly sharp pace, which will probably have to be achieved by means of a few vigorous kicks and a slap down the shoulder with the whip—in the event of explicit instructions from the trainer to 'set him alight', the best prescription is a couple of well-directed and heartily applied cuts of the whip, delivered with the left hand, as far behind the horse's hip as possible.

The real problem horses are those that are highly excitable or very hard pullers.

Horses of the former category may not necessarily pull hard; in fact they are often light-mouthed, and the rider is faced with the difficulty, not of controlling them, but of keeping them calm.

This may often prove impossible, but one's only chance of success with horses of this kind is to ride them as quietly and gently as is possible, handling their mouths lightly and giving them as little intimation as one can that they are going to be called upon, in due course, to go fast. It is best, when occasion allows, to take such horses to the post by themselves, either before or after the other runners, since the presence of other horses round them, and the fact of being passed by them, will increase the tendency to 'boil over'. They should not be allowed to go down too fast, and it is often quite effective to ride with a long rein and an upright stance—such as that often employed by jockeys pulling up at the end of the race—rather than the more stylish method of the orthodox flat race style. The less one bumps about in the saddle, the better, and having arrived at the post the only precept to follow out—it may not be a particularly easy one, as the horse will probably be fidgeting in a manner most trying to the rider's temper—is to 'sit and suffer': kicking him in the ribs or jobbing him in the mouth will only serve to make him worse.

The holding of a puller is largely a matter of knack, practice and knowing the horse. Strength of fingers, wrists and forearms are a help, but they are by no means the whole answer, and when employed in the capacity of mere force are as likely as not to prove useless. The fitness of the rider also comes into the argument, for if he gets out of breath and begins to tire, he will start to bump about in the saddle, change his grip of the reins and thus convey to the horse that he is weakening, of which fact the latter will take full advantage.

There are two ways of coping with a puller when cantering down to the post. The one is never to let him out of a hack-canter, the other to exercise a discreet combination of strength and guile. The first means is best achieved by breaking very gently from a walk to a trot, and from a trot to a hack-canter, pulling him back into a trot at the slightest sign of him wanting to increase his speed. At this pace he can be kept under control, but once he is allowed to get into his stride, he will be the master of the situation. It is sometimes a help to employ the 'pulling-up' stance for this operation, as the rider's upright position, as opposed to the crouch used when galloping fast, will be associated in the horse's mind with decreasing and not increasing his speed, and will not make him think, as might be the case with a rider sitting up his neck, that he is required to go fast.

Whether the rider uses a long or shortened rein must depend upon personal taste and circumstances, but if it is the former he should make sure that he will not need to shorten it once he has set off, since nothing makes a horse take hold of his bit quicker than changing one's hands: to do so on a horse which one is doubtful of holding is to court disaster and may result in 'going for the letters'. If he decides to take a shorter hold of the reins, the rider should do so very quietly and gently, while the horse is still walking, and without intimating to him that any such operation is taking place, since to take a short, firm hold of him before setting off will cause him to begin pulling before he has even broken out of a walk.

The method described above is suggested in the case of a horse

Going to the post; a nice seat, but the rider's back could be straighter

which the rider is pretty certain he cannot hold, if he allows him to get into his full stride, and it is advisable to adopt it when in any doubt about maintaining control.

In the case of a horse who merely takes a strong hold but is not likely to get out of control, the rider does not need to be so careful. His success in taking him down quietly, smoothly and not too fast will depend largely upon the manner in which he sets off.

If he lets the horse jump straight into his stride, as when leaving the starting-gate he will find himself going down a good deal faster than he bargained for, but if he begins gradually, breaking from a walk to a trot, and from a trot to a canter, he stands a good chance of keeping him well under control all the way. When riding pullers it is a help to take the stirrup-leathers up a couple of holes, as this gives one more purchase on the horse's mouth, but that does not mean to say that the objective will be achieved by a mere vice-like pressure of the bit upon the same: the exertion of force in this manner is far more likely to make him pull all the harder.

The benefit which the rider derives from the power acquired from riding with shortened leathers does not lie in the unvarying force which can be placed on the horse's mouth, but in the variation of the force at the rider's disposal, and while the general tone of the pull which the rider exerts on the horse's mouth may have to be both strong and even, the best results will be obtained if it is varied by the periodical and imaginative easing of the pressure at such moments, and to the extent at which the rider feels instinctively that he can give his horse this relief without the latter taking advantage of him.

The term usually applied to this procedure in treatises on equitation is 'ease and feel', but the manner in which the manœuvre is carried out should be so delicate as to be imperceptible to the spectator, and should not consist of the alternate, exaggerated slackening of the reins and heaving, which is not infrequently taken as an interpretation of this term.

To attempt to lay down a hard-and-fast rule for all horses is, naturally, ridiculous, since each horse must be studied according to his individual characteristics, but fundamental principles can be adapted to circumstances, and are therefore, worthy of consideration.

It is, I think, a good plan not to exert any pressure on the horse's mouth until he starts to take hold of the bit of his own accord. This does not mean that the reins should be festooned about the horse's neck, but that they should be in the position of maintaining the fullest, yet lightest, contact with the horse's mouth, being held at the length which the rider has decided to use when he breaks into a canter, and which he has quietly and gently acquired as he walks his horse out on to the course. He can, alternatively, walk out with a long rein and shorten it as the horse breaks into a canter—as described in the chapter dealing with riding work—but he must be quick and skilled in his management of the reins: if he is slow or clumsy in taking them up to the cantering length, he may find that the horse has got first run on him and that his control has vanished.

It is a help, I think, to move the bit about in the horse's mouth to prevent him from taking a dead hold of it, or trying to lock it in one or the other side of his mouth, but this measure should not be translated into sawing his mouth. The difference between a good and a bad rider is that the application of the aids by the former is imperceptible, by the latter, so exaggerated as to be noticeable.

With the type of horse under consideration it is best, when possible, to track a quiet, sober horse down to the post, as one's own horse is more likely to drop his bit when 'covered up' than when allowed to 'see daylight'. But it is important to pick upon the right type to follow, as the rider will not be popular if he picks upon a free-going horse similar to his own, for he will only cause his pilot to go faster, and his own horse to follow at an embarrassingly increasing pace.

In any case, one should not follow too closely upon the pilot's heels, for the obvious reasons, pointed out earlier in the book, that such proximity gives rise to the dangers of striking into the horse in front or getting kicked, and before tracking another horse down to the post in this manner it is only fair to obtain the sanction of his jockey, which will ensure that one does not choose the wrong type of horse to follow. Should one find oneself in danger of striking into the pilot, it is imperative to pull out and chance going down too fast.

By the same token, it is as well to look round before setting off, in case another rider in the same predicament as oneself is preparing to follow one down under the circumstances described above.

Confidence, or lack of it, goes a long way towards success or failure in managing a horse; to make one's mind up that the horse is going to run away is one step towards bringing this regrettable occurrence about, and a firm determination that the journey to the post is going to be accomplished according towards one's own plans, and not at the will of the horse, is a victory in the first round, whatever the final result of the encounter. Horses are very sensitive to the moods and capabilities of a rider, and seem to be able to detect the slightest sign of lack of confidence or weakness, of which they will be only too ready to take advantage. We used to have an old black pony in the stable in which I was a pupil, who was ridden by the head lad and sometimes by the trainer, and was almost wooden in the matter of docility, but he knew straight away when he had an apprentice on his back, invariably running away with the unfortunate lad for his own amusement; having expended sufficient energy as was consistent with his own comfort, he would pull up and return to his usual quietude.

It sometimes comes to pass that, in spite of setting off quietly and calmly, and proceeding at a reasonable speed, one awakens to the unpleasant realization that the horse, and not oneself, is in control. He may not be running away in the sense that he is going faster and faster, but the application of the aids to deceleration will have no effect whatsoever, engendering the unpleasant feeling that one is doomed to circle the course in the manner of the mythical—not the equine—Flying Dutchman. Examples of this predicament occur every now and then, both on the flat and under N.H. rules, and I have a vivid recollection of a horse travelling quietly but relentlessly round Sandown Park, making some two or three circuits before consenting to be pulled up, having taken charge of his rider on the way to the post.

Having landed in this unpleasant situation, the first objective of the rider must be to attempt to conceal from the horse the fact that he is in charge. The more nonchalant the rider's behaviour, therefore, the more likely is this plan to succeed. If he panics and hastily takes a fresh and firmer hold of the reins, the horse is almost certain to go from being slightly the master of the situation to running away in the true sense of the word. The best move the rider can make is, first, to attempt to persuade the horse that he wants to pull up of his own accord, which is possibly most effectively achieved by standing right up in the stirrups (as is often done at the end of a race or an exercise canter or gallop), maintaining a long rein, and talking to him, taking care to keep any tremor of apprehension out of one's voice—which is not always as easy as it may seem, for a horse is very sensitive to inflections of speech. If he sees other horses ahead of him pulling up, he may fall for this, if not the rider will have to think again.

After the failure of the first manœuvre the rider will be left in the position of riding with a considerable length of rein, and three alternatives before him: he must continue on towards the start, hoping that on arrival there the horse will stop of his own accord because the others are doing the same, he must find a way of bringing him to a halt by a combination of guile and the discreet employment of any natural or artificial barriers that may exist in the neighbourhood, or, if it comes to the worst, he will have to resign himself to the Flying Dutchman system of circling the course until fatigue or boredom brings the horse to standstill, which will mean that, so far so the race in question is concerned, he is a spent force.

If the horse shows no sign of wishing to increase his pace the rider will probably find it best not to try to shorten his reins, for any change of hold may cause him to set off in earnest. If, however, he finds that he has inadvertently overdone his persuasion act by giving the horse too much rein, he will be forced to shorten his reins or lose control completely.

He must then set about executing the rein-shortening with the greatest of care and discretion, and without taking any firmer hold of the horse's head while he is doing so. The best way of doing this, I think, is while maintaining an even, firm hold of the reins with the left hand, to slide the right quietly up the rein and take hold of it at the desired length, then to place the right hand gently on the horse's neck, allowing it to rest there for a second or two, and then very quietly and gently taking hold of the left rein with the right thumb and bringing it into the grasp of the right hand, while the left hand, having momentarily been relieved of its task, comes back on to the left rein in its new position. The success or failure of any such change depends upon the lightness and sureness of touch with which it is carried out; the more violent and clumsy the movement, the more likely is it to end in disaster.

Having achieved this fresh hold, the rider can make an attempt to slow the horse down by the judicious employment of force, that is to say, not sawing violently at his mouth or pulling at it as if it was an oar, but by gently moving the bit about in his mouth (if the horse has not already anchored it between his teeth) with as much strength as he can summon. If these tactics are of no avail, or show signs of upsetting him it is better to sit quite still, with an even, strong hold and think out the next move.

During all these operations it is, I think, a help to talk to the horse quietly and persuasively—not that it is likely to make him pull up or even slow down—but it is at least possible that it will keep him from boiling over and from realizing that, sad to relate, he is really in control.

On most courses—except Newmarket where, mercifully, there is no steeplechasing, or loose horses would probably never be caught until they had reached Cambridge—there is some sort of natural or artificial barrier at the start. At Sandown there is a high wooden fence by the 2-mile start—it has proved a good friend to me before now. At Lingfield there is a wood, and on every course there is the bend of the rails to be met sooner or later. Provided a horse is not running away in true John Gilpin style, all such barriers can be brought into use by judiciously facing the horse at them, at the same time intimating to him by the tone and choice of one's words that he is expected to stop.

I have on several occasions been grateful for some of these aids to bring a horse to a halt. At Sandown (as already intimated) by facing the horse at the high wooden fence. At Salisbury, on the flat, by making use of the presence of a thick clump of thorn-bushes at the mile starting-gate, and on various other occasions by turning him carefully into the rails or round in a circle.

A horse will sometimes tend to slow up if guided towards the outside of the track, (as opposed to the inside, according to the way races are run on the particular track) as he associates proximity with the inside rails with going fast, and being pulled towards the outside with pulling up, and one is more likely, on a circular track, to keep a horse calm by taking him down on the outside than by keeping him on the inside rails.

With regard to the type of tactics described above it is important to realize exactly the degree of control the horse has obtained, and the effect it has had upon him, for if he is running away bald-headed and has worked himself up into a state of thorough excitement, he may have little or no idea of what he is doing and be quite capable of crashing into any obstacle that happens to bar his progress. If he is in such a condition and mood it is better to think twice before trying to stop him in this way, since he may be quite capable of crashing through it and injuring himself, to say nothing of the rider.

On some occasions the rider will find that the runners will have to walk past the stands and turn round and canter back in order to reach the starting-gate. Under these circumstances he should avoid engaging in conversations with his friends in the Members' enclosure, or the Silver Ring as far as that goes, nor should he be tempted, as I believe was a bold-betting amateur of a past generation, to pull up and place a bet with a bookmaker, even though the price of his horse, or whatever he wishes to back, may seem too attractive to miss.

The former operation will probably mean that he has to turn round in his saddle and abandon his attention to the business on hand in order to finish the conversation in question, a gesture unlikely to inspire confidence in one's patron, while the latter procedure may quite probably result in the offender being had up before the Stewards.

From time to time every rider will, as he rides out of the paddock, have the somewhat irritating experience of racegoers—probably complete strangers—firing such questions at him as: 'Will you win?' 'Do you fancy yours?' 'Can I have a bit on you?' and so on. Not only is it a gross impertinence on the part of the questioner, who is not infrequently someone who should know better, but it amounts to asking a jockey to betray his patron's confidence.

Such inquiries are best ignored completely, or if made by someone whom the rider feels bound to answer, can be parried by some such Delphic reply as, 'He's doing his best', 'Should run well if the going isn't too hard/soft', 'A fair chance of getting into the first three', which will serve the purpose of having furnished a civil reply without divulging any concrete information.

10

The Start

ON ARRIVING AT the start one should always test the girths to see whether they are tight enough, or too tight, and have a final check-up of equipment in general. Trainers will sometimes tell a jockey not to touch his girths at the post, but he should still check them; on more than one occasion I have had to disobey such instructions and pull up the girths a hole, perhaps more, in order to be sure the saddle remained in place. Even trainers are not infallible, and horses that do not usually do so will sometimes blow themselves out when being saddled, and thus throw out their trainers' calculations.

It is quite common to find the surcingle tight and the girths loose, which is a deceptive state of affairs, as a casual examination might result in the rider accepting the girths as being tight enough. I do not mean to imply that a horse should be cut in half by the tightness of his girths, but that the latter should be tight enough to ensure that the saddle stays in its place, at the same time allowing the horse enough freedom to breathe.

It is always advisable to try one's girths oneself, and then get the starter's assistant to help in pulling them up. One should be capable of pulling up one's own girths, but since the surcingle buckle is usually under the horse's belly it is nearly always necessary to enlist the help of the starter's assistant in adjusting the latter. A number of riders get into the habit of not trying their girths themselves, but of leaving the decision of whether they should be pulled up or not to the assistant. I used to belong to that school, but was cured for life by an assistant who assured me that my girths were in order when, in fact, they were much too loose, as became evident after about four furlongs when the saddle disappeared under the horse's belly, taking me with it.

Starter's assistants are competent, experienced and conscientious individuals and will do all they can to help the jockey, both in the matter of his equipment and in getting a bad starter away from the gate, but when there are a large number of runners they are very busy men, and it is quite possible that, in the heat of the moment, they could make a genuine mistake, and in any case they are only there to help the jockey and are not responsible for the adjustment of his tack.

When a horse is having his girths tried or pulled up he is very apt to kick out in irritation with one hind leg or the other, and it is therefore inadvisable to stand or walk behind him while he is undergoing this operation; indeed, it is a good rule never to pass behind a horse within kicking distance if it can be avoided, for a kick at the start can (and often has) finished a horse's chances before the race, and if the horse happens to have come under starter's orders his backers will lose their money as well, even if he does not take part in the race.

National Hunt racing differs from Flat-racing in the matter of starting, in that on the Flat there is a draw for places at the start, whereas under National Hunt rules jockeys start from any position they manage to secure at the post. This means that there is almost always what might be described as an ugly rush for the place nearest the inside rails, and anyone wishing to secure it is well advised to make certain of getting down to the start early and taking up that position.

The disadvantage of this state of affairs is that, in the case of a restive horse, it is not easy to keep in one position for perhaps five minutes on end; the horse will be twisting and turning every few seconds, and unless the jockeys in the immediate vicinity are gracious enough to let one resume the coveted position by virtue of having secured it first, there is a good chance of the horse backing out of it and thus losing it for good.

But though it undoubtedly has its advantages, it is by no means always the best place from which to start; in fact there are occasions when it may prove a distinct handicap, for instance, if a horse is a slow beginner he may quite probably be unable to keep his place when he has jumped off, with the result that he has to surrender his position to other and faster horses and may get his view of the obstacle obscured, causing his horse to jump it badly, lose ground and expend energy—perhaps even to fall. One trainer at least, for whom I have ridden, always instructs his jockeys not to start on the inside on horses of this type, but to start towards, or even right on, the outside, to make sure of getting a clear view of the obstacle, and then to work their way towards the inside, having negotiated the first hazard successfully.

It is not an easy matter about which to make any firm ruling; so much depends upon the characteristics of the horse, the instructions of the trainer and upon circumstances, but all things being equal the inside is the best place as it affords the shortest path from starting-gate to winning-post, and I have always noticed that many consistently successful riders have always taken the inside place at the start whenever possible.

The advantage of starting on the outside is that, since no one else is anxious to take the place and one has not therefore to stand glued to it for fear of losing it, it is possible to walk in and get off to a flying start, while other horses are flat-footed—provided, of course, one can gauge correctly the approximate moment the starter is going to let the gate up. In this matter it is imperative to keep one's eyes on the starter and not on his arm. There are few, if any, men who can help betraying, by some slight change of expression, the raising of the eyebrows, the twitching of a face-muscle, or perhaps no more than a fleeting light in his eyes, that they are going to press the handle that operates the gate—there have been starters who did everything but announce it verbally—and by carefully watching the starter's face, at the same time keeping oneself aware of what the rest of the field is doing— the gate is unlikely to go up if three or four runners are facing in the opposite direction, particularly if they include the favourite!—one can usually make fairly sure of getting well away on a reasonably co-operative horse.

On the Flat, there probably has never been a jockey consistently better at the gate than Sir Gordon Richards: he was always quickly away, his horse was invariably well balanced and calm, and he made the operation look too smooth and easy to be true. In those days flat races and N.H. races used the same type of starting gate.

By watching him very carefully, I came to the conclusion that his efficiency in this respect was not due to black magic, but to a combination of carefully planned actions perfected by years of practice. In the first place, he always rode with a long rein. This meant that his horse was comfortable, calm and not in danger of being jobbed in the mouth by the sudden surge forward jumping out of the gate. Then, he did not start chivvying his horse in an attempt to get him on his toes until the last few seconds before the gate seemed likely to go up, so that his horse did not get disappointed by false alarms and finally lose interest. Thirdly, he glanced quickly at the rest of the field to see what was happening and, having decided that it was likely to be a 'go', never took his gaze off the starter's face. Finally, he never got his horse right on top of the tapes, instead, he kept him about half a neck behind the horses beside him, which meant that, in that fraction of a second between seeing by the starter's face that he was going to pull the lever and the actual rising of the barrier, he could get his horse on the move, and as the gate went up the latter would be passing underneath it while those with their noses to the tapes would just be starting to jump off.

The whole occurrence was a matter of fractions of a second, but in racing such fractions represent a length, half a length, perhaps no more than a head, but it is by these measurements that races are lost and won, and when a slight lead is established in a sprint-race it is sometimes never broken down, while even in a long-distance race a quick beginning that can enable a jockey to take a good place in the early stages may be the cause of him winning the race. On the flat it may mean going the shortest way by many yards (as at Chester), while over fences or hurdles it may mean a good run clear of inter-ference.

With excitable horses it is best not to let them think they are going to jump off until the last possible moment, but instead, to keep them on their own some yards behind, and away from the other runners, and to sit very still and quiet, riding with a long rein and walking in at the last moment, when it seems certain that the gate will be let up.

In the case of very free horses, with which it is desired to ride a wait-ing race, it is often a good plan to start in the second rank. It means giving away two or three lengths, but if it is going to make the horse settle down and not exhaust himself by running too freely, this sacrifice is well made. Horses of this description are usually more inclined to settle down when started behind the others rather than beside them, as, in the latter case, the competitive spirit in them is likely to be aroused too soon or too violently, with the result that they are a spent force by the time they get to the finish.

Many horses run better when ridden in this way, as they do not use up all their energy in the early stages of the race, and if allowed to go to the front too soon, sometimes jump rather wildly. I used to ride a horse over fences who, on two occasions, fell at the last fence when allowed to make running, but responded so well to the tactics of riding him from behind, having started in the second rank, that he won the first time I employed them.

Under these circumstances I think it is best to start on the inside—since one is in the second rank there will be no difficulty in securing the position—for this helps to counterbalance the loss of ground resulting from starting behind the others, by ensuring that one goes the shortest way.

In the case of horses who are not impetuous, but are best ridden from behind, there is no need to employ these tactics. It is pointless to give away ground when it is not necessary, in fact, even with horses that must be waited with, provided they are not impetuous, one should leave the gate as quickly as possible, as there are certain to be one or two competitors in the race who want to go on. If not, it is quite an easy matter (since he will not be a hard puller) to pull one's horse back into whatever position required.

The riding of a waiting race is often mistakenly associated with getting purposely left at the start, but although this may be necessary in the case of a horse that is a hard puller it is an error of tactics as regards horses who are not difficult to hold.

The manner of dealing with sluggish horses at the start has already come into the book under the heading of an earlier chapter, and it will therefore only be necessary to remark that such horses are best, where possible, brought in to the gate on the move, and that it is advisable to rouse them from their lethargy with a couple of well-directed and sharply applied cuts of the whip, delivered with the left hand, or by getting the starter's assistant to give them a belt round the hocks with his 'long Tom'.

When riding entire horses one should take care not to let them smell other horses when standing at the gate, or they will probably start squealing and striking out with their fore-feet, or getting up on their hind legs. Conversely, when riding other and less fiery animals it is as well to give as wide a berth as possible to horses that show signs of wishing to attack or assault their fellow-competitors.

When riding inexperienced horses it is not always prudent to start right on the inside. They may find the presence of the crowd along the rails, and of the starter up above them on his platform, both distracting and alarming, so that when the gate goes up their attention is fixed on them and not on getting quickly away.

After all the runners have assembled at the start the gate is let down and got ready to be sprung. It usually comes down with rather a clatter, and it is, therefore, advisable to have a young horse at a reasonable distance from it when this occurs, as he may become alarmed and want to back away from it instead of going up to it, when the time comes to line up. Even old horses are not impervious to this distraction, as I discovered by being put on the floor at the start by an old stager, whom I had somewhat rashly stationed a couple of yards from the gate while I was having his girths tightened, and who, when the gate was let down, quite justifiably whipped round without warning and with considerable dispatch.

If by some mischance one gets badly away it is a great mistake to make up the ground too quickly, as it is much more exhausting for a horse to accelerate suddenly and violently than to do so gradually. A bad start does not necessarily mean a lost race, if the jockey keeps his head and does not burst his horse trying to make up the lost ground in the first few furlongs.

The first time I ever rode a winner over hurdles my horse whipped sideways at the start, which was (as is sometimes the case) effected by an elastic tape pulled across the front of the field and released at the appropriate moment, and my horse, having previously been accustomed to more aristocratic racing—he had the distinction of leading the triple crown winner Bahram in his work—found this device strange to him and whipped sideways as the starter beside him let the tape go. Since the first furlong was uphill, I did not encourage him to try and catch the others up while ascending it, and he showed no inclination to do so himself, with the result that it was not until we had gone a mile that we got within striking distance of the leaders, eventually passing them all and winning.

There may be times when one is required to take a horse down very steadily or by himself. On these occasions one should take care to arrive at the post in time. It is better to go down first than last to obtain the necessary isolation, otherwise the wrath of the starter is likely to be felt, and it is quite possible that the rebuke will be followed up by a fine.

One should also be careful, when indulging in any such diversion as having a preliminary jump over the first fence or hurdle, an operation that is not unknown, that one allows an adequate margin of time before the start. This was brought home to me when, together with the late Hywel Jones, I had a trial trip over the first hurdle at Sandown and shared a sharply-delivered reprimand from Major Robertson as, having taken some time to pull up, we came trotting back to find the whole field lined up as if paraded for our inspection, about two minutes after the official time for the 'off'.

I cannot at the moment think of any other aspects bearing upon the start with which I should have dealt, so will end the chapter with saying that success at the starting-gate depends upon riding with a long rein, keeping oneself and the horse calm—or waking him up as the case may be—keeping an eye on the starter's face and intelligently appreciating the general situation.

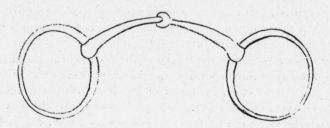

11

Tactics

TACTICS IN A race are the appreciation and employment of the capabilities and characteristics of one's horse, the short-comings of opposing horses and jockeys, the features of the course, the going, and the circumstances that may arise during the race, in order to further one's chance of victory.

To be skilled in this respect is to be a good jockey, and however expert a horseman a man may be, he cannot be considered a good jockey unless he possess tactical skill, while a good jockey in the tactical sense of the word may quite likely be an indifferent horseman. The top-class race-rider is the one who is fortunate enough to combine both qualities.

Skill in tactics depends upon quick thinking and quick decision, a thorough knowledge of the abilities and peculiarities of one's horse—how often does one hear a jockey say after a race, 'If only I'd ridden him before and known him, he would have won'—and experience. Much can be learnt from carefully watching the details of running, as a spectator, and anyone whose ambition it is to become a successful steeplechase-rider, should make full use of every opportunity, both of watching from the stands and of walking out to various points of the course from which he can obtain a close-up view of different stages of the race. He will find this more advantageous and economical than gossiping during the race, or 'watching it from the bar'.

Apart from not falling off or violently interfering with one's horse, tactics are by far the most important aspect of race-riding, and a jockey can often lose a race on the biggest certainty in the world through an error in tactics, while an owner or trainer who has tied a jockey down to orders may find that, owing to unforeseen circumstances arising, the tactics the jockey has been compelled to employ, because of his patron's instructions, will prove the means of defeat.

When a jockey loses a race his tactics are frequently criticised by onlookers, most probably those who have lost their money on the horse he was riding; but no such censure is merited unless expressed by one who knows what orders the jockey was given, what peculiarities the horse possesses, and what has occurred during the race. And since he is unlikely to have any knowledge of the first two conditions at all, and a by no means accurate understanding of the third (some of the running was probably out of sight of the stands, and it is more than possible that he missed seeing a vital incident), the average critic has little or no right to offer adverse comment.

Whatever the natural or acquired tactical skill a rider may possess, in order that he may reap the fullest advantage from it he must be thoroughly familiar with the course over which the race is to be run.

Ignorance of the geography of a course can result in a jockey going many yards out of the way, as was the case with the rider of the French horse, Le Paillon, who was defeated in the Champion Hurdle by National Spirit and afterwards won the Prix de l'Arc de Triomphe against the best flat racehorses in France, and even in going the wrong way altogether, as occurred in the case of Zahia in the 1948 Grand National. And it is of the utmost importance for a jockey to walk the course, not only if he has never ridden over it before, but if he has not ridden over it recently, since it is quite common for slight alterations to be made, without knowledge of which a rider can easily go wrong. If in doubt he should walk it twice.

Having made himself thoroughly familiar with the ground over which the battle is to be fought, the rider must then take thought about the way in which he is going to ride his horse to ensure that the most can be made of him.

Broadly speaking, tactics fall into two divisions: lying up with the leaders all the way, and coming from behind. But before he binds himself to one or the other of these two plans, the rider must learn and appreciate that the dominating factor in all forms of racing is the pace at which the race is run, qualified by such considerations as the state of the going and the wind.

It is not the slightest use leading the field at a hack-canter, under the impression that, through making the running a one-pace stayer is able to benefit from his stamina at the expense of a field of short-runners. Conversely, when riding a horse that must be brought with a run from behind, there is no sense in lying so far out of one's ground that the task of catching the leaders is impossible; under some circumstances (when the going is very heavy or the leaders are horses of doubtful stamina) they may 'come back' to a jockey lying out of his ground, but on good or firm going and in the case of genuine stayers they most probably will not. It is therefore advisable to form a general and flexible plan rather than a narrow and rigid one, so that room is left for adaptability in the case of the occurrence of the unforeseen.

In the world of athletics it is, I believe, generally recognized that the more even a runner's pace throughout a race, the less energy is he likely to waste, and there seems no reason why this principle should not, with reservations to cover individual characteristics and circumstances, be applied to horses. In fact, the frequently used term 'riding a smooth race' suggests an even pace throughout the race, with no periods of violent acceleration or deceleration. The snags to this theory, however, are that horses do not run in 'lanes', but are subject to the rough-and-tumble resulting from the presence of other horses in the race, often to the effects of comparatively steep gradients, and to individual idiosyncrasy and temperament, so that it is frequently necessary to accelerate suddenly and violently, to slow down quickly, or to keep a horse in front or covered up as the case may be. And theory must be sacrificed to practice.

In view of this, therefore, I think that, after acquiring a thorough knowledge of the course, the next most important point a rider must consider is the peculiarities of the horse he is to ride, upon which his tactics in the race will largely depend.

The least complicated peculiarity is that of being what is known as a 'front runner', in other words, a horse who likes to make the running. In riding this type of horse it is fairly obvious that one's tactics must consist in jumping out of the gate as nimbly as possible, securing the rails, going the shortest way round, and remaining in front from start to finish. Nevertheless, there are times when these tactics must be modified, for if another competitor sets out to do exactly the same it is quite possible that the two horses will 'cut each other's throats', that is to say vie with each other to such an extent that they will go too fast in the early stages and be spent forces by the time the finish draws in sight.

When riding a front runner it is essential to be able to gauge the pace one is going in relation to the horse's capabilities, fitness and the state of the going, and to decide, if another competitor draws level or attempts to pass, whether it is policy to increase one's own pace in order to retain the lead, or to allow one's rival to forge ahead, in the belief that he is forcing a pace which he himself will not be able to maintain and which will sooner or later cause him to become exhausted and to drop back, thus enabling one's own horse to reach the front again without having to exert himself to do so.

When horses become well known as front runners, other jockeys frame their tactics to try and make them run themselves into the ground; in fact, the rider of a fancied horse is quite likely to enlist an ally in the shape of a jockey who is considered to have no chance of winning the race but is willing to make the pace so strong that any horse trying to keep with him, or pass him, is bound to exhaust himself before the finish.

Front runners may be inclined to lose heart if they have to relinquish their lead, but if they are over-taxed in being kept in front they will most certainly lose the race, and rather than risk riding his horse into the ground I am sure that it is better policy for a jockey to 'sit and suffer' behind a horse who is attempting to make the pace too fast, for, even if his horse drops his bit for the time being, he will, in all probability, take hold of it again when, as assuredly he will, the leader 'comes back' to him.

I used to ride a front runner over hurdles who reacted successfully to these tactics, for having been beaten on him through riding him into the ground, I sat still on him the next time I met an opponent trying to take him on at his own game, and though he preferred being in front and did, indeed, drop his bit when passed, he raced on with determination when the leader came back to him and fell behind.

When riding a front runner, there is a strong temptation to keep looking back to see what is occurring behind. This is a bad fault: to start with, a rider should have sufficient idea of the pace at which he is travelling to know whether he is going too fast or too slow without having to regulate it according to the proximity of other competitors. Besides this, the fact of looking round unbalances and disquiets his own horse, giving a rider following him the advantage of making his challenge at that psychological moment when the horse in front, and his rider, are off their balance. A rider who keeps looking over his shoulder when not protected by the rails on one side enables his opponent behind him to get first run on him by placing his challenge on the opposite side to which he is looking at that moment.

One can sense the presence and approach of a following rider without looking round to see if he is there, and provided one's horse is balanced, collected and kept up into his bridle, it is possible to take the necessary measures to ward off any challenge delivered from behind, as soon as the presence of the challenger makes itself felt, since the better balanced and the more collected a horse is, the quicker will be his response to any demand of his rider. A rider that is perpetually looking round cannot have his horse as well balanced and as collected as one who is not.

If, then, the particular whim of the horse one is riding is that he likes to be in front, it is advisable to indulge him, but with discretion: to leave the gate with the greatest possible speed—the greater advantage he can gain at the start, the more effort will his rivals have to exert in trying to catch him; to let him run along in front at such a pace as is consistent with his capabilities, condition and the state of the going, but at the same time being prepared to surrender the lead should another horse attempt to force the pace to an unwise degree.

While the front runner is a type frequently met with, the horse who prefers to come from behind is even more common. Such horses are more difficult to ride, since when brought to the front too soon they are either liable to tear away and run themselves out, or become tired of being in front and slow up.

The way in which a horse who likes to come from behind must be ridden depends upon whether he is calm or impetuous by nature. If the former, he presents no great problem: he can be jumped smartly out of the gate, steadied after he has crossed the first fence or hurdle and then be tucked in behind the leaders in about fourth or fifth place, where he can be allowed to remain until turning into the straight, when he can be brought into a challenging position, finally being ranged alongside the leader or leaders going into the last obstacle.

Not being an impetuous horse, there will be no difficulty in putting him in any desired position, and it will not matter whether or not he is 'shown daylight.' He can be kept well up with the leaders, since in the event of one or two of them falling it will not be difficult to pull behind another horse, and it will be possible to start moving up into a challenging position gradually and quite a long way from the finish.

In the case of a hard-pulling horse who must be waited with, however, the correct tactics are not so easily carried out.

One's horse must on no account be allowed to tear off in front from the start, or it will be impossible to get him back, and he will find himself, in spite of the efforts of his rider, occupying the role of a front runner; so that considerable care must be taken as regards the way in which he leaves the gate, an aspect dealt with in some detail in the previous chapter.

The rider's next problem will be to keep his horse covered up behind other runners, without being so close on their heels that he has no chance of getting a proper view of the obstacles or is in danger of jumping into the horse in front, which will be certain to happen if the latter is a 'sticky' jumper and one's own horse a free one. Quite a number of horses, though they will take a very strong hold when they see daylight, will drop their bits when tucked in behind others, when they will be content to lob along calmly and contentedly until such times as they are pulled out and shown daylight. The riding of these horses is quite a straightforward affair and merely consists of not hustling them out of the gate—this does not mean getting left about six lengths—tucking them in behind the leading horses or in the middle of the field, and bringing them out when the moment arrives to deliver one's challenge.

But the real hard puller is a more difficult problem. If one has any doubts about holding him it is (as pointed out in the last chapter) no bad plan to start in the second rank. This will mean that he is covered up from the outset and that, consequently, the rider does not have the task of pulling him back (or trying to do so) in order to get him covered up, which feat, if one is called upon to perform it after the horse has really got into his stride and has seen daylight, is often beyond the task of the average rider.

Before he sets off, the rider should have pulled his stirrup-leathers up as short as is consistent with security in the saddle, in order to have as good a chance as possible of holding the horse. He should be riding the horse on as long a rein as he dares—he will have to take a fairly short hold, but if he overdoes it and 'grabs the rings of the bit' he will be in danger of being pulled over the horse's head if the latter blunders. Having planted himself behind another horse he should endeavour to keep a length or more back, to avoid striking or jumping into him. It may happen that one can just manage to keep far enough behind the horse in front to avoid striking into him but not far enough back to enable one's horse to see the obstacle. This is admirable so far as progress on the flat is concerned, but when it comes to jumping, disaster will be probable unless measures are employed to cope with the situation.

By moving to one side or the other of one's pilot it is usually possible to get a glimpse of the obstacle, even if there is a horse on either side of him, for they are not likely to be jammed right up against one another, and the best plan, therefore, is to wait until the last moment and then let one's horse see the necessary daylight for him to jump. As he lands the rider will have a chance to take a pull at him and bring him back into his covered-up position. This is neither an attractive nor desirable way of riding in the ordinary course of events, but it is one which sometimes must be resorted to if the rider is going to have any chance of carrying out instructions to ride a waiting race.

My most vivid recollection of having to employ these tactics was on the occasion of having the good fortune and privilege to ride National Spirit in an amateur's hurdle race at Fontwell Park, in which the handicapper had given him the astonishingly lenient weight of 10 st. 12 lb. In those days he was not as good or as strong as he later became, as he was still a comparative novice, but he was no weakling, and the combination of his lenient handicapping, his strength, quick jumping and the moderate ability of his opponents made the task of waiting with him rather a formidable one, which I accomplished only by the means described above, resulting in a success which I could not very well have failed to achieve however I had ridden him, my chief satisfaction being that I had been able to carry out the instructions given me, even though the manner of doing so left much to be desired from the aspect of artistic execution.

When the rider finds that he cannot hold his horse at all and is in danger of striking into the horse in front of him, he will have to pull out and let him see daylight, hoping for the best, otherwise he is likely to bring down both the horse in front of him and himself.

When once he has done this he will serve no good purpose by mauling the horse's mouth about in a vain endeavour to pull him back, which he will not succeed in doing. His best plan is to sit firmly but quietly against him, steadying him as much as possible but at the same time not expending his own or his horse's energy in a battle which will destroy any remaining chance he may have had in the race.

Except when there is a 'kink' in a course, in the shape of the track bending inwards and out again, as used to be the case at Newbury and still is at Brighton (which is mercifully confined to flat-racing), the shortest way from the start to the finish is the path followed by the rails, so that the nearer a jockey keeps to these, the more direct will be his route. There is a general idea that to keep on the rails is to court danger, a theory based perhaps upon the competition to obtain this position, upon memories of jockeys being put over the rails—an occurrence met with more often in the realm of fiction than in real life—and the fact that at an 'open' hurdle or fence, that is to say an obstacle placed by itself in the open with no rails running up to the wings, the horse on the inside is more tempted to run out than the one on his outside.

But I do not think that this is altogether correct. When on the rails one is secure in the knowledge that, with regard to the presence of other competitors, there is only one flank to watch, provided, of course, that a gap is not left between one's horse and the rails, in which case it is certain that another competitor will make every attempt to avail himself of the same. Apart from this it is a safe bet, particularly over fences, that the rider in front will jump the obstacle a couple of feet—perhaps more—from the wing, which will enable the horse behind to get a glimpse of the fence, even if he is following closely behind, so long as he keeps as near the inside as it is possible to be. If the horse in front is glued to the inside himself, one can pull back a couple of lengths in order to obtain the necessary view of the obstacle to take off, or jump it slightly to one side or the other, especially over big fences such as at Aintree. If they happen to jump outwards from the rails they can be tracked with safety, as they will veer away each time they take off, leaving a gap between themselves and the rails as they land.

Another reason for being on the rails where practicable is that horses themselves know which is the shortest way round, and when pulled to the outside or middle of the course, will often resent this attempt to make them increase the length of their journey, by hanging towards the inside and paying more attention to getting back on to the rails than to jumping, with at times the most unfortunate results. And even in fields of twenty or more runners, I have often found that a position on the rails offered the clearest run.

Having secured a position on the rails, in perhaps third or fourth place, or even farther back, the problem will eventually arise as to the means of improving this position when the time comes to deliver a challenge. The rider will be faced with two alternatives: pulling to the outside and coming round the horses in front of him, or trying to get through on the inside. The plan he chooses will depend upon the capabilities of the horse he is riding and upon circumstances.

If he is riding a horse that cannot accelerate he will have to think twice about trying to get up on the inside, for he will not be able to dart his horse through a briefly-offered opening, as he could with one able to quicken instantly. If he attempts to do so he will find the gap closed before he has reached it or just as he is getting through, with the result that he will either have to snatch his horse up to avoid striking into the one in front of him, or will find himself sandwiched between the quarters of the horse in front of him and the rails, his horse receiving a violent bump in the ribs which will probably knock all the wind out of him.

If, however, the horse in front of him is obviously tiring or weakening he can probably chance this manœuvre even if he is not riding a horse that can quicken, as the horse in front will be dropping back, thus allowing only a fractional moment in which the one coming up on the inside can be stopped. Since the challenger will be going the stronger of the two he will be more likely to come off best in any *contretemps* that may arise between them.

If, on the other hand, the horse or horses in front show no sign of weakening it is advisable, when the time comes that the rider must improve his position, to pull to the outside and come with an uninterrupted run on the flank. This does not mean that one should pull to the outside coming round a bend; the latter manœuvre is a grave error of tactics, since it necessitates going several yards farther than the horses on the inside, and one should, on principle, keep as close to the inside as possible round all bends, edging to the outside of the leaders when fairly into the straight.

There are, of course, reservations in the case of most principles and precepts, and, in fact, I think that I once lost a hurdle race because I held too slavishly to the rule referred to; for the horse I was riding was a one-pacer who did not get going until the last mile. Having gradually overtaken the opposition except for the two leaders, I found myself about to range alongside the latter as we approached the last bend, but pulled in behind them rather than give away a few yards by coming round them, with the result that I checked my horse's run and could never get him going again until it was too late. And I think that there are times, such as the circumstance I have described, and when there is a short run in after the last bend, when one is bound to come round another horse, perhaps two horses, on a bend.

But one should weigh up the disadvantage of giving away ground against the advantage of not stopping a one-pacer in his run. Whereas it would obviously not be politic to come round the outside of four or five horses running abreast, there may be occasions upon which one should be prepared to come round one or two, and when such occasions arise one should have the moral courage to execute the necessary tactics in spite of the criticism that may arise from those who know a good deal but not everything, and who, in the event of defeat, are more than likely to express their censure.

When in on the rails behind a wall of horses, one is very liable (particularly when inexperienced) to be overcome by a kind of claustrophobia, and to panic because it seems impossible to get out in time to make one's challenge. If on a horse with no turn of speed there may be a certain amount of justification for this sentiment, but it is astonishing how the situation can change in a matter of seconds: tiring horses drop back or begin to hang away from the rails when they come under pressure, and gaps open up where only an impenetrable mass seemed to be, and it is always worth while 'sitting and suffering' as long as one dares, rather than start pulling to the outside before it is absolutely necessary. When riding a horse with a good turn of speed, this is a policy that pays nine times out of ten.

On some courses one can afford to sit in behind longer than on others: when the obstacles are 'open' one can invariably get up on the inside between them, as there are no rails to stop one, and I think that there is usually a better chance of achieving this over fences than over hurdles or on the flat. A certain amount depends upon the ability of opposing jockeys, for what one might successfully attempt against amateurs is not always a wise venture against professionals.

When attempting to come up on the inside, one should never choose the take-off side of the fence to begin operations, for if the jockey in front takes steps to prevent this manœuvre (and he will be quite within his rights in doing so) one is likely to find oneself going out over the wing, baulked or running out. It may be possible to get away with it once or twice—and if riding a fast horse who is going well, this is quite likely—but the day will come when one tries it on once too often, and the results are likely to be far from pleasant.

The best moment to choose is immediately after landing: the next fence is some way away, the horse in front may be slightly off his balance as a result of making a mistake—it may be only a minor one but it will check him for a second and demand his rider's attention—and his rider will be less prepared for the move. When one plans putting it into practice it is advisable to have one's horse going into the fence with a measured, balanced and crescendo approach, so that even if the horse in front has taken off first, one's own will be jumping up to him as he lands.

There are some horses who do not seem to jump well with other horses crowded round them: instead of paying attention to the task on hand they are looking about at the other horses, and tend as a result to jump without freedom, and inaccurately. Such horses almost invariably go best either in front, where they have a clear view of their fences and only one or two horses near them, or on the outside, in which case they only have other competitors on one flank to contend with. If they are not fast enough to take up the running from the start it is as well to begin on the outside, clear of the ruck, and, after jumping the first two or three obstacles without interference one can then work towards the inside, which will quite likely offer a passage free of interference in the second division of the field. If such horses are unsighted or interfered with at one of the first two or three obstacles, they tend to lose confidence and jump badly throughout the race, but if they get over them successfully they gain courage and jump better and quicker as they go along.

It is inadvisable to try to come between two horses just before taking off: a good many horses jump slightly to one side or the other by nature and thus there is a chance of being jumped into and sandwiched between the two, one's horse having all the breath knocked out of him. Moreover, a jockey sensing this move can pull slightly towards his neighbour, blinding the horse behind to the obstacle, causing him not to take off at all, to hit it hard, or to check himself almost to a standstill, lurch over it and lose many lengths. Instead, manœuvring for position should be done well before the fence is reached, so that in the event of being thwarted one has time to pull back and give the horse a view of the fence.

When riding a fast, accurate jumper every use should be made of his ability to confuse and dismay any less fortunate opponent who threatens danger. By getting about half a length in front of such a competitor and encouraging one's horse to stand back it is sometimes possible to delude the other horse into taking off at the same time, with the result that, since he left the ground several yards behind, he will probably either hit the fence hard and lose ground, fall, or put in a couple of short strides, buck over, and consequently take about twice as long over the procedure as in the case of a good jump. Conversely, when opposed by a really good jumper it is not advisable to try to jump stride for stride with him on a horse that is not experienced and skilled.

The situation sometimes arises that the riding orders have not allowed for the particular circumstances that have come about, so that if rigidly adhered to they will bring about certain defeat. The rider must then make up his mind whether to take it upon himself to disobey his instructions, or to stick to his orders regardless of the result. His decision must depend entirely upon his understanding of the trainer, or whoever gave him directions, and upon the certainty that he has made a correct appreciation of the situation.

It is quite possible that the owner or trainer in question would rather have his orders carried out exactly, regardless of the consequences, than see the jockey taking matters into his own hands. On the other hand, and if he has backed the horse this will be his view, he may expect the jockey to use his initiative where necessary for the achievement of victory. But it is certain that, if he wishes to retain the confidence and patronage of his employers, a rider should make quite certain that his action is essential, before he goes against the instructions given him before the race.

Neither horsemanship nor tactics are of any avail without determination and the will to win, which was one of the qualities responsible for Gordon Richards' phenomenal success on the flat. One should never give up persevering until it is quite obvious that the horse cannot win. A number of horses are lazy by nature, and though quite willing to exert themselves to the utmost when called upon to do so, are equally happy to slouch along unambitiously if the rider is prepared to let them, and the weaker, more unfit and gullible the rider, the quicker will they be to realize and take advantage of his shortcomings. A jockey is usually warned about any such tendency in a horse, but even then it is not difficult for an inexperienced rider to be deceived by a cunning horse, and he should always shake him well up, if necessary giving him a couple of reminders with the whip, before he lets himself be convinced that a horse of this type is a spent force.

Some horses have a habit of giving themselves a breather about half a mile from the finish, dropping back several places as they momentarily relax their efforts. In such cases it is as well not to bustle them for a stride or two, so that they may have every chance of getting their second wind, but once they have recovered they can be urged on with impunity, and a rider should not take it for granted that, because a horse drops back a place or two during the race, he has shot his bolt.

Horses that have this habit of giving themselves a breather present their riders with a valuable tactical weapon, for an opponent that has seen a horse range upsides about half a mile from home and then drop out may easily be deluded into thinking that the latter is done with and will not trouble him again, and—particularly if there is no other horse in the offing—start to take matters easily in the belief that the race is as good as won. This enables the rider of the horse that has momentarily fallen back to use his horse's second wind to great effect, by attacking with a late, strong run, which gives the deluded one no time to get going again before the winning-post has been reached and the race lost and won.

Similarly, a horse should never be 'let down' after striking the front, even if it seems that victory has been secured, in case something comes from behind with a wet sail and catches the leader unawares.

12
The Finish

I SUPPOSE THAT the Finish, like the Start, could claim to belong to the chapter on tactics, but that somewhat indigestible section seemed quite long enough as it was, and since both starting and finishing are an art in themselves, I think it is right to make the separate divisions as has been done.

In steeplechasing and hurdle-racing the finish can be considered to begin with the last obstacle. In this respect N.H. riders learn to regard this as a recognized landmark which is, I think, the reason why good riders over fences and hurdles are not necessarily good jockeys on the flat, where they have no such guide and consequently tend to make their effort too soon, or too late, until they have had sufficient practice to accommodate themselves to the different conditions.

A jockey who can ride a flat race finish is worth several pounds from the last fence, when opposed to one who cannot, which is borne out by the fact that ex-flat race jockeys always make better hurdle race-riders than those who have had no experience on the flat, hurdle-racing being a matter of jockeyship rather than horsemanship. When a rider is both a horseman and a jockey he comes into the top class, and it is notable that most jockeys in the top flight of their generation, over hurdles or fences, could ride on the flat.

But before the question of 'scrubbing them out' arises a jockey has to get over the last obstacle, and the manner in which he does so will contribute about as much to the result as will his skill—or lack of it—in riding a finish; this applies even more to fences than hurdles.

To the case of a horse coming into a fence unchallenged the remarks in earlier chapters on riding over fences may be applied. His rider's only task will be to get him safely over, which he will be most likely to achieve if he employs the recognized methods I have already endeavoured to expound, and provided his horse is not unduly exhausted he should be able to carry it out with success.

But it quite often occurs that the horse who comes into the last fence unchallenged and comparatively fresh does not get over safely. And there is a reason for it.

The rider's mood is reflected in his actions, which in turn pass on that mood to the horse, and when—as is only too easy when one is in the pleasant position of approaching the last fence, 'a winner without a fall'—the rider signifies, by loosing the reins and making no application of the legs, that he has ceased to bother about the proceedings any longer, the latter is liable to catch his mood and do little about jumping the fence, with the result that he falls, goes on his nose and shoots the jockey off or makes a bad enough mistake for him to lose the race to the horse lying second, even if the latter may be some dozen lengths behind.

The moral is that one should always collect a horse when going into the last fence, no matter how far away the nearest opponent may be, and ride him into it with sufficient determination to make him realize that his task is not over until he has cleared it, and there is every chance that he will then pay attention to what he is doing and will jump it properly.

But no one goes through a race-riding career riding horses that win unchallenged, and the aspect of more hardly contested battles must now be approached.

When coming into the last fence side by side with one or more opponents, one of three situations arises: one's horse is going the best, there is nothing in it, or he is not going as well.

All three cases are governed by further factors. One's horse may have more, or less, finishing speed than his rival. If he has more finishing speed, and is going the better, one can afford to make certain of clearing the last fence by riding him with what might be described as 'discreet determination'—keeping him well up into his bridle with the legs, but not loosing his head, giving him every chance to jump it cleanly—on the principle that it is only necessary to get over without making a bad mistake to be certain of winning, by virtue of having the better speed in the run-in.

If he has less finishing speed, or is going no better or not so well as the other horse, it is essential to get over first to have any chance of winning, so that everything must be sacrificed and risked—even a fall—to try to bring this about.

Riding a horse into the last fence falls into two phases: the approach, from the landing side of the last fence but one up to two strides outside the wings of the last, and the strides from that point to the take-off. The first consists of riding as one would ride a finish on the flat, which, as it has not yet been discussed, had better be considered forthwith.

In what is known in the profession as 'scrubbing a horse out' there are three forces of propulsion that are brought to bear on the horse: the legs, the hands and the whip. For the time being the subject of the whip will be laid aside.

The principle of riding out a horse with hands and heels is that, as the hands go forward the heels go back, the two motions being synchronized with each other and with the stride of the horse. When the horse's legs are fully extended the hands should be forward and the heels back, when his legs are doubled up beneath him the hands come back and the legs return to the vertical—one will quite often see them swung right forward, when a jockey is using his legs with the greatest possible vigour. During this procedure the reins should, if possible—and this is very difficult and not essential if the horse is running straight—be just taut. I think the best way to prevent the reins from flapping about is to keep the wrists and hands in the same relation to each other as is taught when playing tennis, that is to say the fists bent as far back as possible and as nearly perpendicular to the wrists as they will go, their action being forward, and at the same time slightly upward—as the heels go back, returning to a position level with the horse's neck and about six inches in front of the withers as the heels come forward again.

When starting to 'scrub' a horse one should begin gradually, as opposed to rushing into a whirlwind motion of hands and heels, which will probably be out of time with the horse's stride and each other. The first step is to 'pick the horse up', a term which signifies shortening the reins to the length most suitable for riding a finish (dependent on the build of the horse, whether long-fronted or short-fronted), collecting the horse, and poising him for that increase of pace which is about to be demanded of him.

Having picked him up, the next move is to begin working hands and legs gently and gradually, while doing so picking up the rhythm of the horse's stride and fitting that of the actions into it. If this is done suddenly, violently, or out of time, the chances are that the horse will swerve, or be thrown out of his stride and begin to roll, and as a result he will not progress as well as he ought to. If in difficulties, it is best to stop scrubbing, give the horse a couple of strides to recover his balance and get on an even keel, and then start again; to keep on riding when out of time and with the horse unbalanced will only make matters worse—it is often noticeable in the case of amateurs and apprentices that, as soon as they stop riding their horses run on.

Meanwhile the seat should be just clear of the saddle, the body leaning as far forward as is consistent with the jockey seeing where he is going, and the back as straight as is compatible with smooth and rhythmic movement.

This, then, will be the manner in which a jockey will be riding as he urges his horse towards the last fence with his hands and heels, Two strides from the wings he should sit up a shade, drop his hands on his horse's withers, keeping a light but none the less definite contact with the horse's mouth, and continuing to apply the legs and heels with determination and vigour—unless it becomes unpleasantly obvious that the horse has met the fence completely wrong and is going to hit it hard, in which case the rider's only hope is to resort to the measures suggested in an earlier chapter.

The object of bringing the body to a slightly more upright position is that the rider can see what he is about and where the horse is likely to take off, while the idea of dropping the hands on his withers and keeping contact with the horse's mouth is to give him a chance of maintaining control in the event of the horse attempting a last-stride swerve, and of being in unison with him as he takes off; the action of the legs and heels prevents him from slowing down when the movement of the hands is stilled.

The rider will probably be riding with a flat-race shortness of rein while he is approaching the last fence, which will be too short to be altogether advisable when he actually jumps. As he lowers his hands and ceases their motion he should slip the reins the extra few inches necessary to forestall the eventuality of interfering with the horse's mouth, or being pulled over his head. When he lands the rider will find himself in the position of having a slightly longer rein than he wishes to use for riding his horse out from this point to the winning-post, so that he will have to pick him up again, and then get down and scrub.

It has already been mentioned that some critics give as a reason for supporting the forward seat the fact that its principles, which include riding with a very short rein, enable a jockey to go straight from landing over the last fence to the flat-racing position. In point of fact this offers no advantage, for it is essential, after a horse has landed, to give him at least a stride's pause before beginning to ride him out, and the fraction of a second taken by a good jockey to shorten his reins occupies no more than that necessary time for him to 'get on his legs'. A jockey who 'flies at him' without giving him this respite will only throw him off his balance so that by the time he has adjusted himself and is running on an even keel the race will be over.

Even if a jockey has landed with a short enough rein to enable him to go right into his 'scrub', he should not be tempted to do so until he has got his horse properly poised. This is even more important when the horse has made a mistake.

From the moment of starting his final run to reaching the winning-post the rider becomes, for all practical purposes, a flat race jockey, and it is from those of the latter categories, rather than from steeplechase-riders, that the learner should take his example.

I once asked Charlie Elliott, as brilliant a jockey and as good a stylist as could be found, what he considered the most important factors in riding a finish and he said:

'Always pick your horse up and get him balanced before you start your run.

'Never look about you, but keep your eye on the winning-post.

'Don't try and go faster than your horse; in other words, do not increase the rhythm of your "scrub" to a tempo greater than that of the horse's gallop.'

I do not think I can do better than repeat this advice. These principles are the framework round which the rider should build personal style and adaptation to circumstances.

In the heat of the moment it is very easy to become over-excited and start throwing the reins at the horse in a desperate attempt to urge him on, but such tactics will not make him go any faster, and though the vigour of the rider's efforts should not flag, enthusiastic effort must not be allowed to take precedence over rhythm.

It is easy to forget that the vital factor in winning or losing a race does not lie merely in getting the horse's nose in front of his nearest rival's, but in getting it in front at the winning-post. And it is not the slightest use winning the race ten yards before, or after, passing the post, when the only place at which the verdict is given is the winning-post itself.

Thus it is essential, not only to realize exactly where the post is, but to keep one's eye on it as well, and not on the horse who appears to be the danger. It is quite possible that the horse in question will prove the wrong one and that the eventual winner will come from another quarter.

One can sense the approach of a horse from behind, and while he is alongside it is of no use looking at him: in neither case (unless endowed with hypnotic powers) will it be possible to influence his progress by looking at him. But by gauging one's horse's powers, and using them in relation to the position of the winning-post itself, it may sometimes be possible to win a race at the place that counts, when a rival may have won it too soon or too late.

Besides looking round there are two other heinous crimes which jockeys can commit. Pulling up before the winning-post has been reached and showing off by trying to win by a short head when a couple of lengths could have been achieved.

Some horses, once they think their task is over, pull up in about two strides, so that even when winning a race easily it is a dangerous action to drop one's hands about twenty yards from the winning-post. When a horse has begun to pull up at the end of a race it is impossible to get him going again until too late, and an enterprising and energetic rider in his wake could snatch the race out of the fire, after all seemed lost. Having been beaten under such circumstances, even if surviving the rain of bottles which will not improbably emanate from the less pretentious enclosures, a jockey is unlikely to be patronized by the same owner again.

Trying to win by a short head when it could have been three lengths is liable to produce similar results. An opponent may not be as stupid as he seemed, and the stone one believed one had in hand might turn out to be only 10 lb., a discrepancy that a two-length margin would cover, but which would not be answered for by a short-head. When riding a 'good thing' some thought of future handicapping should be taken in not winning by a street, yet it is as well not to cut matters too fine, for besides incurring the wrath of a patron an answer for the action might be demanded by the Stewards.

In the case of having orders not to win by more than a certain distance, it is always advisable to come from behind rather than to hit the front early and then take a pull, for in the former case one can see exactly what is occurring, and thus be master of the situation, but in the latter it is impossible to tell what is going on behind, and it is far easier to get caught napping when slowing up than when approaching the winning-post at an increasing speed.

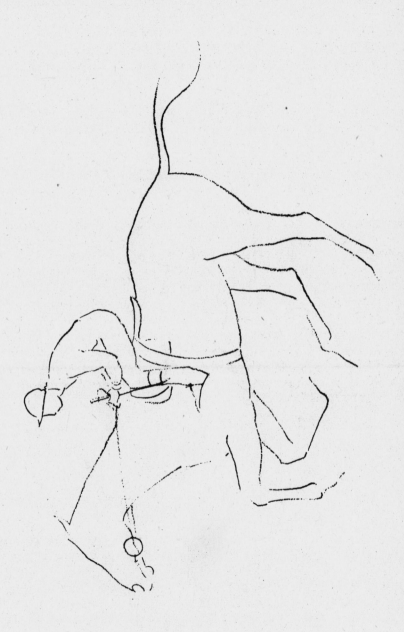

Picking-up a horse

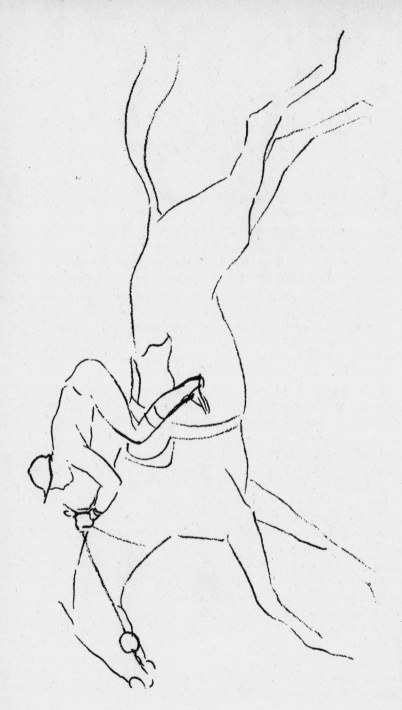

Scrubbing a horse out

13

The Whip—Its Use and Abuse

THE USE OF the whip falls into two categories, a means of correction and an aid to propulsion.

Since this book is not a treatise on horse-breaking, the use of the whip as a means of correction does not enter into the argument, and any references to this department that may be thought necessary will be made in the chapter on schooling. The present chapter, therefore, deals solely with the use of the whip during a race.

The first matter the rider must decide for himself is in which hand he is going to carry his whip. This will depend upon two factors: whether he can transfer his whip easily and quickly from the carrying position to the operational position, keeping it in the same hand, and whether or not he can use it in both hands.

The opinion has already been put forward that a jockey should be able to use his whip with either hand, and it is very seldom that a good jockey cannot do so, the only exception I can think of was the late Brownie Carslake, who was left-handed and could not so much as swat a fly with his right.

The easiest way of getting a whip into action is to carry it in the opposite hand to which one intends to use it and when the time comes to grasp it with the disengaged hand, pull it through the carrying hand and proceed from there. A jockey who intends to use it in this way should remember to start off with his whip in the opposite hand to the one he intends to employ.

But circumstances may arise that cause the rider to wish to carry his whip in the same hand as the one in which he is going to use it, and the problem then arises as to how he is going to change it from the passive position to the active.

There are two ways in which this can be achieved: the one is a kind of gear-changing movement in which the top of the whip is brought backwards and the grip is changed by an under-arm motion of the hand, during which the elbow involuntarily shoots outwards. This is rather an unsatisfactory and clumsy method, as the thumb is somewhat of a hindrance during its execution and tends to cause the whip to be dropped altogether.

By far the best way—although it requires considerable practice to perfect it—is to swing the whip sharply forward and upwards, so that it is grasped between the first and second fingers and the thumb (the third and fourth fingers automatically release their grip), the top of the whip pointing straight backwards towards the elbow joint and the whip itself being parallel to the forearm, which becomes almost vertical to the ground. The next stage is to bring it downwards with a strong enough swing to enable the whip to pivot right round, between the first and second fingers, until it arrives in the position in which it is going to be used; while it is pivoting between the two fingers it is momentarily separated from the thumb, which meets it again as the shaft of the whip comes to rest against the heel of the hand, the final movement being to bring the index finger across into position on the same side of the whip as the second finger. This is the recognized method used by all English jockeys, and with practice it becomes second nature, though it sounds rather complicated when one attempts to put it into words.

When practised on the ground, or while riding along on a quiet horse, it seems comparatively easy, but when tried in a race it is more difficult, owing to the force of the wind-resistance set up by the speed of the horse.

The best way to overcome this is to swing the whip forward and upward with some force, ensuring that it goes far enough to make certain of an equally good swing back, the arc that it describes being parallel to the direction in which the horse is going. If the swing is not straight and true the whip will not pivot properly between the fingers and is liable to be dropped, and it is sometimes a help to give it a couple of preparatory swings before turning it right over; this also warns the horse that you are going to ask him to increase his pace.

When once the whip is ready for action, which in the case of an expert will be in a second, one should begin to swing it in rhythm with the horse's stride and with the movements of one's own hands and legs. That is to say, as the hand holding the reins goes forward and the heels go back the whip should be swung forward, coming back with the bridle-hand and as the legs go forward.

Before hitting a horse the whip should always be swung two or three times to give him fair warning that he is expected to go faster if he can. If he responds, it will not be necessary to hit him at all, but it is advisable to keep on swinging the whip, otherwise he may, if the whip is returned to the carrying position, take it as a sign that he is expected to slow up.

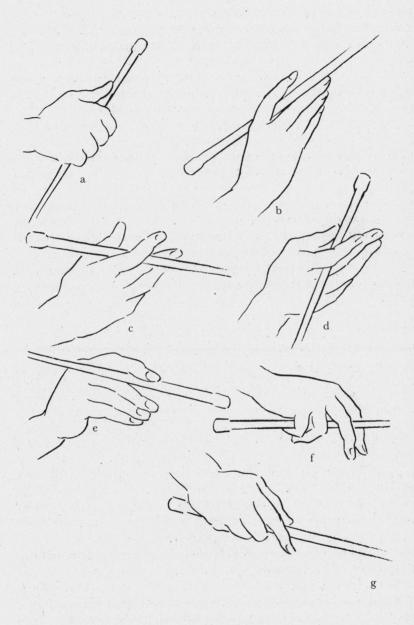

Bringing the whip from the 'carry' to the 'operational' position

When a horse is hit, the whip should fall as far back as possible, the hand coming in the neighbourhood of the horse's hip; he should on no account be hit in the stifle or ribs. The action of the hand and arm should be forward and backwards, rather than out to the side and inwards, as the latter movement, besides tending to make one hit a horse in the stifle or ribs, is liable to result in hitting another horse or jockey.

A horse should be hit when he is at that stage of his gallop when his legs are curled up underneath him and he is about to start a fresh stride, because when he feels the sting of the blow he will tend to react to it by increasing the vigour and length of his stride, but if hit when he is fully extended there is nothing more he can do, and he will be more inclined to to curl up than stretch himself out. Therefore the fall of the whip should take place as the bridle-hand goes back and the legs forward.

The next point is the return of the whip from the position of action to that of being carried. It consists merely in letting it fall vertically downwards, pivoting between the first and second fingers, and bringing the thumb, and the third, fourth and little fingers into the position round the shaft from which they originally started. Americans carry their whips in what we would call an upside-down position, namely in the same position as when in action, but in England this is one of the first signs of an amateur or inexperienced performer. It has a clumsy and inartistic appearance and should never be resorted to by a rider who wishes to be considered anything of a jockey; it is not uncommonly met with in the case of an amateur or inexperienced rider who has arrived at the 'action' position but cannot get back to the 'carry'.

The severity and frequency with which a horse is hit—or whether he is hit at all—must depend upon the characteristics of the horse and the discretion of the jockey.

Some horses are by nature thick-skinned, tough and idle, and seem to show little or no resentment of the whip, in fact, horses of this description invariably need a couple of good cracks at some stage of the race to bring to their notice the fact that they are supposed to be racing. When riding them one should not be deluded into thinking they are spent forces when in reality they are not fully extended—but it is not necessary to punish them.

But the average horse will either do his best if ridden out with hands and legs, while the whip is waved at him or with the addition of a comparatively light tap every few strides, or he will resent being hit to such an extent that he will swerve or slow up when it falls. If an honest and

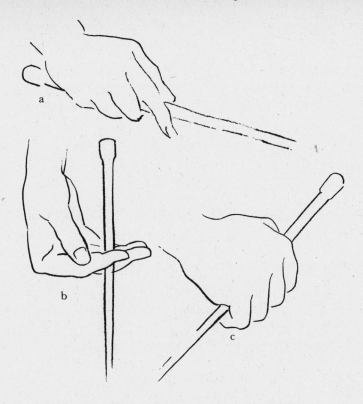

Returning the whip from the 'operational' to the 'carry' position

high-couraged horse is given a thrashing when he is doing his best in a
race, it may break his heart and turn him into a rogue, and the longer
a horse's racing career is expected to last, the less should he be hit at
the finish of his races. To hit a horse in the middle of a race is not quite
the same thing, since he is still capable of pulling out a bit more, and
will not, therefore, feel the same resentment that he would when hit at
the end of a race, when he is doing his best and has nothing more left.

Because a jockey gets out his whip some considerable way from the
winning-post, it does not follow that he is hitting his horse: he may
only be swinging his whip and will quite probably never hit him at all.

It would be safe to say that the lower the standard of riding, the
more are horses punished, and one quite often sees competitors in
point-to-point races thrashing tired horses from the first fence to the
winning-post in order to obtain the doubtful privilege of sixth or
seventh place. While it is both necessary and desirable to get a place if
this should be the owner's wish—some owners have no ambition for
their horses to be placed if they cannot win—there is no sense

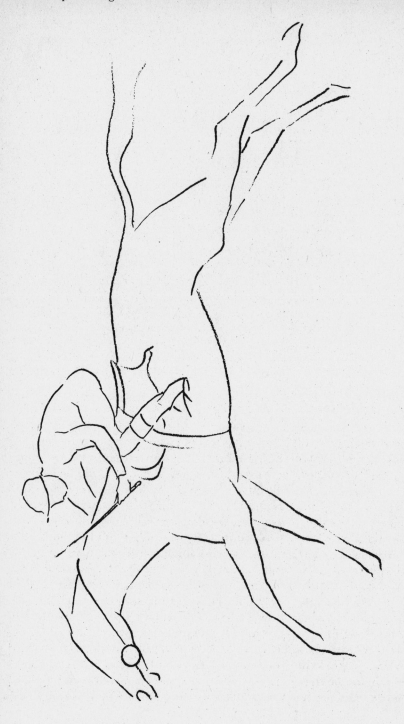

in flogging a horse that has no chance of finishing in the first three.

If, when the jockey brings out his whip and starts to swing it, the horse hangs or swerves in the opposite direction, he should immediately return it to the 'carry' and ride the horse out with his hands or pull the whip straight through and begin swinging it with the opposite hand; to continue to use a whip when the horse is going away from it is worse than useless and will result in the horse veering right across the track or cannoning into another runner, incurring the risk of disqualification in the event of him winning and, in any case, the censure of authority and the umbrage of the rider interfered with.

As has been mentioned earlier in the book, use of the whip should always be perfected at home before experimenting with it on a racecourse. One can practise getting it from the carrying to the active position while out for a walk, and can get into the way of swinging it by doing so while sitting on a gate, a chair or a saddle-horse. Nothing looks worse than the unskilled use of the whip, and it is better not to use it at all than to use it improperly.

When it is necessary to give a horse nothing more than a reminder in the shape of a tap from the whip, it is quite a good idea to give him what is known as a 'back-hander', that is to tap him with the whip used in the carrying position. When hitting him in this manner it is difficult to hurt a horse unless he is hit in the stifle and as a means of encouragement at the finish one can wave it at him held thus, which is often seen done by professional jockeys.

When riding a horse that hangs or veers to one side or the other, or is inclined to try to run out—or when running on the inside on a track on which there are 'open' fences or hurdles—it is often advisable to carry the whip on the side to which the horse is likely to veer, and when approaching an obstacle or a bend, to tap him down the shoulder to remind him of its presence, so that he will think that, if he tries to run out he will be met by the whip to stop him. Under such circumstances should the rider wish to use the whip in earnest he will have to be able to get it into action with the hand in which he is carrying it, since, if he pulls it through with the opposite one, he will have the whip in the wrong hand, thus causing the horse to swerve or veer even more violently in the direction from which it is desired to prevent him going.

The situation may arise that the rider has got out his whip before getting to the last fence, and finds himself approaching the obstacle with his whip in action. He must then decide whether he is going to keep it out when he jumps, or return it to the carrying position before he takes off.

When riding a horse over a fence with the whip up it is essential to have him balanced and going straight. If he is approaching it rolling, sprawling or veering to one side or the other, he is liable to make a mistake or fall, and if there is any sign that the horse is unbalanced or hanging to one side or the other, it is better to return the whip to the carrying position, try to collect him and keep him straight, when he will be more likely to jump quicker and get into his stride again sooner, than would be the case if he jumped the fence unbalanced and at an angle. This does not mean that the jockey should stop riding him: he should drive him on with his legs and heels, keeping him straight with the help of the improved control which the use of both hands will afford.

Whether or not a horse should be ridden into an obstacle under the whip is not always an easy matter to decide. One must be guided by the way he is going, and must weigh up the possibility of 'knocking him down' by using the whip at an inopportune moment, against that of gaining ground by availing oneself of the additional aid to propulsion that a skilled and appropriate use of the whip can sometimes supply.

In the case of a rider who has got out his whip, but is in any way doubtful of his ability to use it or of his knowledge concerning when to do so, he should put it back and ride his horse out with his legs and hands.

When using the whip in a finish with another horse it should always be between the two horses so that it prevents one's own horse from rolling on to—or hanging towards—the other. When sandwiched between two horses one should use the whip on the side towards which he is likely to veer, which, in nine cases out of ten will be the left.

In recent years the undesirable habit of hitting a horse down the shoulder, other than merely tapping him without taking the hands off the rein (to keep him straight) has developed. This is more likely to make a horse swerve than go forward, and, when delivered going into a fence, to distract rather than encourage him. In some cases, this may be due to jockeys riding too short to use their legs, at the same time not wishing to hit him hard. By and large, I found it best to give the horse a couple when well outside the wings and then kick him into the obstacle.

14
Returning to Scale

THE FIRST POINT to remember, after having passed the post in the first three, is not to dismount until reaching the unsaddling enclosure, since this action results in disqualification. It seems a simple rule, but it is astonishing how often placed riders, particularly those who have finished second or third, forget themselves and dismount outside the appointed place, and one should always make quite sure that the unsaddling enclosure has been reached before getting off. I heard of a case of some unfortunate amateur who, having finished first in front of an experienced and not too scrupulous rider on a heavily-backed favourite, was deluded by the latter into dismounting before he should, whereupon the jockey who had finished second objected to the winner on the grounds of dismounting before he had reached the winner's enclosure, and the stewards were forced to award him the race.

Having reached the appointed place, the rider unsaddles the horse himself, and does not (as I once saw) stand by with his hands on his hips waiting for the trainer to do so. It is always possible to tell if a rider knows anything about his business or not by the way he unsaddles a horse, mounts, or settles himself in the saddle, but whereas he will quite probably pass unnoticed when getting up to leave the paddock, he certainly will not do so when he is in the unsaddling enclosure for one of the placed horses.

When he dismounts he should—if he has not already done so while still on the horse's back—pull the near-side stirrup-iron up as far as it will go, or throw it over the saddle so that it is out of his way. He can then proceed to undo the surcingle and then the girths and take the saddle off; if encumbered by his whip he can lay this down. If the horse is wearing a breast-girth he must detach this before trying to take the saddle off otherwise he will find, having removed the latter from the horse's back, that the breast-girth is still attached to the horse itself. If the horse has also been wearing blinkers, while the rider has been dealing with the saddle, the trainer, or lad in charge of the horse,

In the earlier editions, only diagrams were used as illustrations to the text. These are admirable, but in view of the favourable reception of the addition of photographs to the latest edition of 'From Start to Finish', the flat-racing companion to 'Steeplechasing', a similar feature has been introduced in this edition.

Press Association

The leading jockey presents a neat, stylish and effective
appearance. He is not riding excessively short, so that scope is
allowed for the use of his legs. He is in accord with his
horse—evident in the latter's contented expression—and is so
poised as to adopt the flat-racing position the moment the horse
lands. The rider could be criticised, however, for not giving his
horse a little more rein, in case the latter pecks on landing. The
position of the second rider is also good, but he, too, could give
his horse more rein. 'Go forward over your hands' is not a bad
dictum to keep in mind.

Press Association

An example of a jockey riding with ultra-short leathers over fences. He is kept in position by a combination of pressure on the horse's mouth, weight in the stirrup irons and the small area of grip afforded by the lower part of his leg. His weight is behind the centre of gravity and, when he lands, his only method of getting forward into the flat-racing position is to pull himself there. Should the horse land awkwardly, his rider will come down on the animal's loins possibly injuring his back. In any case, the length of his stirrup leathers prevents him from using his legs at all as a means of propulsion and guidance, leaving him thus entirely dependent on his hands and whip.

Control Press Photos Ltd

This picture is of the historic Cheltenham Gold Cup of 1935 when
Golden Miller ridden by Gerry Wilson (No. 6) just beat
Thomond II (Billy Speck), here lying second. Third was
Kellsboro' Jack (Danny Morgan), who is following Golden Miller
and is outside Fred Rimell (black cap) on Avenger. The leading
horse is Southern Hero, ridden by Jack Fawcus. All these jockeys
were top class, Danny Morgan the most stylish. They rode a
medium length, Wilson a little longer than the others, thus
achieving maximum security as well as having their weight
correctly placed. This was essential, as the fences were
appreciably stiffer than they are now. Here, Fawcus and Morgan
are riding with an ideal length of rein, Wilson and Speck with
slightly too short a hold.

Press Association

An excellent example of a horse being given every chance to recover from a blunder on landing. Here the jockey is letting the horse have the full freedom of his head and neck while at the same time maintaining contact. He has not moved in the saddle and, at the next stride, will be able to balance the horse and continue, losing little or no ground. The jockey on No. 8 shows how to ride a horse into a hurdle under the whip. The horse is collected and balanced, the rider is going with him and has good contact without too short a rein. He also has his whip in the correct hand, that is between him and the challenger and against the direction in which his horse is hanging.

V

Press Association

The jockey on No. 5 has too short a hold of his horse's head. Though
not interfering with him, he would be in trouble if the horse pecked
or blundered. It is not easy to tell whether he is 'calling a cab' or has
hit him to take off; if the former, this could be due to his over-short
rein, without any compensating bend in his arm. He is riding short
for his height and, should the horse land awkwardly, might come
down on his mount's loins. The jockey on No. 3 has a nice length of
rein. He is, again, riding a little too short, but has a more suitable
build for this style than the jockey on No. 5.

A champion giving a faultless exhibition over hurdles: John Francombe wins the Daily Express Triumph Hurdle on Rodman. He is riding a practical length—short enough to distribute his weight correctly but long enough to allow him full use of his legs for propulsion and guidance; a sensible length of rein, with sufficient bend in his arm allows his horse further freedom if necessary; a straight back and low crouch that is not so low as to prevent him from seeing where he is going.

The author on Kami in the Grand National of 1947 (in which he
finished third) endeavouring to demonstrate the precepts,
expounded in the text, of a practical seat for landing over
Becher's: the body approximately perpendicular to the
ground—neither leant back nor inclined forward; sufficient rein
for the horse to have the necessary freedom of his head and neck,
but with contact maintained and a short enough hold to obviate
'winding up' at the next stride; medium length leathers, short
enough for correct balance on the flat, but long enough for
security, propulsion and control.

will probably have removed them. Having achieved all this the rider should (if he wants to see it again) pick up his whip and go straight to the scales.

He discards his whip, passes the Clerk of the Scales and then—and not before—he can consider himself the official winner of the race—unless he has to survive an objection.

Besides the winner and the placed horses—and jockeys are always being fined for forgetting to do so—the fourth has to weigh-in, and a jockey who has finished anywhere near the first few horses should always check with the Clerk of the Scales to make sure that he has not been placed fourth by the Judge, before he returns to the dressing-room.

Having passed the scales the number-cloth should be detached from one's tack and handed back to the official appointed to issue and collect them, as one passes him on the way back to the dressing-room. To forget to do so means that the latter who, when there are big fields has quite enough to do otherwise, will have to hunt through the dressing-rooms to retrieve it, or the valet will have to take it back to him. Riders who are new to the game are apt to think that they are going to be waited upon hand and foot by all concerned, but the efficiency of the service can only be preserved if they will co-operate to the extent of making everything as simple as possible by doing these little things for themselves, which are no trouble to them but are of the greatest help to the staff. The dressing- and weighing-rooms on many of the smaller courses are too small for the number of riders present-day fields produce, and valets and all concerned work under considerable difficulties, so that the more streamlined the work can be made, the better will the result be for everyone.

Under such circumstances, riders who are not actually changing should avoid getting in the way by sitting about on the benches and gossiping: if one wants to see the valet with regard to arrangements at a future meeting, the time to do so is just after the riders have left the dressing-room for the paddock; the room will then be comparatively empty and the valet will not be so occupied, and will therefore be more likely to appreciate and remember what he is told than if he is approached during the furore of his busiest moments. Soldier riders should avoid bringing their batmen to valet them, even if it saves paying the valet. The average soldier knows nothing about racecourse procedure, and besides taking up too much room (particularly if he is a guardsman of a build proportionate to that particular arm of the service and is wearing army boots) he will probably send out his master improperly equipped and turned out.

Having returned to the dressing-room, a rider should put down his saddle on the table used by the appropriate valet—not on the bench, where it will get in everyone's way—remove the colours, unless using them in the next race, and roll them up in the cap, tying up the bundle with the cap-string, and either putting them back in the colour bag to which they belong or leaving them on the bench by his pitch; scattering them about the room only means that the valet or travelling lad responsible for them has to search all over the place for them, and it is not improbable that someone looking for a particular coloured cap may appropriate the one belonging to them. This is more likely to happen at a point-to-point meeting, where there are not usually any official valets and where unauthorized borrowing and appropriation sometimes goes on.

When riding at such meetings it is advisable to keep one's kit under lock and key, as articles such as whips, weight-cloths and the lead panels for the latter, have a knack of disappearing the moment one's back is turned.

If one has no further ride that day one can dress and depart to watch the rest of the racing. When due to ride again, in a later race, it is as well to get the valet to adjust the weight on the trial-scales, so that there will be no last-minute rush when the time comes to weigh out. After that one can go out and watch the racing, or if in a state of exhaustion sit in the dressing-room to recover.

Most jockeys hand their wallet and any such valuables as their watch to their valet before they go out to ride; this is a matter for individual choice, but as I seldom carried enough money on me to be worth stealing, and am not given to wearing expensive watches, I always trusted to the general honesty of the occupants of the dressing-room and never had any reason to regret it.

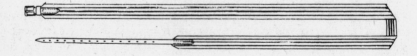

15
Falls

OF ONE THING a steeplechase-rider can be certain: he will not go
through his career without having a fall. He may not have many, he
may have more than his fair share, but no serious one among them, or
he may both fall frequently and hurt himself badly, and he may even
be crippled for life or be killed, but into one of these categories he will
come, and if he thinks that he will not he is under a grave delusion.

If a rider keeps in the game long enough he is almost certain to have
a serious fall sooner or later, and there are few jockeys I can think of
who have been fortunate enough to escape this fate. Bruce Hobbs
broke his back, Alec Marsh his neck—both survived. Fulke Walwyn
fractured his skull, Gerry Hardy was lamed for life, Lord Mildmay
had more bad falls than I can enumerate. I myself survived about four
seasons unscathed and then spent nine months on crutches as a result
of an injured leg.

About the only rider of my generation that I can think off who did
not have a serious fall during his riding career—I cannot even
remember him breaking his collar-bone—is Bobby Petre. But to show
the tricks that fate can play, the latter broke his leg so badly when step-
ping a couple of feet down from a breakwater on to the beach—I
believe he did not even fall—that he had to have it removed.

In all aspects of life there are two distinct forces that direct a man's
life: the hand of fate and his own actions.

There are strokes of fortune and misfortune, which are brought
about through circumstances over which we have no control, and
there are likewise others for which we have only ourselves to thank.
And it is the presence of the former strange, unpredictable and, at the
same time, frightening and exciting power that, in the case of those
whose profession or calling is in any way overshadowed by danger or
death, tinges the mind with—according to the individual—superstition, fear, excitement, or delight, or, to be more accurate, with a mixture of these sensations, varied according to the physical and mental
characteristics of different people, and according to circumstances.

No steeplechase-rider can help feeling, at the back of his mind, that there is a possibility that he will have a bad fall or that he will even meet his end. The awareness of this sentiment must vary with the individual and with the time and place, and it is so closely allied to the nervous excitement of taking part in a race, which brings with it the thrill of possible victory, the fear of making a fool of oneself or failing to carry out one's orders, and all the other influences attendant upon performing in public, that it is not always easy to diagnose or distinguish the different influences, even in oneself. And there have been occasions upon which I have felt more nervous before riding on the flat, than when waiting to take part in a race at Aintree.

A rider's frame of mind and outlook is bound to be affected directly by the falls he incurs. Apart from the mental aspect of the situation, falls affect the nervous system, muscles and the working of various parts of the body, and can therefore have their repercussions in such ways as being too stiff to ride a finish properly, loss of grip, or slowness in thinking and acting, according to their severity and nature, quite apart from any direct fear of their recurrence that may have been implanted in the rider's mind.

If, therefore, a rider is fortunate enough to avoid having a fall during his first few rides it will greatly increase the confidence with which he starts upon his career; on the other hand a couple of fairly severe shakings, even if no specific injury has been sustained at the outset, are liable to have a discouraging effect, though such an experience does at least reveal to the rider whether or not his heart is really in the game. If it is, he will struggle on regardless of his discomfiture and apprehension, if not he will soon drift out of steeplechase riding.

If a few good rides come his way a keen rider will recover his confidence and never look back, but even the most enthusiastic cannot go on falling indefinitely and retain their zest. After a series of hard falls it is advisable to take a rest for a week or two before starting again.

Before embarking seriously on the career of a N.H. rider I think it is a help to work out a set mental attitude towards the risks attendant upon the calling, for upon the thoughts that lurk subconsciously at the back of one's mind a great many of one's actions depend. A clear-cut mental foundation goes a long way towards preventing that hesitation and vacillation of thought that is liable to have a repercussion in one's actions, with unfortunate results.

One must first decide whether one is morally justified in embarking on such a career at all. In the case of a professional this is a comparatively simple decision, provided he has no illusions concerning his ability. If he is a competent rider and not likely to come to grief through his own inefficiency, he is merely taking the risk of injury through bad luck, or what might be termed fate, which is the lot of everyone belonging to any form of hazardous profession. If, however, he is an indifferent rider he should, in fairness to those dependent upon him, think twice before choosing a career that is likely to be of little service to himself or his family.

The outlook of the amateur is, in the same way, moulded by his responsibilities. If he is a single man with no one but himself to worry about, he has no cares and can throw all his energies into the sport with a good heart. He will get falls that he cannot help, and he will incur others through his own ignorance and incompetence, and since a great proportion of mishaps are due, directly or indirectly, to the latter cause, a rider should thrust the idea of the former eventuality to the back of his mind as something over which he has no control, and which is therefore not worth worrying about, and make up his mind to improve his riding to the extent of having as few falls as possible through his own inefficiency and lack of knowledge. And I think it is noticeable that first-class riders, though, it must be admitted, they usually ride the best horses, have comparatively few falls, compared to bad riders.

When the fear of falling becomes uncomfortably persistent, it means that the rider's system is arriving at the stage when it will be incapable of bearing the shock of falls without damage and that the time of retirement is close at hand. It may be averted by cutting down the number of one's rides, or tying oneself down to riding only over hurdles, nothing but one's own horses or for one stable alone, which is well enough for an amateur, but which, for a professional, signifies to the world that he has reached the evening of his career.

After innumerable falls some riders reach the stage of being 'punch-drunk', which is when their minds have become numb to the normal subconscious apprehension, and while they may have lost the realization of the risks they incur, they have also lost the quickness and keenness of thought that is essential to a good jockey.

When an amateur rider becomes responsible for a wife and family he must view riding over fences from a different aspect than that of the free abandon of a bachelor—one trainer used to make a point of employing only unmarried jockeys—and though there is no reason why he should give up altogether, he should choose his rides with some care or tie himself down to riding a set category of horse, as suggested above.

After passing through the earlier stages of an amateur rider's career and arriving at the one in question, I can present the aspect with a certain authority, although fully realizing that no two people are the same, and after a period of confining myself to riding over hurdles on the principle that, though falls over hurdles can be worse than those over fences, they are less frequent, I retired from the fray altogether. Such an attitude is dictated by circumstances and personal inclination.

What, I believe, is important with regard to a personal mental attitude is to stick resolutely to the rule one has made for oneself, otherwise the hesitation and change of mind that comes into deciding whether or not to accept a ride outside the category fixed creeps into one's riding, at a period when it can least stand it. It is also difficult to accept one ride but refuse another without giving rise to a measure of bad feeling among those people who have been refused, some of whom have probably just as much moral right to one's services as those that have been accepted.

I seem to have strayed somewhat from the subject of falls themselves to a kind of psychological dissertation, but the mental side of a rider's career is so closely allied to the direct or indirect fear and effect of falls that I think it deserves the attention it has received.

As regards the practical side of falls, horses fall for six main reasons, or through a combination of these reasons:

(1) Bad riding—lack of control, going too fast, allowing them to swerve, interfering with their jumping, letting them slow down approaching the fence, getting them blinded on the take-off side, and so on.
(2) Being asked to race at distances beyond their capacity.
(3) Being unfit.
(4) Interference from other horses.
(5) Being naturally bad jumpers or improperly schooled.
(6) The rider being out of condition.

While some of these causes are beyond the rider's control, unless he happens to train the horse as well, incompetence and unfitness are his direct responsibility, and in the interests of himself, his patrons, his fellow-competitors and the public, he should do his utmost to improve his riding and keep himself fit.

In falling there is one precept which the rider should never forget, that is to lie still when he is on the ground, until the rest of the field have passed by. It quite often happens that a jockey falls unhurt, but is injured through being knocked down by a following horse, because he has risen to his feet before all the horses following him have passed by. Horses will not tread on a man if they can help it, but they cannot always avoid doing so if he is moving.

Falling is, to a certain extent, a knack, and an experienced rider will sometimes fall without hurting himself, where a novice would incur a broken arm or collar-bone.

So far as it is possible, and the whole thing is often over so quickly that one has no chance to think, a jockey should try to fall with his muscles relaxed, arms, elbows and head tucked in. The stiffer the body, the more likely is a broken bone to result; arms and elbows stuck out are liable to injury, while to hit the ground with the point of the chin is to chance a broken neck. It is best to tuck the head into the chest, try and land on the back of the shoulder and roll over, rather than to hit the ground with the point of the shoulder, which is liable to result in a broken collar-bone, or a broken or dislocated shoulder. A course of ground-training as given to parachutists would, I think, prove beneficial as a preparation to falls.

So far, I have only referred to falls from the aspect of the horse himself coming down, but the occasion frequently arises that the horse does not fall himself but shoots his jockey off.

Often the rider has no chance at all of staying on the horse—though this is not a view that is always held by his backers—but it is sometimes possible to get back into the saddle from the most improbable positions, and one should never give up trying to do so, no matter how hopeless the predicament may seem. 'You're never off till you're on the floor' is a sound principle.

In the case of falls during the early stages of a race when there are a reasonable number of runners the pace will be fast, and there will be little chance either of keeping hold of the horse or of serving any useful purpose by remounting and continuing, an action which has often ruined a young horse's confidence. But there are times—at the end of a race when perhaps only one or two horses are standing—when it is possible to remount and gain a place, or even win, in which case it is always advisable to keep hold of the horse and jump on him.

It is a good plan to learn to vault on a horse, as it can be done in an instant and is a much neater and quicker method than scrambling up his shoulder. The best way is to place the left hand on top of the horse's neck, about half-way up, the right on the pommel of the saddle, and then, springing from the left leg to swing the right leg right over the saddle. It is possible to practise this by vaulting gates and trying it out on quiet horses, and it is a most useful accomplishment, particularly in getting on fidgety horses at any time.

Some owners and trainers are against a jockey jumping up and continuing after his horse has fallen, particularly if he has a long way to go. The horse may have hurt himself, or he may incur another fall. If the former has occurred, to go on may ruin him physically; if the latter, his confidence may be shaken irreparably though one's actions must depend on such factors as: proximity to the finish, the possibility of gaining a place, or winning, the apparent condition of the horse, the value of the race and whether or not the stable has backed the horse. I can remember being instructed by an owner, before getting up to ride for him in a three-horse race at Sandown, that I was on no account to let the horse go if I fell, as there was £10 for third place, a position which I fortunately succeeded in achieving without falling off.

One of the first precautions a N.H. rider should take is to secure the name of a reliable and efficient osteopath, whom he should visit whenever he has had a hard fall, even if he has not necessarily broken a bone, for it is possible to put a bone out of place slightly without feeling more than a certain amount of stiffness or mild periodical discomfort, but which, if not put right, will cause trouble years afterwards. I found myself getting severe attacks of lumbago every time I got on a horse (and often when I had not been near one) after I had had a fall which, at first, seemed of no consequence. After some weeks of massage, with little or no improvement resulting from it, I went to see an osteopath, who put me right in one sitting.

Racecourse doctors do not always have the opportunity to examine a jockey thoroughly, particularly if he has had only a minor fall, and it is therefore as well, if in any doubt, to be examined again at home. I remember, on one occasion, a jockey was allowed to drive home after having had a fairly hard fall, a further examination of his condition on the following day revealing that he had fractured his skull!

The treatment of the injuries of N.H. riders is a specialized business and it is always better to go to a doctor who understands what riding over fences means, otherwise he may either pass one fit to ride too soon, or be so cautious that one is kept hanging about for weeks; if asked whether one was fit to ride again some doctors might interpret it as going for a hack in the Row.

A jockey, after falling, must always get permission from the doctor before he rides again. Unless there has been a bad fall in a race the doctor usually stands in or about the weighing-room, so that jockeys who have fallen can report to him as they return. If he is not there it is the jockey's responsibility, whether he is a professional or amateur, to find the doctor and get his leave to ride again.

If through a fall, refusal, running out, pulling up, or any other cause a rider does not complete the course, he must report the fact to the Clerk of Scales when he returns to the weighing-room.

Having recovered from a fall that has kept him out of the saddle for some time, a rider should always make sure he is really fit before he starts riding again. If he is not, besides laying himself open to the

The wrong way to fall

The right way to fall

Never get up too soon

possibility of hurting himself again, any shortcomings in his riding are liable to be attributed by the critics to loss of nerve.

One of the worst experiences that can befall any rider is for him to be caught up by the foot in the stirrup-iron and dragged, and one should never, under any circumstances, set out with stirrup-irons that are too small for one's feet, which should be able to slip in and out of the irons with ease.

Falls do not necessarily have a bad effect on the nerve; in fact, a soft fall can go a long way towards both restoring and creating confidence, as it brings home the fact that it is quite possible to hit the ground without getting hurt.

'A fall's a hawful thing,' said Mr. Jorrocks, and in many cases it is, but anyone who takes Mr. J.'s statement too much to heart should never think of riding over fences.

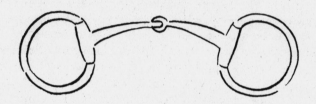

16

Aintree

THERE IS NO steeplechase course in the world like Aintree. Apart from its geography and construction, it is the seat of the most famous of all races over fences, the Grand National, and it has about it an atmosphere and individuality that is peculiar to itself.

I think that one of the most attractive and characteristic features of English racecourses is their variety, both of surroundings and of design, and while Aintree may not differ greatly in the former circumstance from some courses, in the latter it is quite unique.

Whether the average racegoer approaches the course by train or by car he is met with a long, dreary succession of streets belonging to the suburbs of Liverpool, which, gradually and relentlessly, has eaten up the surrounding countryside until it has reached and swallowed Aintree itself, once the little Lancashire village around whose open fields were run, over a hundred years ago, those cross-country races that were the forerunners of our Grand National.

Now, with its tram-lines and its villas, the railway and the canal, it is difficult to picture Aintree in its rural guise, and one wonders (as I never cease to do when approaching a metropolitan racecourse) how it can be that, at any minute, the barriers behind which is hidden that huge triangular expanse of the racecourse itself are reached.

In those remote days when Aintree was nothing more than a country village, and when the smoke and grime of Liverpool itself was still far distant, the atmosphere was probably rather sharper and clearer than it tends to be now. But it must still have been prone to those Atlantic mists, which, in varying degrees of intensity, roll inland, rendering an incident more than a hundred yards away a matter of complete conjecture. And there were probably occasions upon which our ancestors (as we do, from time to time, today) cursed themselves for being foolish enough to make what was then a far more tedious—but much less expensive—journey to Aintree to see the Grand National run, only to find their view of the race blotted out except for a couple of hundred yards in the immediate vicinity.

But Aintree is by no means the only part of England liable to fog, and there are occasions moreover when, with bewildering and inexplicable suddenness, the mist will lift, the sun will shine down, and every detail of the course will be visible with the clarity of crystal, which pleasant conditions can, with similar despatch, revert to a state of Cimmerian gloom.

Such was the case at the Grand National meeting of 1947. It was the first year in modern times upon which the 'National was run upon a Saturday, instead of the traditional Friday, and, as if to pronounce disapproval of this tampering with established order, while the Friday was a day worthy of May at its best, the Saturday broke in a thin, cold drizzle of rain, and a grey, clammy mist crept in from the sea and hovered over the course all day.

It always strikes me that, at Aintree, the direction of the traffic and the car-parking arrangements are better than at any other jumping meeting. The police there are particularly competent, and though, as a result of their presence in force at the meeting and its approaches, crime in the various areas of Lancashire from which they are drawn may be given a greater, if temporary, scope than is usually the case, their good-humoured and intelligent supervision is a boon to race-goers. The car-parks—at any rate the élite ones—are divided up with military neatness, each vehicle placed over a stud numbered according to the owner's ticket.

The Aintree crowd is a distinctive one; apart from the professional element in English racegoers, it always includes a large number of Irish owners, trainers and riders, for the journey across is an easy and convenient one, and the Irishman's love of steeplechasing will draw him to Aintree with a power he finds hard to resist, whereas Epsom and Ascot leave him unmoved. The fact, too, that Ireland is the home of the 'chaser, and that almost all the best jumpers come from there, places Irish trainers in the strong position of being able to make frequent and successful raids on our courses, the most convenient for them being Aintree, and in the years that have elapsed since the war, many have taken Aintree races across the Irish Sea, and with few exceptions the winner of the 'National itself is Irish-bred.

While the English parson is a rare visitor to the racecourse, his Irish counterpart is a keen follower of racing, and one of the most notable features of an Aintree crowd is the heavy sprinkling of Irish priests that are to be found in it, and however sombre the traditional black of their clothes, there is nothing gloomy about their faces, as they inspect and criticize—often with considerably more judgment and skill than their lay brothers—the horses in the paddock, occasionally stopping one of their racing flock, to exchange the time of day, discuss the forthcoming race, and if he happens to be an owner, trainer or rider concerned in it, to glean a hint as to what to back.

From the spectator's aspect, Aintree offers a wide and delightful variety of places from which the jumping can be watched. On a clear day the roof of the stand is about the best, since from here it is possible to follow every detail of the running over the whole course, and to look down on one of the most imposing of all Aintree sights, a field of 'chasers going over the 'Chair'—the big, open ditch in front of the stands.

But when visibility is poor there is much to be said for walking down to one of the fences, perhaps Becher's Brook, or the last fence, and seeing the battle from the front line. From the top of the stands the race gives the impression of a play being acted before one's eyes, a play, it is true, that is both accurate and thrilling, but one that seems to lack some vital element that robs it of a spice of reality. Such an impression has often come upon me when watching racing from this lofty and distant position—not only at Aintree but at other important racecourses such as Ascot or Doncaster, during the Royal Meeting at the former, and the St. Leger meeting at the latter—and for a long time wondered how it came about.

Eventually I came to the conclusion that it was as a result of the silence, not, of course, the silence of the crowd, which, as the finish of an important or thrilling race approaches, gives voice as when, at a football match, it seems that a goal will be scored, but of the horses themselves, for one is too far away to hear the gradually increasing drumming of their hooves, that starts with a barely perceptible rumble and swells into an almost frightening *fortissimo*, much in the same way as does the approach of a train, except that there is none of the metallic clanging, as in the latter case; nor is there to be heard the hissing of the horses' breath, the grunt of effort as they jump, the creak of leather, the clash of steel, the exclamations of the jockeys, and all the other sounds that comprise the discordant orchestra of a field of steeplechasers taking a fence. But by the fence itself, all this stands out, and creates a picture of what is really happening.

In the background, the noise of the crowd swells and dies as the various incidents in the race develop and occur, and every now and then the harsh, piercing bellow of a bookmaker breaks through the waves of sound from the stand. But all this is only the accompaniment to the true theme, the music of the race itself, which by proximity is brought into its own.

Before proceeding to discourse upon the various points of vantage from which the spectator can view the racing at Aintree, it seems appropriate to describe the course itself.

As has been mentioned, the course is roughly triangular in shape, the stands running along the shortest side, which faces approximately due east and comprises the run-in, the longest side stretching from the end of the run-in to the Canal-turn, the remaining one running due east and west to meet the shortest side at its northern extremity.

The steeplechase course is two and a quarter miles round, the Grand National itself being run over two circuits.

It is left-handed, and the start for the Grand National is in the southern corner, close to the paddock.

There is a run of nearly four furlongs to the first fence, which in a race such as the 'National is a great boon, as it enables the field to sort itself out by the time the fence is reached, so that there is not too much of a crush when jumping it.

The foundation of every Aintree obstacle is a natural thorn hedge. This is packed and faced with, as the case may be, gorse, fir or spruce, to a thickness of three feet. The fences vary in height, but are much more upright than on other courses. At one time they were completely upright but after the 1939–45 war were modified, being bellied out at the bottom and bevelled at the top. Many of them have a drop on the landing side, that is to say, the take-off is on a higher level than the other side of the fence.

They are much wider than is the case elsewhere and stretch right across the course, this being necessary to accommodate the large number of runners that always take part in the Grand National.

On the way to the first fence there are a hundred yards or so of 'plough', this being a strip of unturfed soil that has the appearance of having been ploughed and harrowed and is a relic of the days when quite a considerable part of the course was actually plough-land. The first fence is of gorse, four feet six inches in height, with a small drop on the landing side. It is not a very formidable obstacle and gives horses a chance to accommodate themselves to a type of obstacle which, if they have not been to Aintree before, is strange to them.

The next fence is similar but an inch higher, and has a slightly greater drop. The following one is an open-ditch, the fence itself being made of fir and four feet eleven inches in height. The fourth is a gorse fence, four feet, ten inches, the fifth another but two inches higher.

The sixth is the formidable Becher's Brook, so called because a certain Captain Becher fell into it in the days when it was a brook in the true sense of the word, remaining there while the rest of the field jumped over him. It is made of fir, four feet ten inches in height and has a very big drop on the landing side, the distance from the top of the fence to the ground being over six feet. All that is left of the 'brook' is a narrow, dry ditch, about four feet in width, which constitutes no menace unless a horse jumps so half-heartedly that he has not the impetus to enable him to clear it. Every now and then a horse lands in it, but most falls at Becher's are due to horses being unable to accommodate themselves to the drop on the landing side.

From the first fence until Becher's the contour of the course is such that, on the extreme sides of each fence the ground slopes down towards the wings. The result is that at these parts the fences are slightly higher and the drops slightly greater than in the middle, for which reason some riders make a point of keeping towards the middle rather than holding to the inside.

The seventh fence is one of the trickiest on the course: after Becher's the course begins to bend slightly to the left, the seventh fence being actually on the elbow of a further and sharper bend, so that it is met at an angle, horses being on the turn as they jump it and having to turn again on landing, in keeping with the trend of the course. It is five feet in height and made of gorse.

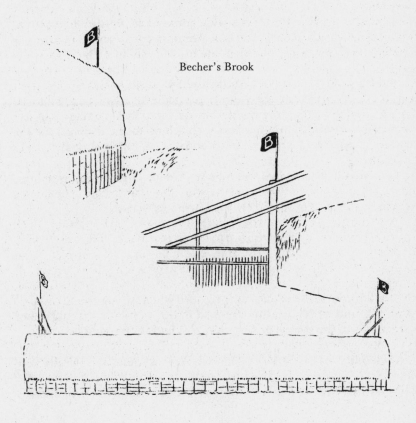

Becher's Brook

The eighth fence comes very soon after the seventh (which follows close on Becher's) and is the famous Canal Turn fence. At one time it was an open ditch, but after Easter Hero had landed on top of it in 1928, causing almost the whole field to refuse, the ditch was removed and it has since been a plain fence.

Immediately after the fence the course bends to the left at a right angle and runs parallel to the Leeds and Liverpool canal. In the past, if a horse failed to turn he was bound to finish in the canal, and it was not uncommon for a loose horse to do so—one rider who had backed himself to get round was bold enough to jump in after his horse, swim up to him, catch him, lead him out and finish the course—but there is now a barrier to prevent this. The fence itself is five feet high and made of fir.

After the Canal Turn fence comes Valentine's Brook, the counterpart of Becher's in that it shares the same 'brook', which runs across the narrow eastern extremity of the course from the one fence to the other. Valentine's has much in common with Becher's, except that it is made of spruce instead of fir and has not so great a drop on the landing side.

Following on Valentine's is a plain gorse fence, five feet high; then, what many jockeys consider to be the most formidable fence on the course—the eleventh—which is an open-ditch to a five-feet fence made of fir, with a big drop on the landing side. The reason why it is feared is that horses are always inclined to stand back and put in an extravagant leap at any open-ditch, particularly at one facing a fence six inches higher than the regulation size on 'Park' courses, but are not always able to accommodate such a leap to the drop on the far side, with the result that they land at too steep an angle and fail to keep their balance.

The twelfth fence is five feet high and made of gorse and is the last one 'in the country', that is to say, soon after jumping it, the horses return to the area occupied by the hurdle racecourse.

First they cross the tan road that leads to the Anchor Bridge over the canal, and then they come on to the former flat course, but instead of continuing round the latter they swing left in a sharper turn. The course is railed off, so that it is impossible to go wrong, but if one is not careful it is easy to swing wide through instinctively trying to follow the old flat course—as I once experienced when, somewhat to my surprise, I found myself leading the field in the 'National, having never ridden round the course before, though I had been round on my feet, a reconniassance which, perhaps because I was so overcome by the formidability of the obstacles, did not prove as useful as it should have done.

From the twelfth fence to the thirteenth is something like half a mile, for it is about two furlongs to the turn and a further two to the fence. The most notable point concerning this obstacle and the next is that neither has a drop on the landing side, in spite of which quite a number of horses fall at them—even on the first lap, when they are still comparatively fresh. In search for an explanation of this phenomenon, I asked one or two jockeys about it, and gathered that, after having become accustomed to encountering a drop after each fence, horses are sometimes taken by surprise to find a fence at which the take-off and landing are on the same level, and stumble as one sometimes does when expecting to take a step down and finding none there.

I have fallen once at this fence myself, though I cannot say that this was the cause of our downfall, as my horse hit the fence very hard before landing at all, but I do remember that the first year Kami ran in the 'National he got as far as this fence without putting a toe wrong, but fell there—the year afterwards I rode him and he must have realized what had brought him down before, as he jumped it perfectly. The fence itself is not a high one, being only four feet seven inches, and it is made of fir.

The fourteenth fence, the last fence on the second circuit of the Grand National, is an inch lower and is made of spruce. Like its predecessor it is not a formidable one, and the horses that fall there usually do so, either for the reason propounded above, or because, on the second circuit, they are very tired, a reason for many falls in the 'National.

On the first circuit of the 'National the fourteenth and fifteenth fences are the 'Chair' and the water-jump, which of course are not jumped on the second, as they occur after the last fence.

The Chair is the biggest fence on the course. It consists of a big open-ditch to a five feet, two inches spruce fence, but the fact that there is no drop to it, and that by the time horses have reached it they have become aware of the fact that they must not take it for granted that each fence is a drop fence, comparatively few falls occur there. The 'Chair' derives its name from the small iron seat perched up at the end of the fence; how or why it came to be placed there, and for what reason I have never been able to discover, but it has been there as long as any riders I have known can remember.

The water-jump is fifteen feet wide from the take-off side of the fence, which is two feet six inches high. This makes it rather bigger than the water-jump on the average course, which is about fourteen feet, but the take-off slopes slightly upwards in the form of a ramp, so that horses obtain a very good chance of getting over and, in fact, usually do so.

Since, on the last circuit, the water and the Chair are not jumped, there is a long run-in from the last fence, the thirtieth this time and the fourteenth on the previous circuit, to the winning-post.

The length of the run in has often been debated, it being argued in some quarters that it is too long, as it places at a disadvantage the horse whose chief talent is his jumping, for such a one often lands first over the last fence but is run out of it on the flat. However, it must also be appreciated that, at the end of a steeplechase at Aintree, horses are usually tired, and whereas the long run-in enables jockeys to ride their horses into the last fence with a certain amount of discretion—since they have plenty of time to get them going after they have landed, and in any case must reserve something for the finish—if the fence was placed nearer the winning-post, jockeys would be forced to ride at it a great deal harder, with the result that there would be more falls. And although it may favour the horse that can gallop—as opposed to the one that can only jump—if the latter has succeeded in getting as far as the last fence, he is surely entitled to reap the benefit of his superior ability on the flat; if he were unable to jump well he would never have got so far.

There is a smaller steeplechase course, with ordinary 'park', fences, inside the 'National course, known as the Milimay course (see map).

The Foxhunters' chase used to take place over the whole four and a half miles of the 'National course, but has now been reduced in distance.

The hurdle races take place on the flat race course, which lies within the area bounded by the Melling Road, running from between the start for the 'National and the first fence, to the Anchor Bridge, and a line running along the front of the stands to the canal, parallel to the Ormskirk Road.

One of the chief characteristics of the Aintree course is that the going is almost always good. The soil is sandy and as a result the track is never too hard in dry weather or too soft when it is wet—at any rate on the steeplechase course, for on the hurdle racecourse it tends to become appreciably heavier. But for this phenomenon Aintree would become almost unjumpable in wet weather.

To return, then, to the subject of watching racing from places other than the stand itself.

There are, I would say, three main points of vantage to choose from, or, what is better, to sample in turn: Becher's, the Canal-turn and the 'Chair'. Each has its own attractions, each its own individuality, providing quite different aspects from each other.

The most impressive of all sights is, I think, to watch the field come over Becher's. To appreciate its magnificence one must stand on the landing side, just about level with the 'brook' and as close to the course as possible. The dark green mass of the fence towers above one's head like a cliff, with the 'brook' at its base gaping, narrow, but ominous, a trap for the unwary, the pitfall of the faint-hearted. At each end, where the white skeleton-like wings meet the fence itself, flutters a small red flag, with a white 'B' displayed upon it, a vivid splash of colour against the slate or the blue of the sky. If the race is the 'National itself the rails and area on the right of the course will be packed tight with humanity, the inside of the course being empty, except for a policeman or two, some ambulance men and photographers, and the high tower of scaffolding from which some of the TV cameras dotted at different points on the course operate.

When the 'National is being run a position once taken must be held during the whole race, or be surrendered for good; there is no wandering up and down the rails to see when the horses are coming or what is happening at a previous fence, and the approach of the field is therefore out of sight. From the point of view of one wishing to follow the course of the race with detailed and mathematical accuracy, such a point of vantage will obviously be of no use, but, as has already been pointed out, there is only one time and place for such a design—a clear day and the top of the stand—and the fact that the horses cannot be seen until they surge over the crest of the fence, only adds to the dramatic quality of the moment.

Before the reverberation of the hooves warns the spectator from this pitch that the field are approaching, the voice of the crowd farther down the line and up on the embankment will make it clear that this is the case. Here is no dignified hush as is usually present on the top of the member's stand—though the traditional freezing silence, and appearance of misery, with which the English élite are wont to take their pleasures, is less evident now than was the case before the war—the Lancashire crowd is not afraid of using its voice and it does not think it has had its money's worth unless it has done so, and as the runners near the fence it will not be difficult to become aware of the fact.

The volume of sound becomes deafening, rising to its height as the leading horses soar up from the take-off. First appear the horses' heads and the jockeys' caps, then the horses' necks, shoulders, forelegs, and finally their whole bodies; the forelegs are folded tight as they top the fence, and then gradually stretch out as the horses begin to descend in the ever-steepening arc in which the drop on the landing side brings them.

Tufts of fir, knocked out by horses that have brushed through the top of the fence, begin to shower down as the horses descend. The colours of the riders' jackets make a rainbow against the sky, their bodies moving in relation to their horses and according to individual style. Both horses and jockeys seeming to dwell for a moment in mid-air, before landing with a thud, collecting themselves and then galloping on.

The whole scene gives an impression of real jumping, not the flippant skimming of fences so often seen on Park courses or abroad, but a leap that must be made high, wide, cleanly and boldly, over an obstacle that is truly worthy of the name. It is a feat that is something in itself and which, well executed, is one to be remembered.

In that brief, but seemingly ageless, moment between a horse reaching the top of the fence and landing, it is possible to see different expressions flickering across the face of the rider: relief at realizing that he is over safely, horror at knowing his horse is going to fall, delight at the exhilaration of it all, or the tenseness of the strain of the race reflected in a look of grim, harsh tautness.

As they land horses will sometimes pitch, stumble, and then either recover or over-balance; sometimes they will slither or totter for several yards before finally losing their legs and rolling over, taking with them the ambitions of their riders and the hopes of their owners and backers. The polished performers will float over in a graceful, even arc, their riders sitting as quietly and easily as if jumping Becher's were an everyday occurrence, the horses themselves with ears pricked, poising themselves for landing, finally touching down and galloping on with the lightness of gossamer and the skilled assurance of the technician—no awkward lurch on landing, or violent contortions on the part of the rider, but a rhythm as smooth and musical as water flowing over a weir.

Soon the last horse will be over, the leaders will be jumping that tricky fence that follows close after, and the landing side of Becher's will be deserted, except perhaps for a dismounted jockey walking towards the rails, or the injured, stretched still and limp where they fell, or twisting in pain, or getting slowly and stiffly to their feet. Perhaps there may be a loose horse trotting round in circles, bewildered, and trying to find the quickest way back to the paddock without having to jump Becher's from the landing side; other horses that have fallen and got up, or whose riders have fallen off, will be galloping after the field towards the next fence.

Everywhere will be little sprigs and bunches of fir, some that have been knocked out of the fence as the horses came over, others that have clung to a boot or bandage for a stride or two and have then been flung off. And the noise of the crowd will have sunk to the low, soft murmur of conversation.

In a few minutes the injured will have been removed, the loose horse caught, and the scene will be one of quiet, the odd bits of fir and the ragged edge of the top of the fence fretted against the sky being the only reminders of the field having passed on.

Then comes an interminable wait for the horses to come round for the last time. The gap is filled in by discussions and arguments as to what was leading, the names of the horses that fell, the extent of the injuries of those jockeys who have been removed in the ambulance, and speculations as to the probable winner.

Possibly someone in the crowd may be armed with a portable wireless, from which can be followed the course of the race; otherwise it will be a case of waiting in ignorance.

At last the growing volume of the voice of the crowd will give warning that the runners are coming near, and in a few minutes they will be streaming over Becher's again. But not in a dense and long-drawn-out pack as on the first circuit. By now many will have fallen, pulled up, refused, run out, or have been put out of the race in one way or another, and perhaps only a dozen or so will be left standing. The chances are that a loose horse will be first over. Lightened of some ten or eleven stone his advantage in the weights will have taken him without difficulty to the front, and with his reins dangling, his stirrups bumping about, but the spirit of competition still keen within him he will sail over with his ears pricked, and forge on towards the next fence. He may peck slightly as he lands, but it is unlikely that he will fall—jumping with no weight on his back, except the bare saddle, is a very different affair from having to carry eleven stone or so.

Then will appear the leaders of the brave band that are still in the race. Probably two, side by side, then a batch of three or four, then the rest of the field, strung out at varying intervals, many of them with little hope of ever finishing the course.

As opposed to when they passed on the first circuit, they will be showing signs of the battle. Horses will be sweating and flecked with foam, and their heads will be lower as they slog along, doggedly but with none of the fire that was evident as they came by the first time. In the some cases the saddle will have slipped back towards the horse's rump, kept from going too far—if the trainer has been wise enough to take the precaution of putting one on—by the breast-girth or breast-plate. An odd plait of a horse's mane may have come undone in the struggle, and both horses and riders will be splashed and spattered with mud if the going is wet.

The riders' faces will be more firmly set—either through determination to make the most of a winning chance, or, if such an eventuality seems too remote, because they mean to get round having already got so far. Some will show that mixture of apprehension and indecision that is a sign that it will not be long before they pull up.

This time the horses will not be jumping so well. The few that are still comparatively fresh will not be making such heavy work of it, but those that are beginning to tire will be saving themselves to the utmost, not going any higher than is absolutely necessary, hanging towards any gap in the fence, screwing in the air, lurching as they land, bringing big lumps of fir out of the fence, or perhaps stumbling on landing and toppling over because they are too tired to keep their legs.

It is almost certain that the eventual winner will be among the first three or four at this stage. He will be one of those that still show no sign of tiring, and he will be jumping with a freedom and power beyond that of most of his opponents.

At this stage the final drama begins to take shape. 'When you're over Becher's the second time, make the best of your way home' is an instruction many a 'National rider must have received before he went out, and any with a chance in the race, once they have landed safely, will be pushing on to get within striking distance of the leaders.

Soon they will all have passed for the last time, and for the spectator on the spot the race will be over.

A brief, fleeting glimpse of the race will be all that he has seen, and his friends who have watched from the top of the stands will doubtless look upon his choice with a mixture of surprise and scorn. But he will have experienced something that they have missed, no detailed panorama, it is true, but the flesh and blood and the very spirit of the race itself, a live, thrilling impression of what really goes on, and a feeling almost of having ridden in the race himself. His waiting and discomfort will not have been in vain, he will carry away the memory of an episode he will not easily forget.

In some ways it is pleasanter to stand by Becher's during one of the less-important steeplechases, when there is no 'National crowd and it is possible to move about in comfort between the fences, see more of the race, and study the style of the riders better. There is not the same electric atmosphere of excitement as prevails when the 'National is being run, nor yet the sense of drama, but from the point of view of one who wishes to study the art of riding, or the jumping of the horses, the situation is less overwhelming and bewildering, and it is easier to pick out the various points of interest. There is no noise, and the sur-roundings are calmer and more peaceful. The picture is one of grace and clarity rather than of strength and vigour, a Watteau as opposed to a Turner.

From the point of view of watching the 'National, the Canal Turn is one of the most advantageous positions on the course.

As opposed to Becher's, where the final issue has sometimes hardly begun to take shape, the Canal Turn is quite often jumped with the eventual winner in the lead—on the second circuit, of course.

The stand there affords a very good view of most of the course, particularly the stretch between Becher's and Valentine's, and though the fence itself cannot compare with Becher's as a spectacle, the position has much to command it from the aspect of seeing the race, as opposed to obtaining the full and exciting dramatic effect which a close-up of Becher's can best give.

For a horse who has never run at Aintree before it must be something of a surprise to come charging down at the Canal Turn and, having arrived on the other side, find himself facing the Canal at a distance of what seems only a few yards. The old hands know all about it and will steady themselves as they take off, bearing slightly to the left as they jump, so as to be on the right leg to make the turn quickly and smoothly on landing, but the novice is inclined to make a clumsier job of it, perhaps starting his next stride after landing with the off fore leading, so that he begins to swing wide and has to change legs as his rider heaves him round.

It is a strange and impressive sight to see a big field of horses taking the Canal Turn, the mass change of direction seeming reminiscent of a movement during a cavalry display at a Tattoo, except that there is none of the ordered neatness of such a manœuvre, instead a jostling and scrimmaging to get round as quickly as possible, and sometimes a certain amount of bumping and boring, as one horse endeavours to cut in towards the inside while the horse on his left is still swinging out.

Occasionally a horse falls and on getting up charges straight on, but usually they keep going with the rest of the field.

When they come round for the last time, well strung out, it is almost certain the winner will be among the first two or three, and as they start to go away from the Canal Turn spectator and make their way down the long stretch from the Canal to the racecourse, getting smaller and smaller in the distance, the first three quite often assume the order in which they will eventually finish. This was the case in 1947 when Caughoo, Lough Conn and Kami had sorted themselves out in this order by the time they had reached the racecourse—to be exact, Prince Regent was a couple of lengths in front of Kami approaching the last fence but one.

The Canal Turn spectacle is one worth seeing, if only because it is so unusual, even for Aintree. Becher's has its similar, if less spectacular, counterpart in Valentine's; the 'Chair' is not the only formidable open ditch on the course, but there is nothing else like the Canal Turn, either at Aintree or at any other course in England, and no follower of steeplechasing can say truly that he knows Aintree until he has stood at the Canal Turn during a race.

While the characteristic of Becher's is its dramatic quality, and that of the Canal Turn its uniqueness, the 'Chair' I think provides the most thrilling spectacle on the course. To approach it on one's feet and look over into the moat-like chasm of the open ditch, in front of the huge, wide, uncompromising fence is an awe-inspiring experience—particularly for those who are about to ride over it—and gives some idea of what a horse has to cope with, not at the easy, collected gait of the hunter or show-jumper, but at racing pace after he has been going for two miles.

Whereas the only place to stand at Becher's is the landing side, the 'Chair' is best viewed from the take-off, for it is then possible to see the ditch jumped, and the whole quality of the sight afforded is in the distance some horses stand back to take off, and the way they reach up and out at the fence itself. Seen from the landing side it is much the same as any other fence.

To see a good jumper negotiate the 'Chair' is one of the finest sights at Aintree. Twenty yards away he will know exactly where he is going to take off, his last strides bringing him with powerful and quickening stroke to that spot, which will be well back from the ditch itself, perhaps only just inside the wings. Then he will leave the ground in a high, graceful parabola, its zenith bringing him well over the top of the fence. If he has taken off unusually far back his forelegs will have unfolded before he has reached the top of the fence and his toes will be out in front of his nose in an almost heraldic position. For a fraction of a second he will seem to hang in the air over the top of the fence, then he will complete the downward arc, his tail waving in rhythm with the movement of his body, land truly and collectedly, and then gallop on.

Sometimes a horse, overawed at the formidability of the obstacle facing him, will lose heart at the last moment and either try to refuse and finish up in the ditch, or leave the ground with no impetus, hitting the face of the fence and coming down on the other side, or landing on top of it and sliding over.

A clever jumper who finds himself meeting the fence wrong will shorten his stride, putting in a couple of 'quick ones' to bring him just close enough to the guard-rail to miss it as he leaves the ground, and will pop over in a less spectacular but none the less effective manner than the horse that stands back.

All these different phases and movements are doubly clear to the spectator down on the spot, and I think, of all the fences on the

'National course, the 'Chair' is the one I enjoy watching most. It has the further advantage of not being too far from the last fence, so that it is possible to walk back to the latter in time to see the horses come over it on their way to the winning-post.

As opposed to the last fence on a Park course, that at Aintree is not always the best value from the spectator's point of view. By the time it is reached the field is often strung out, with one horse far ahead of the others, and perhaps only two or three still left in the race. They are tired and jump with none of the zest and abandon they show at, say, Becher's or the 'Chair', which they meet when still comparatively fresh, but often crash through the top of the obstacle and land amidst a cascade of gorse.

Occasionally one is lucky, and I can remember few more thrilling or dramatic experiences than that of seeing from the spot—as a result of having parted company with my horse on the first circuit—Zahia, First of the Dandies, Sheila's Cottage, Happy Home and Cromwell, in a bunch, landing over the last fence but one and heading for the last, with Zahia suddenly mistaking the course and regardless of our shouts and warnings running out to the left, leaving First of the Dandies, with Sheila's Cottage on his heels, racing all out for the last.

So much for the 'view from the ground' aspect of watching steeple-chasing at Aintree. To the man who races for purely speculative or social reasons, it is one which will make little or no appeal, but to the real lover of the game, and to the rider, it is an experience which will prove as enjoyable as it is valuable.

Looking back on my racing life I cannot think of anything I enjoyed more than a good ride round Aintree, and I think that everyone who has had this experience would say the same.

The atmosphere and sensation is entirely different from that of a Park course: there is more room, the size and quality of the fences cause horses to jump differently, and the sharp turns, together with the spaciousness of the track, give the impression of something between hunting and racing. All this is brought out in particular emphasis in the 'National itself.

In the world of flat-racing there is no great event open to the amateur rider. Competition against professionals is barred, so that there is no chance to emulate Sir George Thursby and ride in The Derby, nor is there even an equivalent of the National Hunt 'Chase. But in steeplechasing the amateur has as much scope as the professional, and can therefore take part in the greatest of all races over fences, the Grand National, thus experiencing that especial thrill of playing a part in an event of world-wide importance to all interested in racing.

For the rider in the race, 'National day begins early. By about half past seven a sizeable stream of cars and taxis begins to roll up to the course, emitting numbers of owners, trainers, jockeys and supporters, the jockeys, clothed in the various garbs adopted for the purpose of riding work which according to individual taste, may be jodhpurs and a golf jacket, or that combination of a thick, blue woollen sweater and a pair of flannel or corduroy trousers which gives the wearer an air of being connected with the fishing industry; the spectators, macintoshed or coated according to the weather, the casual, unshaved, the meticulous already washed and barbered.

The stables themselves will have been active for some hours: at six the horses will have been fed and by seven they will be in the course of being groomed and saddled preparatory to going out to exercise. Some trainers never work their horses on the morning of the race, but the majority like to give them a final 'pipe-opener', and almost every runner in the race will be seen out.

Besides those directly connected with the competitors and belonging to the profession are a heterogeneous crowd, made up of newspaper reporters, racegoers who have no connection with any particular runner but enjoy seeing the morning work—some who, having been dragged out by their friends after sitting up half the night playing poker and imbibing, do not look as if they were enjoying themselves at all—and spivs, touts, stable-boys, motor horse-box drivers, paper boys, and all the many other sorts and conditions of humanity which the fascinating mosaic of the racing world comprises.

At this early hour the sun has hardly risen. Sometimes when the thin, misty rain with which the district is so familiar shrouds the morning it never appears at all, and people and horses loom out of and disappear into the gloom like so many ghosts of the many predecessors that have been before them. Sometimes it rises in a fiery, red ball behind the mist, 'shorn of its beams', later to break through, glittering in reflection on the dew, causing a peeling off of overcoats and horse-rugs, and changing the whole atmosphere from what might well be November to Spring.

On the wide, bare patch of ground beside the stables, horses will be walking or trotting round before they work; others, having already finished, will be strolling about, their lads leading them, to cool off before returning to their boxes.

A continuous stream of horses, in twos and threes will be moving between the walking ground and the paddock, the flat racers (particularly the two-year-olds) looking small and frail compared to the burly, big-boned 'chasers, a similar comparison offering itself with regard to the respective flat race and steeplechase jockeys.

Out on the course, the working horses will be going round the inside track used for that purpose singly, following each other in single file or in pairs or threes. When they swing into the straight and come down the stretch lying parallel to and on the inside of the 'Chair' and water-jump, they are usually allowed to stride along fairly fast, and when they pull up and come trotting back, owners and trainers run anxiously towards them to see that all is well, and to hear the jockey's final opinion.

Riding in the 'National, especially if one is on a fancied horse, is a considerable strain on the nerves. Weeks and months of effort have been put in with this one day in view; the owners' and trainers' money, hopes and work all devolve in the end upon the rider, on whom rests the added burden of knowing that a great deal of public money has been betted on his horse. No matter how calm and imperturbable a man may be by nature, this responsibility must affect him consciously or sub-consciously, and as the day approaches the strain is bound to tell.

By the evening before the race the nervous excitement of anticipation tends to reach a high pitch, and this, roughly speaking, shows itself in one of two ways: either the rider feels that he cannot face the prospect of going to bed early and tossing about unable to sleep, and he therefore goes on a party and stays up until two or three in the morning, or else he goes to the other extreme and goes to bed about nine or ten o'clock. My personal experience is that the best results are obtained by the latter method, but I have known of jockeys riding a brilliant race after having been up all night, and having gone to bed for only a few hours and by no means sober.

It is, I am sure—whatever one's individual characteristics may be—a great help to have a ride on the morning of the race. It clears the lungs, keeps the muscles tuned, gets the circulation going and rests the mind by giving it something active to work on, besides producing that sensation of well-being that pleasant and not too violent exercise gives.

If the horse one is riding goes well it is an added fillip to confidence; after riding Kami and Cloncarrig on the morning of the respective 'Nationals in which I rode them, the impression of fitness, keenness and well-being that they gave me was a tonic in itself, and I went off to breakfast with an easy mind and a good heart, knowing that, whatever else occurred, they would not fail because they were unfit or out of sorts.

Many jockeys stay for the meeting in Liverpool itself, but others prefer lodgings near the course itself, which I think is the pleasanter alternative. It is quieter, more convenient from the point of view of riding work—and less expensive. The food is plainer, but more plentiful and better, and there is a homely and restful atmosphere which the turmoil of the average hotel never possesses. I shall always look back happily on my sojourn in those rooms near the course which I occupied before I rode Kami—rooms from which at least three jockeys have gone out to win the 'National.

But such a matter, again, is one of personal taste, in which each man must choose for himself.

Unless compelled to waste, a good breakfast is a sound basis. One need not eat anything else afterwards, and it provides a power upon which nervous and physical energy can draw.

It is a good plan for a rider to arrive on the course in good time: to start late and cut it fine is only to use up an unnecessary amount of nervous energy worrying about arriving in time, and in this lies the advantage of staying on the spot, as one can walk to the course in a few minutes and is not dependent either upon a lift from anyone else, or any other hazard of transport, and it is not necessary to start outrageously early in order to make quite sure of arriving on time, and to avoid being held up in the traffic.

By the day of the race one should have walked the course. It is, of course, possible to do so on the day itself, in which case the early morning, before the crowds have gathered, is the best time, but a previous inspection can I think be conducted in a calmer atmosphere and a more suitable frame of mind.

On arriving at the dressing-room it is advisable to see that one's equipment is in good order: that stirrup-leathers, girths and breast-girths are not likely to break, and that, in the case of riding a horse with a deep body, the girths will be long enough. There are usually some forty runners in the 'National, and as a result the situation tends to become somewhat hectic as the time for weighing-out approaches: valets are running about trying to attend to six or seven riders at the same time, and may have some difficulty in coping with last-minute demands for different pieces of equipment. They have not got a limitless supply of girths, breast-girths, and so on, and if a need is discovered too late it may not always be possible to fulfil it.

On 'National day there is an electric atmosphere of anticipation that pervades the whole course. It spreads through the people on the stands, in the paddock, the crowds along the railway embankment and the Canal, and even through the officials, whom one tends to regard as emotionless. In the jockeys' room, too, it is evident—perhaps more markedly than anywhere else, since here are to be found those most directly concerned in the event itself, the actors in the play.

To start with, there are many more jockeys crowded into the changing-rooms than usual. Besides all those riding in the race, and there may be forty or fifty, there are hurdle race and flat race jockeys who are riding at the meeting. Travelling lads leaving their little leather satchels containing the racing colours, and trainers in search of their riders, or wishing to leave some instruction with the valet concerning equipment, hover round the door.

It is a scene and an atmosphere which will always be clear in my mind—possibly because I have not experienced it often enough to lose the illusion, but, even so, I cannot think that the hardiest veteran of the profession can remain quite unmoved by the environment.

Almost the sole topic of conversation is the 'National: what will win it and what will not, how it will be run, whether or not there will be many falls, anecdotes of horses and jockeys past and present, and personal views about one's own and other riders' probable fate in the race. Jockeys who have never ridden in the race before will be seeking advice from the experienced, some of those who have taken part in it (perhaps only once, getting no further than the first or second fence) will, like a second-termer holding forth to a new boy, address the inexperienced with the patronizing assurance of one who has ridden over the course many times.

In the weighing-room is to be seen the unusual sight of TV cameras perched up in various corners, aimed at the scales and ready to take the jockeys as they weigh out, a scene that comprises part of the news film of the race. In odd places arc-lamps are being set by to provide light for photographers, and technicians and cameramen, strangely out of place in this environment, flit about among members of the racing world making adjustments to their equipment.

On this day the weighing-room board is almost completely covered with telegrams: messages of good wishes to jockeys riding, from friends, relations, and fans, with a few letters among them from those wishing to express their sentiments more fully or solicit information about a jockey's chances in the race.

Outside, the approaches to the weighing-room, too, are crowded, and a jockey on his way into this building will find many well-wishers—as likely as not complete strangers—among the bystanders, who will give them a word of encouragement, and perhaps a pat on the back as they pass through. The 'National crowd is distinctive. In the Members' Enclosure and Paddock are to be seen a sprinkling of bowler hats, a great proportion of their wearers being hunting men who, except for the National Hunt meeting at Cheltenham and the 'National and possibly their local meeting, never go racing at all.

It also comprises many non-racing people who have come to see it, as one would go to see the Aldershot Tattoo, the Tower of London, or any other of our national scenes or spectacles. Most of these are tourists from abroad, who comprise quite a number of Americans, many of whom are keen followers of English steeplechasing, possibly because the scope of the sport in their own country is rather limited, except for hunt-racing.

The 'National is the third race of the day, being due to start at 3.15 p.m. Owing to the large number of runners and to the fact that there is a parade for the race it is necessary to weigh out in good time, and most riders begin to get ready before the first race.

The sense of excitement and anticipation increases—it always made me think of the time of preparation before doing a parachute jump: the procedure of adjusting attire, drawing parachutes from the store, checking that they have been correctly put on, and then the tension of waiting until the time comes to emplane, having a sharp similarity to the procedure in the jockeys' room, where in a like manner racing clothes are put on, saddles are got down and given to the appropriate jockeys, and all the procedure of preparing and checking equipment is gone through.

There is the same feeling of comradeship that arises among those who share a common danger, however remote and slight that risk may be, the same feeling of thrill, and the vague apprehension that is born of awaiting the fulfilment of fate which, whether or not it is pre-destined, cannot be foreseen. In an hour or so's time, someone's fortune will be made, someone's reputation enhanced or created; there will be disappointments, surprises, shocks, comedy and perhaps tragedy, but how—and to whom—such things may happen no one can tell.

The atmosphere affects individuals in different ways. Some become garrulous, others silent, some unusually cheerful, others morose. The face of one will be pale and set, of another flushed and animated. Some will appear unaffected, except perhaps for some mannerism such as a tendency to yawn; others will be unable to stop their muscles quivering as if stricken with ague—I have seen jockeys of iron nerve and brilliant dash in a race so affected, and have noticed in my own case—though I lay no claim to the latter qualities—that I have often ridden best when particularly nervous and jittery in the dressing-room.

Some of the most amiable of characters, in the ordinary course of events, will snap their valets' heads off for no apparent reason, others will become unusually hearty and sociable. One man's speech will become pedantic, another's blasphemous. Whatever the nature of the individual, and no matter how calm or undisturbed he may be, he will almost certainly betray the effect of the nervous tension within him by some expression or action to which he is not usually prone.

As time passes there is a tendency for conversation to veer away from the subject of the race—even from steeplechasing itself—and to circle round such more distant topics as the cinema, women, domestic affairs, clothes and so on, and in spite of its ever-nearing presence the race itself seems to become something remote and unreal, almost a dream to which one does not belong and, as one sometimes finds in dreams, there arises the wish to awake in order to discover whether or not it is a phantasy.

When a jockey is ready he moves along to the weighing-room and joins the queue leading to the scales, which stretches the whole length of the room, its tail winding into one of the changing-rooms, so many riders does it comprise.

Here the unreality does not cease, for by now the arc-lamps will be blazing, with a white, slightly violet-tinted glare, lighting up the racing colours with a brilliancy foreign to them, glinting from stirrup-irons, and turning the scene from an ordinary part of racecourse procedure to one that might be taken from some theatrical production such as *Ali Baba and the Forty Thieves*.

The line gradually moves forward, stopping while each jockey steps on to the weighing-machine for his weight to be passed as correct. During this respite the others will lean up against the wall, their saddles under their arm, every now and then shifting the load from one arm to the other, their skull-caps stuck carelessly on their heads, the strings of their racing cap dangling down like a pair of pigtails, the small squares of paper given them at the trial scales and bearing their number on the race-card and the weight they should carry, stuck into a fold of the girths wound round the saddle, and transformed to a starchy whiteness by the glare; or they will stand in their place in the closely-packed line, their saddles balanced on their hips, or rested momentarily on anything within reach, to ease the burden of the weight.

Every now and then the cameras will whirr and click in action as the rider of a fancied horse steps on to the scales, and then return to silence as less publicized contemporaries take their place. Soon the jockeys who have been riding in the previous race come in. Those who have finished in the first four hold up the line as they pause to weigh-in, the others break through the queue on their way back to the dressing-room, exchanging a quip or letting fall a word of encouragement on the way: 'Hope you haven't forgotten the glue; good luck and get round safely,' or some such remark.

Most trainers like to get their jockeys weighed out in good time, even if they do not actually put the saddle on the horse till the last possible minute. It allows time for changing the girths, going back for a pad to put under the front of the saddle, or any similar contingency, so that, after he has passed the scales, a jockey will probably have at least half an hour on his hands before being called out for the race.

This spell is, I think, the most unpleasant of all. There is nothing to do: one is dressed and ready, except for tying up the cap ribbons, which is a matter of seconds, and the only occupation is sitting aimlessly on the bench and talking—or just sitting. Some adjust and readjust their boots, wristlets, or some other part of their equipment; others sit on the table swinging their legs, or tapping their boot with their whip; some smoke, suck sweets or chew gum, others stretch themselves out when and where there is room, relaxing until the last moment.

For all, the time drags on as if the hour of the race would never come.

There will probably be a cluster of jockeys round the fire, availing themselves of all the warmth and comfort they can before going out into the cold, and perhaps one will go over to the wash-basin and rinse out his mouth with cold water to remove that unpleasant dryness that sometimes seems to accrue.

Jockeys who are not riding come into the room to tender their good wishes and pass the time of day—'Wish I was coming with you' is a remark often passed by those for whom circumstances have made its fulfilment an impossibility—and the valets sort out and distribute whips to those who have not already got them.

So the minutes gradually slip away, until at last the official assigned for the purpose enters the room and announces the 'Jockeys out, please,' which is the call to move to the paddock.

A cat pitched into a dovecot could hardly cause more disturbance than these words. There is an immediate scuffling to find and put on coats—if they have not already been donned—one man has suddenly lost his whip, a second is asking the valet to let him have a last puff from the latter's cigarette, and a third has broken his cap-string in his eagerness to get it tied securely, and is bawling at the valet's assistant to give him an elastic band to take its place.

Finally, the last man has been attended to, and the jockeys are streaming out of the weighing-room into the paddock, leaving the valets hastily putting on their jackets and diving under the benches, or into the hampers, for race-glasses, preparatory to jostling for a place on the stand to see the race, as eager for one of the jockeys they look after to win the race as are their patrons themselves.

After the stuffiness of the changing-room, the cool air of the paddock is a refreshing tonic—I always liked to take two or three deep breaths of it to get rid of the smoke and fustiness of the last half-hour—and it seems to bring one back to reality and the task on hand.

In the paddock the density of the crowd increases as one nears the parade-ring, and walking up the slope of the bank which surrounds the latter enclosure, it is necessary to elbow one's way through a tightly packed throng which, however, opens up to allow a passage through with cheerful readiness, as soon as those in the way are aware of the riders' approach. Friends, acquaintances and even strangers will be free with their good wishes and greetings, which are a heartening pleasantry to those at whom they are directed, however commonplace and meaningless they may be as regards the speaker.

There is something rather impressive about large numbers of people, especially when one can view their massed formation from a position of comparative isolation, and though, containing as it does many groups of owners, trainers and jockeys, the centre of the parade ring could hardly be termed isolated, in comparison with the mass of people ringing its perimeter, and packing the bank in solid tiers, its oval of grass with the beautifully laid-out bed of scarlet flowers in the centre is a veritable oasis. To one who is little accustomed to such circumstances, the sight and experience is remarkable and not a little awe-inspiring.

The runners for the race are being led round the inside of the perimeter, each with a white sheet bearing his name over his stable clothing, and on the way towards the owner and trainer for whom one is riding, the inclination is to search for the horse one will soon be mounting. Sometimes it is a minute or two before he can be picked out—in 1947 there were so many runners that the horses were walking round two deep—but soon a familiar feature or trait catches the eye: perhaps a white blaze or star, a particular way of walking, the set of his ears, or merely the name on his sheet, but I would say that most racing men instinctively look for natural means of identification before they fall back upon this last, simplest, and most accurate clue.

When speaking of my own feelings I by no means impute that other riders experience the same—one owner who was gracious and courageous enough to avail himself of my services in the 'National, on my appearance in the parade-ring enquired feelingly after my health, admitting to me afterwards that from the colour of my face he feared that I was suffering from a bilious attack.

However, by paying strict attention to the advice and instruction of whoever is responsible for delivering the same, and a well-regulated stable will always see that either the owner or the trainer, never both, do this, otherwise their directions are apt to be confusing, occa-

sionally contradictory, and concentrating upon forming a clear con-
ception of the plan of campaign the feeling of apprehension gradually
passes, so that when the rider is finally in the saddle it has gone. He is,
as it were, in a new atmosphere, with no time for apprehension,
superstition or thoughts beyond the actions of the moment.

While it is important enough to see to one's equipment in an
ordinary race, it is doubly essential to do so in the 'National, and
though the trainer will take pains in such matters himself, it is as well
to cast a quick eye over everything. It is not the trainer that is going to
be the direct sufferer as the result of any carelessness, and it is possible
that one may be riding the least-fancied of several runners, in which
case it is unlikely that the horse in question will be given quite the
same careful scrutiny as will be the case with the more fancied
candidates. In fact, it is more than probable that the saddling of it has
been assigned to an assistant, and it will be little consolation to the
rider of a horse whose saddle finished up round its belly, owing to
carelessness or lack of adjustment in saddling, that the accident was
not really his fault.

On leaving the paddock, the horses assemble just by the gate leading on to the course and sort themselves out into the order in which
they appear on the race-card. On such occasions, when there are a
considerable number of horses milling around in close proximity to
one another, it is not difficult to get a horse kicked, and it is therefore
advisable to avoid taking up a position that might enable such an
occurrence to come about, and to keep clear of any horse that shows
signs of letting drive.

Whether the day was clear or misty, I have never failed to be moved
at the vista offered from the back of a horse in the 'National parade.
Straight down is the long, green avenue of the course, neatly hemmed
by the white rails. On the one side the tightly-packed stands soar up
towards the sky—in contrast to the empty stretches of the track, they
seem bigger and more densely thronged than when seen from among
the crowd itself or from any part of them; on the other, a thinner
gathering, spread out along the far rails, and the trim, formidable
outlines of the water-jump and the 'Chair'.

On a clear day every detail stands out as if viewed through a
telescope; when it is misty the course vanishes into nothingness and
the stands become indistinct dark masses against a background of
grey, the horses themselves an endless snake, whose head, or tail
(according to one's position in the line) disappears into the greyness.

When about level with the end of Tattersall's enclosure, the horses
turn round and canter back past the stands. As each arrives at the
point of departure, the lad leading him slips off the rein, gives his

horse a pat, the rider a word of encouragement or exhortation, sometimes of warning—'You won't get far on this one,' was the somewhat
dampening farewell offered to me on one occasion—and he is swinging down to the post.

The repetition will doubtless infuriate the lay reader, but as this
book is primarily designed for those who are contemplating embarking on a career as a steeplechase-rider I will take the risk of incurring
the wrath of the former in the hope that I may be preventing a fall to
the latter, by saying that on arriving at the post he should always see
that the girths are tight enough (or not too tight), and that stirrup-
leathers are neither twisted nor the loose ends likely to ruck up and get
in the way.

I am not, on the whole, superstitious, but have always avoided
making discouraging or disparaging remarks to fellow-competitors
before a race, as a result of a jockey once observing to me at the post
that my horse did not look the type likely to get round Aintree, adding
that he was bloody glad he was not riding him himself. He fell at the
first fence, and I got round.

There are several schools of thought with regard to what style of
riding and what tactics are most successful at Aintree, and in dealing
with this matter I have endeavoured to be as open-minded and as un-
dogmatic as possible.

I think it advisable to ride about a hole, or two holes longer at
Aintree than on a Park course, the degree depending upon the shortness with which one is wont to ride in the ordinary course of events,
and the characteristics of the horse. I have heard a first-rate Aintree
jockey of a past generation quoted as having said that he always rode
shorter at Aintree than at any other course, but I would attribute this
to the probability that his idea of riding short would differ very considerably with that of today, and that, therefore, his Aintree length
would approximate—proportionately to the individual of course—to
that of the average jockey riding over this course today.

The first time I rode at Aintree I let my leathers down about five or
six holes, just about to hunting-length, only to find that I almost
strained my thigh muscles through riding too long. The next day I
rode the same horse, having pulled my leathers up to within about
a hole of my normal length, and found the result much more
satisfactory.

Concerning the length of leather with regard to the old and new
schools, I think it may be of interest to record the gist of a conversation
I once had with the late Sir George Thursby, who competed with outstanding success against the best flat race professionals of his day and
who, though he did not ride over fences, was a good man to hounds.

He asked me if I rode 'short', and when I told him that I did he remarked that I was quite right in doing so, since, in his day, before the new style of riding had been introduced, it was no uncommon thing for jockeys to wrench the 'tailor's muscle', the muscle that runs down the inside of the thigh, which he attributed to riding 'long', the custom of his time.

As has been mentioned earlier in the book, the finer adjustment of the length of one's stirrup-leathers must depend upon the individual characteristics of the horse one is riding. I have found myself riding what seemed like about three holes too short, though in fact the length of my stirrup-leathers was exactly the same as that I had used, in perfect comfort, on the horse I had previously ridden, the reason being that while the first horse took a strong hold and had a long stride, the second barely went into his bridle, and had a short, scrappy action. But if in doubt it is better to ride a hole too long than a hole too short, particularly at Aintree.

With regard to the best position to take at the start, different jockeys have different ideas. Some prefer the extreme inside, others the middle, a few the extreme right, and in the long run I do not suppose one's place at the gate has much effect on the ultimate result. The jockey's two aims are a clear run and going the shortest way round. If riding a horse that is a quick beginner, I think that the best place to take is about twelve from the inside. This avoids the scrimmage that tends to develop among those of the leaders who are competing for the inside itself, places one on the line down the first half a dozen fences and Becher's where the drop is not quite so marked, and does not mean going too far out of one's way.

On a slow beginner I think it is as well to start as near the inside as possible, since he will not be fast enough to jump off and vie with those bunched up on the inside, and will thus have a very good chance of finding a clear run on the inside behind the leading group. Both Lord Mildmay on Cromwell and Sandy Scratchley on Pencraik told me that they found this to be the case, and the photographs of Caughoo's 'National show the American rider, F. Adams, to have followed this procedure, securing a wonderful run all the way round, at the same time going the shortest way.

The first time I rode in the race I started on the extreme right, under the delusion that I would find least interference there. Such, however, did not prove the case, and since the drop to the fences on this side of the course is greater than that in the middle, and it means going the longest way round, I can see no object in beginning on or pursuing this path.

Whether one jumps off slowly or quickly in the 'National must depend upon the horse's capabilities and characteristics. If he is naturally a slow beginner, nothing will stop him quicker than trying to make him race away from the start with faster horses, but if he is able to strike off quickly without effort, there is nothing to be gained by getting slowly away—unless he is the very hard-pulling type of horse that must be tucked in behind others in order to prevent him from running himself to a standstill. But even the latter are not so impetuous at Aintree, the size of the fences causing them to slow up whether they want to or not, and, in most years, the winner is usually in the first six all the way round.

Concerning the rider's seat at Aintree, most of what has been written before is applicable. It is best to go into one's fences with as long a rein as goes with complete control, to sit as still as possible, the body leant slightly forward as the horse leaves the ground, the lower part of the leg a little advanced—particularly if the horse seems likely to hit the fence. As the horse comes down there is no need to lean back, it is quite enough to sit still and let the horse pivot beneath one, if necessary, slipping the reins sufficiently to give him the full freedom of his head and neck as he lands—horses that land steeply, even though they may jump perfectly, often like to stretch their heads and necks out so far that they almost touch the ground, and when Battleship returned after winning his 'National his nose was covered with mud, even though he was never in danger of falling.

It would obviously not be impossible to get round Aintree using the forward seat, or any of its variations, but from practical experience I am convinced that, on the whole, the method described above is the best to adopt. At the same time I would emphasize that the strap-hanging, back-seat style of riding, in which the rider leans back as he takes off, finishing with his head somewhere near his horse's tail, does not tend to improve his horse's chance.

On Park courses one can usually chance letting an experienced jumper have only a fleeting glimpse of the obstacles—often there is no option than to do otherwise—but if a horse is expected to get safely round Aintree, it is essential that he has every opportunity of seeing what he is at, and that he has a clear view of each fence.

On a horse that has never been to Aintree before it is as well to sit tight over the first fence, as he will not be prepared for the drop, and though he may jump it perfectly he is more than likely to peck or stumble on landing, as a result of meeting the ground before he actually expects to do so.

A few strides from the fence the horse is certain to need squeezing with the calves of one's legs, to ensure that he maintains his impetus and is kept up into his bridle; I do not say that it is necessary to kick him with one's heels, as this may be too severe in the case of a sensitive horse, but I am sure it is essential to give him some indication that he is expected to concern himself with jumping the obstacle, particularly if there are any doubts as to his resolution.

While the Aintree fences may seem strange to the horse that is new to them, they are no more so than to the rider who has never undergone the experience before, and I can still recall that odd sensation of being suspended momentarily in mid-air the first time I rode over them, a sensation described as well as anything by a line borrowed from *The Lotus Eaters*, 'to pause and fall and fall again did seem'.

It is as well to make quite certain that the horse has landed properly before going forward to the flat-racing position. On one occasion my horse appeared to have made a perfect landing, but, possibly because it was at the first fence and he had not yet accustomed himself to the drops, stumbled on to his knees just as I was expecting him to gallop on, and but for sheer luck I would have fallen off, as he shot me right up his neck.

The first fence is never the happiest stage of any race, and in the 'National there is the added uncertainty of how a horse is going to cope with the drop, unless he is a seasoned performer round the course. Once over it I always feel conscious of a considerable sense of relief.

By the time the second fence is reached the field has already begun to string out. The quick beginners have formed a spearhead of their own, the rest of the field stretching out behind in an ever-lengthening train.

The third fence is the first open-ditch, and—especially if one's horse is inclined to pitch on landing over the drops—it is advisable to be prepared for a mistake on landing, as the ditch makes horses stand well back and jump big, so that they are inclined to land at a steeper angle than in the case of a plain fence.

Two more fences, and then Becher's. Riding towards it, this obstacle does not look any different to the others, but if one glances up at the flag above the wings, besides the ordinary red one, there will be seen another with a white B upon it. This warning, fluttering as nonchalantly in the breeze as a buoy rides carelessly upon the waves—signifying, too, approaching danger—always sent a slight, cold tremor down my back, not that Becher's has proved a disastrous fence for me, as I have always been fortunate enough to cross it safely, but because it is something out of the ordinary, and one is even less certain than in the ordinary course of events what is going to happen on the other side.

When nearing it I think it is a good plan to slip the reins to as long a length as one reasonably dare, for of all the fences on the course this is the one at which a horse needs the full freedom of his head and neck on landing, and it is better to go into it with a long rein and make sure that he will have this freedom, than to take the risk of slipping the reins too late and as a result interfere with his balance, which can easily occur through having too short a hold of a horse's head on taking off. It is just as easy to get 'left behind' with a long hold as a short hold, but in the former case there is less chance of interfering with the horse's mouth, as there is more play between it and one's hands than in the latter, in which there is a danger of being pulled out of the saddle as well.

At the tricky fence, met at an angle, that follows Becher's I am certain that it is best to approach from the middle of the course, which narrows considerably at this point, than from close to the inside, the reason being that the turn is so sharp that, when on the inside, one is almost bound to swing wide on landing, unless virtually pulling up and starting again, whereas from the middle of the course it is possible to cut in after landing and keep an even pace, which is less tiring to a horse than stopping and starting.

The same applies at the Canal Turn, which fence I think is best jumped at a slight angle, so that on landing the horse has almost made the turn, and does not have to be wrenched round, as would be the case if he were going straight on.

At both these fences there is usually a good deal of jostling and bumping, owing to different horses veering one way or the other, and one must be alert in trying to avoid trouble.

I do not know why, but horses tend to jump to the right rather than to the left at Aintree, and thus, if following directly behind another horse, I think it is as well to keep just to his left, though naturally making sure that he is not a horse that always jumps to the left.

Valentine's is a less formidable edition of Becher's. The fence following it, except for the drop, has nothing unusual about it, but at its successor, the last open-ditch before the 'Chair', it is wise to watch that a horse does not over-jump himself, as the obstacle consists of a big fence with a substantial ditch in front of it and a very considerable drop on the far side.

After that comes another ordinary fence, with a less severe drop, and then the two fences, the last but one and the last on the final circuit which, as has already been noted, must be given attention by reason of the fact that there is no drop to either, and horses are liable to expect one.

All the way from the first fence until reaching the solitude of the racecourse, one is conscious of the dense crowd along the railway embankment and the Canal. In spite of all powers of concentration being fixed on the task, its roar rises and falls as each fence is approached and left behind. It beats on the ear like the throbbing of the sea, and it is impossible not to be stirred and encouraged by its strength and power.

Every now and then a single word or phrase detaches itself from the main mass of sound, as a meteor might leave the huge, molten globe to which it belongs—the name of a horse or jockey coupled with some exhortation shouted by a supporter—and reaches one or two of the riders, but usually nothing can be distinguished in that deep, booming accompaniment that follows as far as the turn on to the race-course. Then comes, in contrast, a blank silence, all the more marked if one is making the running, in which case it leaves a queer sense of loneliness; the other forty odd runners seem to have vanished, the noise of the crowd lining the course has died and the voices of those on the stands are still out of hearing. The mind is only conscious of the green of the grass, the flash of white rails, and the steady rhythm of the beat of one's own horse's hooves and the even inhalation and exhalation of his breath, interrupted, perhaps, as he misses a beat to take a single, deep gulp of air to charge his lungs for his 'second wind'.

Turning for home and the end of the first circuit, the noise from the stands begins to be heard. First only a faint whisper, then as each stride brings it nearer a gradual crescendo leading up to the same familiar roar.

By the time the two plain fences, the thirteenth and fourteenth on the first round, are reached the loose horses have come to the fore. They have probably got rid of their riders some time ago, but by now the loss of this burden has enabled them to move up without undue exertion to themselves, and approaching the 'Chair' the chances are that it is a riderless runner that is in front.

Even including Becher's and the last open ditch before the race-course, the obstacle that made my heart beat fastest was the 'Chair.' It stands up against the skyline, grim, tall and formidable, the rail before it a reminder of the veritable moat that it guards, the fence itself seeming as impenetrable as a prison wall.

That it is not as formidable as it appears has already been said; however, it never looks less alarming, and it is a relief to be over it.

Provided a horse is not faint-hearted—if he is of this nature he is unlikely to be standing at this juncture—he should be given every chance to get a good view of this fence, and it is essential that the impetus of his last few strides is a crescendo and not a diminuendo. The guard-rail will prevent him getting too close to the fence, and he can be ridden into the fence with considerably more freedom than in the case of an obstacle with no ditch before it.

After the 'Chair' comes the water, concerning which the same rules apply as with the water at any other course: never loose the horse's head until he is in the air, get him back on his hocks and going into his bridle some way from the fence, and squeeze him hard with the legs right up to the time of taking off. Once over the water the end of the first lap has been reached.

By now the field will be well sorted out. There will be, at the most, twenty horses standing, and as the second circuit begins to be eaten up, more and more will fall by the wayside. Lack of stamina and exhaustion as a result of jumping one big fence after another start to make themselves felt, and loose and tiring horses will be wandering and rolling all over the course.

From here onwards, ground must be saved as much as possible, keeping clear of trouble at the same time. There is often a strong temptation to accelerate suddenly in order to get in front of a batch of loose horses, but I think it is better to sit and suffer behind them, as any such effort takes a great deal out of a horse at this stage, and the more level his speed throughout the last lap, the more likely is he to last out. Besides, it must be remembered that a loose horse has anything between ten and a half and twelve stone the best of the weights, which, together with the inclination for him to accelerate as one tries to pass him, makes the tactics of passing him of doubtful value, and it is therefore better, I think, to keep behind and watch which way he is tending to veer at each jump, so that it is possible to place a horse at his fences in a way that precludes the likelihood of jumping into the loose one. There is no harm in drawing level with or passing him, provided it does not entail asking for an extra effort to do so. Loose horses seldom fall, and so long as they are not followed closely, there is a reasonable chance of avoiding trouble.

On the second circuit it is possible one or more of the fences will have a gap in them, where a horse has charged at a fence and knocked a hole in it. At all costs these should be avoided, as a horse jumping a gap never jumps properly, with the result that he either falls, stakes himself, or lands on the horse who has caused the gap.

At Becher's a rider should begin thinking about making the best of his way home—as opposed to being concerned merely with avoiding trouble and keeping the horse upright and staying in the saddle—and at the Canal Turn it is best to be not more than three or four lengths behind the leaders. Horses cannot sprint at the end of four miles, and though something should be kept for the final run-in, it is not wise to expect a horse to make up ten or twenty lengths from the last fence. Horses that do so succeed not because they themselves are going faster, but because those in front are tiring quickly. Provided the horses in front do tire all is well, but if they are at no greater stage of exhaustion than the horse a number of lengths behind, the chances are that they will manage to hold on to their lead.

Another factor is the physical state of the rider. No matter how fit he is, a jockey is bound to be feeling the strain by the time he is approaching the finish, and he is unlikely to be able to ride a rigorous finish for the whole of the long stretch of the run-in, so that the handier he is at the last fence, the more likely is he to be able to help his horse in the final stage.

I have only completed the course in the 'National itself on one occasion, and as a great deal of that season had been lost owing to frost—in fact, racing was only resumed a few days before the 'National—I was probably not quite as fit as would otherwise have been the case, and by the time I was half-way round the second circuit, exhaustion was beginning to creep gradually and relentlessly over my limbs and muscles, causing a tightness in the chest and an unpleasant fear that I would be finished before the end of the race. I was quite unconscious of the crowd at the fences, only of what was going on in the race in the immediate vicinity of myself, and of the anxiety of getting over each fence, mentally ticking them off one by one, a great feeling of relief following each one safely cleared.

I have noticed that exhaustion in a race, in the case of anyone who does not ride a great deal, is as much mental as physical. If a rider thinks he is going to get tired he gets tired, even if he is really quite fit. On the other hand, provided he is reasonably fit, if he makes up his mind that he is going to last out the race he will do so, though he may feel utterly exhausted afterwards. In the particular race of which I write, I found it a great help taking one or two deep breaths as I was coming round the last turn; it seemed to revive me and enabled me—I think I can fairly say—to ride my horse out to the full advantage to finish third.

I have never been in the happy position of going into the last two fences in the 'National in front and going well, but should this enviable situation ever be experienced each fence should be negotiated with the same care and determination as in the case of a horse that might be expected to fall or refuse. It has already been pointed out that it is a fatal error, at any time, for a rider to let a horse 'slop' into the last or last obstacle but one, no matter how easily he is winning, as it encourages the horse to become careless, and when a horse approaches the end of the long and tiring course of the 'National, he does not need much encouragement to relax, in which case he will quite possibly fall, and until a rider has literally passed the winning-post, he cannot afford to let his concentration waver an iota.

After he passes the post his work is done and, except in some of the more trying circumstances of war, I cannot think of any moment of greater relief, mental and physical, than when I realized that at last the race was over and my horse had secured a place.

With it came the mingled sensations, of exhaustion, thankfulness, and disappointment at not having won. Returning to scale, it seems that a river of humanity has burst its banks and is tearing across the paddock in flood. Hardly has the winner entered the paddock gate than he is surrounded by an admiring, cheering mob—the winner of The Derby is received coldly by comparison—and but for the mounted policemen who swoop down upon him and escort him to the winner's enclosure, it would seem impossible that he would ever reach it at all. As it is he is entirely surrounded, only the jockey, the horse's head, and the top of the latter's back being visible, seeming to float along in the stream of people like a raft on the waters.

Around the second and third are small eddies of faithful supporters, those connected with the horse or jockey, people who have backed them each way, or those left behind by the main throng surrounding the winner. Nearing the weighing-room, crowds are still pouring down the stairs of the stands and joining the ever-widening group round the unsaddling enclosure itself, to cheer, congratulate and admire the winner—and rightly so, for whatever a horse's or jockey's past or future performances, in winning the 'National he has triumphed in the noblest and most testing of all turf ventures.

The placed jockeys have only to slide off their horse's backs, unsaddle, sink for a second on the weighing-machine chair, and the last procedure of the race is over. Gradually the others drift in: some who have fallen on the first circuit are already back, and the dressing-room becomes full of the chatter of what happened at different stages of the race—how one must have won had he not fallen at Becher's the second time, how another had two double-handfuls when he was knocked over at the Canal; how one jockey's horse 'never lifted a ruddy leg' at the 'Chair', while another never put a foot wrong all the way.

The winning jockey will be finding it difficult to wash and change with all the handshakes and congratulations that his fellow jockeys, the valets and others are showering upon him, and as he sits in his usual place on the bench, gulping down his cup of tea, which has probably been preceded by some stronger source of revival—the trainer, for whom I rode, most thoughtfully brought me half a glass of neat whisky—he will be made to recount the story of the race to all and sundry. Outside the weighing-room door the Press correspondents will be gathering, anxiously waiting to get the story from the jockey himself as soon as he reappears.

The placed horses will have been led away a few moments after the jockeys have disappeared into the dressing-room, and the crowd round the enclosure will then start to disperse. Before long the jockeys for the next race will come out, and the 'National of the year will already have become an event of the past.

Every year the 'National is always discussed in the press from various angles. It is argued that it is too severe, that it should be a weight-for-age race and not a handicap, that it should be a handicap with more rigid restrictions, that it should be a handicap with no restrictions. It therefore seems that this book would not be complete without some reference to these matters.

To the charge of undue severity it can be said that, provided the horse is suitable the 'National is a perfectly fair course.

This raises the question of what is, or is not, a suitable horse for the 'National, which is not an easy one to answer, since so many different types have proved good Aintree horses. Battleship was very small, Moifaa a giant, Double Chance looked like a flat racer, Master Robert at one time worked in the shafts. But there are several qualities that he must possess: he must be able to jump, that is to say, in a manner calculated to get him safely over the fences at Aintree, for a horse that jumps in a style that would prove highly successful at, say, Auteuil, where a horse can go straight through most of the fences, would, if he tried to use it at Aintree, be certain to fall, and even horses that are good Park fencers are by no means sure to get round here.

A horse must jump the fences, as opposed to brushing through them, and if he makes a mistake he must have the weight and power to enable him to get away with it. Thus, a horse must either be a good, clean jumper, or he must be extremely well-balanced and of great strength and weight—as was Troytown, about the only horse who ever succeeded in taking any real liberty with an Aintree fence without falling—if he is going to get round. Apart from this he must have the conformation to enable him to cope with the drops, and while a horse with a straight shoulder might quite possibly get on excellently over a Park course, he would almost certainly be doomed at Aintree; I cannot think of any good Aintree horse that did not have good shoulders, and would say that, so far as conformation is concerned, the first qualification is to be truly made in this respect.

A horse need not necessarily be massive or heavy, as long as he is an accurate jumper, and many thought that Kami, who carried me into third place, would prove a most unsuitable horse over the course, owing to his frail build, but in actual fact, owing to his brilliant jumping ability, he was as good a performer over these fences as one could wish for.

Then, a horse must be bold. A number of horses are brave enough to take on Park fences, but find the Aintree obstacles too alarming, and as a result either refuse, or jump with no heart and fall.

Finally he must be possessed of endurance; I say endurance as opposed to stamina because it is the ability to keep on jumping rather than staying-power on the flat, that enables a horse to last out at Aintree. A French 'chaser might be a better natural stayer than, say, a horse such as Davy Jones, who would almost certainly have won the 'National, but for running out at the last fence, and did not get more than about a mile on the flat, but whereas jumping Aintree took nothing out of the latter, the effort of heaving himself over the fences would take so much out of a horse of the build of the average French 'chaser, that he would be exhausted long before the end, though on the flat he might be the better stayer of the two.

Horses such as Lutteur III, the only French-bred winner of the race, and Kami, were exceptions, but both had a wonderful hind leg, which many good French 'chasers have not, quite a number being decidedly weak behind the saddle by our standards.

Finally he must have the ability to carry weight. To have to go on lifting about eleven stone or so over the Aintree fences for 4½ miles is a feat of considerable strength, and if a horse is ever to become anything approaching a top-class Aintree performer, in which case he will find himself carrying about twelve stone every time he runs, he must possess the ability to do so, which is another reason why many French horses fail, the scale of weight in their races being some two stone less.

It is often impossible to tell how a horse will react to Aintree: Russian Hero had fallen round a Park course just before he won the 'National. Some, however, are doomed before they start: that good French 'chaser, Symbole, who was unfortunately killed at Becher's was one, since, either because of their style of jumping, their conformation, or their physique, they are unsuited to the task. For the right horse Aintree is a stiff but fair test; for the wrong one it holds certain disaster.

The argument in favour of the 'National being turned into a weight-for-age race is based on the fact that it is the richest and most important 'chase in the world, and should therefore go, if possible, to the best horse rather than to the best horse at the weights. The answer is that if it were not a handicap it could not possibly be as rich a race, since the greater proportion of the stake money is made up from entry fees, and whereas innumerable owners are willing to enter a horse in a race in which, theoretically, every competitor has an equal chance, a vastly smaller number would be prepared to subscribe a similar sum in order to send to the post a horse that, at the weights, had no earthly chance. The race would, in fact, develop into an Aintree replica of the Cheltenham Gold Cup, in which some of the best horses might not run.

Originally, or rather from the time that the race became a handicap, there were no restrictions, otherwise Tipperary Tim could not have won, but with the huge increase in the numbers of starters it was felt that some attempt should be made to limit the size of the field without destroying the traditional character of the race. The present conditions seem fairly satisfactory.

Another subject of discussion with regard to Aintree in general is that of the construction of the fences.

At the present the foundation consists of the remains of the original thorn fences, which have in some parts grown into thick arms, many of them dead, and have on one or two occasions caused horses to be badly staked, such a case being that of Platypus in the 'National of 1948. As a result of this state of affairs it has been suggested that the original thorn should be substituted by birch, which would be covered with spruce, fir, or gorse, as is the case now, built to the same strength, and in fact, be indistinguishable from the fences as they are now. The objection to this is, again, tradition. But if the nature of the original foundations has changed, it seems reasonable to keep pace with it to the extent of preventing any unnecessary risk to the horses, and unless some means can be devised to pack or replant the present foundation fences so that they do not present the danger described there seems little practical object in not changing them to birch. As mentioned earlier, the fences have been modified since the war, being bellied out at the bottom and bevelled at the top.

Aintree is the finest and greatest test of the steeplechaser in the world—and of a steeplechase-rider, too, but as a result of the many valuable races over fences on other courses which have appeared since the 1939–45 war, the National has lost the unrivalled prestige it held in former times. Then, it was the aim of every top 'chaser, now horses of this calibre are not risked in the race. As a result, the

standard of the competitors is far lower than in the golden age of the
'National and, though a magnificent spectacle and a great sporting
event of worldwide fame, its unrivalled supremacy as a magnet for
every 'chaser of the highest calibre has gone forever.

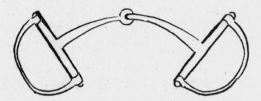

17
Hurdle-racing

SOME FOLLOWERS OF National Hunt sport look upon hurdle-racing as an effeminate and inferior alternative to steeplechasing, in which many of the participants, both equine and human, are too soft and frightened to indulge in the more robust activity of racing over fences.

This, however, is a somewhat extreme view. Certain horses, it is true, make good hurdlers but dislike 'chasing, just as some top-class flat racers have no heart for hurdling, while the professional who has to make a living out of riding cannot be blamed for choosing the least dangerous branch, if it is best suited to his inclinations and abilities. And to condemn a N.H. jockey for riding over hurdles but not over fences is akin to criticizing the champion flat race jockey because he confines himself to riding on the flat, or a Derby winner because he never ran over hurdles.

Concerning the amateur who has never ridden over fences and will only take part in hurdle races, this is a matter for his own conscience, but the chances are that, if he rides only over hurdles, and has no experience of steeplechasing, he would be a menace to himself and his fellow competitors if he turned his attention to fences.

In some ways hurdle-racing provides better competition than steeplechasing. It attracts a higher class of horse, produces closer finishes, more skilful jockeyship (as opposed to horsemanship), and results in fewer falls—to a lower order of spectatorship this may be considered a disadvantage—and I would as soon watch a top hurdle race as any ordinary steeplechase. In a steeplechase the issue is often cut and dried a long way from home: mistakes in tactics are smothered by good jumping, while there are sometimes only one or two horses left standing by the time the last fence is reached, and it is the exception rather than the rule to see four or five horses coming over the last two obstacles with nothing in it between them. Over hurdles, however, the issue depends upon jockeyship rather than horsemanship, upon racing as well as jumping ability, with the result that there are more close finishes and it is no uncommon sight to see half a dozen horses going into the last two hurdles heads apart, no more than a couple of lengths covering them at the winning-post.

There is something thrilling about standing by the first or second hurdle (which will be the last but one or the last on the second circuit) and seeing a field of twenty or so hurdlers rattle over it, the noise of them hitting the top bar sounding like a burst of machine-gun fire, then, as they come round for the last time, seeing them go all out over the last two. A good jumper over hurdles is naturally less spectacular in action than his prototype over fences, since the lower obstacle necessitates a flatter trajectory, but none the less he is impressive in his own way—the distance he stands back from the hurdles as he takes off, the speed with which he leaves the ground, and the skill with which he either skims the top or hits the bar in such a way as to make not the slightest difference to himself or his rider, landing well out on the far side.

The ability of a hurdler is dependent upon the shortness of time he takes between leaving the ground and landing; he does not need to get any higher in the air than about three feet, so that he must develop the trajectory of a missile from a gun rather than from a mortar, the fact of him hitting the obstacle (provided he has acquired the knack of doing so properly, with his forelegs as he goes up, and does not either put his fore feet between the top two bars as he is coming down, or catch his hind legs on the hurdle when he is in the air) making considerably less difference to himself and his rider than would be the case over fences.

At the first sight it might seem that to obtain a good hurdler all that is necessary is to buy a high-class horse out of a flat-racing stable. This, however, is not the case, such horses often proving grave disappointments. Besides coming under the same category as the steeplechaser to the extent of being able to carry weight, stand up to winter weather, cope with the rough-and-tumble of the game and jump, he must have a fair measure of stamina, be active and have speed, otherwise he will be unable to keep out of trouble during a race. Like the 'chaser he must be able to act in soft going, the top-of-the-ground conditions of some seasons being an exception to the ordinary going during winter racing.

He may be a stayer, but he must not be a 'plodder', and if stamina is his strong suit he must be able to keep up a fast enough pace from the start to enable him to hold his place during a race, even if he cannot accelerate quickly and suddenly.

Thus good hurdlers fall into two categories: either they are milers who can be ridden from behind (in this way preserving their speed) and are nippy enough to avail themselves of opportunities and avoid trouble during a race, or they are stayers who can keep up a strong, steady pace from the start; in both cases they must be bold, quick jumpers.

If a miler cannot be ridden from behind, he will run himself out before he has gone the two miles; if a stayer is devoid of speed, he will continually find horses beating him from the last hurdle.

For a horse to get two miles over hurdles, it is usually sufficient for him to get a mile on the flat—occasionally a good hurdler does not get a yard beyond six furlongs—but the really good hurdlers have all been able to get at least a mile and a half on the flat.

Many good hurdlers take a strong hold.

A certain amount of what has been written concerning riding over fences is applicable to riding over hurdles. A horse should always be going well into his bridle approaching a hurdle; he should not be ridden on a loose rein; he should be squeezed with the legs as he comes into the wings, and it is advisable not to ride with too short a hold of his head, or a similar fate is liable to be incurred as results from riding with too short a rein over fences.

Regarding the position of the body there is no need to do more than lean forward in about the same position as is adopted on the flat, but it is, I think, important to lean forward with a straight and not a rounded back, otherwise the rider's head tends to go down and his seat up, with obvious detrimental results to security and balance.

The lower part of the leg can be advanced slightly forward, as described in the chapter on riding over fences, but if it is allowed to remain more or less perpendicular it should answer the purpose, even though the horse does hit a hurdle.

On horses that are inclined to pitch on landing it is advisable to sit a little more upright than when using the flat race crouch, and to ride with a slightly longer rein. If a horse makes a bad mistake he should be given all the rein he needs towards making a full recovery. It should never be necessary to lean back over hurdles, though it is not enough, on the average horse, merely to sit 'up his neck' and hope for the best, as he will then tend to slow up approaching each hurdle, consequently losing ground instead of slightly increasing his impetus as he reaches the wings, which is achieved by riding him into each hurdle with one's legs. Flat race jockeys who take to hurdle race-riding are often incapable of riding a horse into a hurdle properly, being under the erroneous impression that they can make a horse jump quicker by keeping their legs still—they are probably riding too short to use them in any case—and slapping the horse down the shoulder by flicking the whip without taking their hand off the rein.

With regard to the length of the stirrup-leathers I found that I rode about the same length as on the flat (which was not markedly short), depending upon the horse's action and whether he pulled or not.

Whereas it is sometimes unwise to ride a horse into a fence vigorously—for instance, when he is meeting it 'wrong'—a horse can be ridden into a hurdle with impunity, since the harder he hits it the more likely is it to fall down, and one cannot afford to give away a fraction of a second at any hurdle in a closely contested race.

The most likely way for a horse to fall over hurdles, short of galloping straight into one, is when he stands too far back, reaches for it and puts his feet between the top two bars. For this reason it is advisable, in the case of horses that tend to stand too far back, to ride them in the manner suggested for riding over the water: namely, to take a strong, even hold of their head some way from the obstacle, apply the legs with a considerable measure of power and vigour, neither ceasing the application nor loosing their head until the moment of taking off. This procedure tends to prevent a horse taking off too soon.

Hurdle race tactics approximate far more to those of the flat than do tactics in steeplechasing, as the obstacles do not merit the same regard—an experienced hurdler can go into a hurdle 'blind' and will take off according to the horse in front of him—and, with reservations governed by the ability, experience and characteristics of the horse in question, one does not need to take the same precautions about letting a horse have a clear approach to his hurdles. Some inexperienced hurdlers need a clear view of their hurdles until they have had enough racing to adjust themselves to taking off without actually seeing the hurdle, and there are others who do not jump properly unless they are allowed to 'see daylight' and are kept clear of the mêlée, but such matters can be decided only through knowing the horse.

One trainer, for whom I had the privilege of riding, sometimes instructed jockeys to jump the first two hurdles towards the outside in order to be certain of giving the horse a clear run—some horses, particularly fillies or entires, are completely put off by being baulked early on in a race and jump badly throughout as a result. Provided a horse is impervious to interference, or is a quick beginner, or pulls so hard that it is advisable to start him in the second rank, the nearer one starts to the inside the better, but I have often found that it is possible to jump the first two hurdles on the outside and then move on to the rails when the field has sorted itself out, without losing an appreciable amount of ground. A small, light-framed horse is better given a clear run, even if it means going a slightly longer way round, than be knocked about in the mêlée, as he will come off the worst in any altercation with bigger and heavier horses.

Whether on the flat, over fences, or over hurdles, there are two pre-

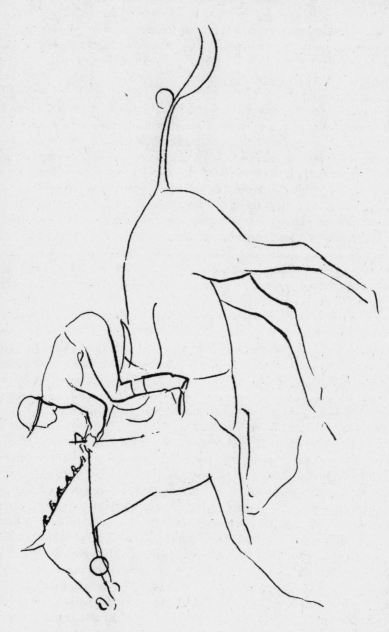

About to take off

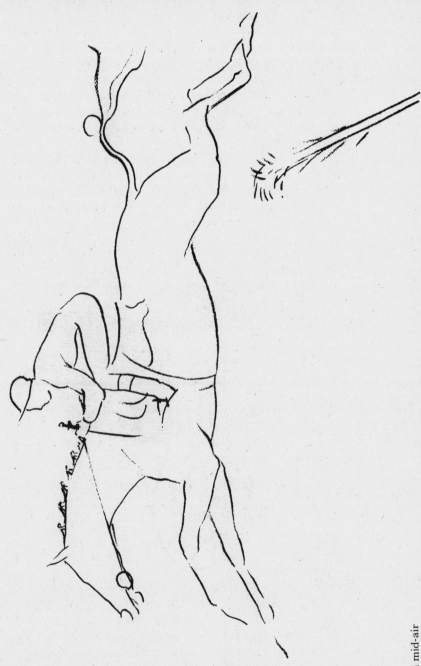

cepts that must be regarded: when the going is firm one cannot afford to let the leaders get too far ahead; when it is soft one can lie further out of one's ground. On top of the ground horses bowl along and do not 'come back', but in the soft ground front runners are apt to exhaust themselves and often slow down almost to a trot by the time the end of the race is in sight.

One can afford to lie further back over hurdles than over fences, as a mistake does not tend to have so grave an effect in the former case as in the latter, but it is unwise to wait as far behind over hurdles as is sometimes possible on the flat.

A course of riding on the flat is a good school for a hurdle race jockey, and any amateur who has ambitions towards being a jockey over hurdles, or over fences, as opposed to merely going round without falling off or making any grave tactical error, will be well advised to get as much riding on the flat as possible. N.H. flat races serve this purpose well.

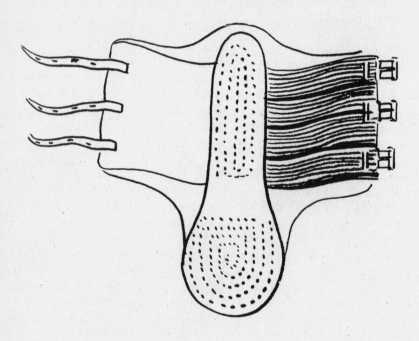

18
Training

GENERALLY SPEAKING, TRAINING falls into three stages: conditioning, slow work, and fast work, to which is added schooling over hurdles and fences.

Conditioning is one of the most important aspects of the art. If a horse is not in really hard condition, and at the same time big and well, when he is put into fast work he will not last out the season. He may go through a couple of races without showing any particular ill-effect, but the first time he has a hard race he will begin to fall away, and it will be necessary to put him by for some weeks, or his appearance and form may continue to deteriorate.

When a horse comes into a trainer's yard the latter should first thoroughly examine him, looking to see if his teeth or feet need attention, finding out if he has worms—red-worm can cause a horse to lose his form completely and may even kill him in the end—and ascertaining what exercise he has been doing during the last few weeks. If a horse's teeth are wrong he will not be able to eat properly and will suffer from indigestion. If his feet are hurting him, or are too long, he will not be able to gallop as he should, and if he has been doing nothing except light exercise—has been recently gelded, or is just off grass—he can be completely ruined by putting him into fast work too soon.

In these days of high expenses owners are apt to become impatient if a trainer wishes to give a horse time, but it is false economy to hurry horses in their preparation; nowadays a trainer makes no profit out of a horse's keep and cannot therefore be open to the accusation of persuading an owner to give a horse time for no better reason than to swell his own bank balance. 'It's the trainer, not the horse, that wants time' is a quip of pre-war days that has now died a natural death.

If a horse is not looking well and there is no apparent reason for his condition, it is as well to have him treated for red-worm whether he shows a large count from a test or not, as such tests are not infallible. Sometimes a horse will come into training looking a picture, but will fall away as soon as he begins to do strong work. If he has been given ample time to get into hard condition (so that his falling-off cannot be attributed to getting at him too soon), it is quite possible that he is suffering from red-worm, the effects of which have not appeared until he has begun racing and doing strong work. It is not a bad plan to treat horses for red-worm at the beginning of the season, regardless of whether they appear to be affected or not, otherwise it may be necessary to interrupt a season through the horse losing condition and having to be treated when racing is at its height.

Thus, the first move is to make sure the horse is in order, from a veterinary aspect, and a good vet. is worth anything to a stable.

The next step is to get the horse ready to go into work. If he has come straight off grass and has been having no corn, this will take a long time, six to eight weeks, perhaps. He cannot suddenly have his diet changed from one of grass to one of from twelve to twenty pounds of corn a day, or be put into anything more than very gentle walking and trotting exercise while he is on a light diet without ill-effects: his corn must be increased gradually, and his exercise lengthened by stages from an hour to two or three hours a day, depending upon the horse in question and the staff available.

One of the difficulties of training under modern conditions is to give a horse the required time out of the stable; in the old days horses were never out less than two hours a day, and though horses that are fit, particularly if they are fillies or geldings, can often keep their form on very light exercise and short hours, long, steady work is essential to getting a jumper ready for an arduous season. One solution is to find a keen amateur who can be entrusted to take the horse out for the required time, but some trainers solve the problem by sending him out two lots a day.

I do not suggest that it is impossible not to employ completely different methods, say, start cantering a horse gently after he has been in a week—some horses are tough enough to survive almost any treatment—but I am convinced that, in the long run, it pays to get a horse really hard by walking and trotting for some weeks before he goes into cantering work. This does not refer to yearlings, but though some flat-race trainers do not like trotting exercise, I cannot say that I have ever found it did a flat racer any harm, in fact an old-time method which often proved most successful with bad-legged horses was to get them half-fit by driving them in a dog cart.

The length of the conditioning stage of a horse's preparation depends, of course, upon his state on coming into training. He may have been hacked about before he came in and be ready to start steady cantering straight away; he may be a horse that does not need much work at any time—one that gallops about when he is out at grass will obviously come to hand much quicker than one that merely stands and eats—and his preparation must be guided by observation and experience.

Similarly the matter of feeding cannot be fixed by rule-of-thumb. A horse should be kept neither too loose nor too hard inside—his droppings are the guide—and while one may thrive on 14 lb. of corn a day, another may need 20 lb. One horse will do better on four, even five feeds a day, another on two. The skilled and conscientious trainer will study the peculiarities of each. In the winter, when there is a lack of sunlight, some horses are the better for a spoonful of cod-liver or halibut oil every day (if it is rubbed on their noses first, they will not notice it in the feed), in the case of others it might make them too fat round the heart. Some horses thrive on steamed food, others do just as well if they are fed dry with the addition of kibbled linseed cake or some such equivalent, according to the time of year. The best plan for the complete amateur is to be guided by an experienced head-lad.

In the matter of feeding I would say that the first essential is to have food-stuffs of the highest quality—good hay being just as important as good oats; next, to feed a horse regularly, and finally to regulate the amount according to the work he is doing, and to supply any variations and additions which appear suitable and necessary to the individual. Some horses dislike carrots but love apples, in others the reverse may hold; one horse may eat better during the night, another during the day; some have to be coaxed to eat at all, others would, if allowed, over-eat themselves.

It is as impossible to set out a rule for feeding a horse (unless one is personally acquainted with the peculiarities or otherwise of the individual in question) as it is for a man; successful feeding depends upon intelligent observation, imagination, experience and knowledge.

Horses appreciate such additions as carrots, apples, dandelions, lucerne and even mangels, in their respective seasons, and linseed cake provides a variety from the ordinary linseed mash, which most trainers feed twice a week, while I have heard of sugar-beet pulp being used with success in some cases. Like many other things, feeding is an art, and, besides knowledge and experience, the best feeders are possessed of an instinctive understanding of what will or will not suit a particular horse, which the ordinary man does not possess; the trainer who is fortunate enough to employ a really good feeder has solved half his troubles.

Nowadays many people feed nuts. The advantage of this is that they are easy, the disadvantage that it is not possible to tell the quality of the ingredients in them, unless these are personally supplied to the manufacturers, and there is no scope for individual feeding. My inclination is to use them only for hacks, or ponies or hunters, but preferably not at all.

A few trainers do their own feeding, but this is not easy with a big string of horses, and when the racing season necessitates them being away at meetings, and though they may be able to supervise the feeding of their horses closely, trainers will be largely dependent upon the ability, punctuality and reliability of the head-lad in this respect.

However fortunate a trainer may be in his head-lad he will get the best results if he shows a real personal interest in every department of his stable, every now and then appearing to see his horses fed first thing in the morning and looking in at them late in the evening to see how each is doing. The most reliable of men will tend to become slack if they realize that their employer is an over-keen adherent to the practice of decentralization, and the better a trainer can get to know his horses as individuals, the more successful and enjoyable will be his profession—that is to say if he has chosen the calling because his heart is in it, and not merely because it is one way of making a living.

The routine in different stables varies considerably, and is also dependent upon the time of year. In winter most jumping trainers get the first lot out at eight o'clock. They will have been given a small feed at six, will remain out for about an hour and a half, come in, be dressed over and fed, and then the second lot will go out. Some trainers give the first lot a small feed when they come in, and another one when the second lot are fed after exercise, the latter having been given a somewhat larger breakfast than the first lot, and in several stables the six o'clock feed is not given.

From mid-day to about 4.30 p.m. the horses are left to rest. When the lads return to evening stables some trainers give their horses a small feed of corn, others wait until they have all been dressed over and are ready to be shut up for the night at about 7 p.m.—in the former case the horses will of course, have their 7 p.m. feed as well—and the few that may need an extra feed later will be visited again, perhaps about nine or ten o'clock.

In the case of gross horses, some trainers believe in giving no hay the night before they run, and with such animals it is certainly advisable to muzzle them when they arrive at the meeting and are loosed in their box, in case they stuff themselves with straw; another measure is to stand them on moss-litter instead of straw.

Some trainers water their horses at set times, but I think that most of them have water left permanently in the box, so that they can drink when they feel like it. The only snag with regard to the latter system is that idle stable-lads will not take the trouble to change and clean out the water-manger unless they are compelled to, but under the former method it is, of course, possible that an indifferent stableman will forget to water the horse at all.

A good head-lad will always make a practice of going round the horses after the lads have left, in order to see that all doors are shut—it has not been unknown to find a horse walking about the yard or passage as a result of this precaution being overlooked—to ensure that a horse has not been left tied up, that all have been fed and watered, and that articles such as stable-forks have not been left in the boxes. An efficient trainer will make a practice of doing the same from time to time, when occasion allows.

When a trainer is satisfied that a horse is ready to go into faster work, the next stage of his training begins.

This will consist of steady cantering every day, except for Sundays, when most trainers either give their horses walking exercise only, have them led out in the paddock, or leave them in altogether.

The number of canters a horse will do a day depends upon the nature of the training-ground—at Newmarket, which is almost completely flat, horses need far more work than on the downs, where horses have to walk up and down hills from the time they leave the stable—and on the individual characteristics of the horse; it is never an encouraging sign in a trainer if he makes such remarks as, 'I believe in giving all my horses plenty of work—or very little work', since horses vary a great deal in the amount of work upon which their best form is produced. Although some seem impervious to the way they are trained, adapting themselves to the methods of a different trainer after being in his charge a few weeks, a considerable number are not, and it is quite common to find a horse showing entirely different form with one trainer from that which he displayed with another—as I have no wish to be sued for libel I will not endeavour to give any examples.

With regard to the contrast in the type of work required by different horses, I have in mind the cases of two horses I used to ride, the one required a sharp canter every day and at least two good gallops a week, otherwise he blew up during a race, the other won a two-mile steeplechase after having done no more than go out on a long rein for the last five days before he ran.

After a horse has been cantering steadily for a week or two he can go on to faster work. Nearly all trainers begin this stage by letting horses start off at a steady pace and work up to a faster one over the last furlong or so—'finish running away' was an expression often used by the late Tom Coulthwaite, one of the most successful trainers of jumpers of his day, in giving instructions before an exercise gallop, to signify that he wanted his horses to be full of running at the end of their work, rather than that they should tear away at the start and finish 'sold out'. This method makes horses enjoy their work and ensures that they are not overdone. The secret of keeping horses from becoming stale at home is always to (except for trials) have them 'on the bit'; if he is perpetually being ridden right out a horse will soon lose enthusiasm, a state of mind he may carry to the racecourse, to the detriment of all concerned with him.

When stable-boys cannot be relied upon to go the correct pace the gallop can always be regulated by making the lads keep behind a horse chosen for the fact that he cannot go too fast whether he wants to or not, and forbidding them to pass the pacemaker until they are signalled by the trainer to do so.

A good trainer always goes about his business quietly and efficiently. His horses (except those who are impossibly excitable by nature) are well-behaved and happy out at exercise—the obdurate will have been put in their place, the highly-strung will not have been over-taxed. He will know exactly how he is going to work his horses and who is going to ride each horse in the different gallops, so that there will not be a lot of unnecessary changing and re-changing of riders, a shouting for one horse to come back and another to take his place just as a bunch of horses are going down to work, and the general waste of time and confusion that can result from lack of method, incompetence or an over-fiery temperament. 'Where the hell is—' bellowed a well-known trainer of a past decade, referring to a horse he wanted to work, but could not see among his string. 'You're riding him, sir,' pointed out the head-lad when he was able to get a word in edgeways.

A horse can be made or marred by unskilled riding at exercise, and bad mouths, nervousness, whipping round, fly-jumping and other such unpleasant traits, are often due solely to this cause.

It makes a great deal of difference to the success of their combined efforts if a horse and rider can get to know each other, and a jockey that is keen on his job will be as anxious to come and ride out a difficult horse every morning he can, as will be his trainer to have him do so. Once a rider has got into a certain way of riding it is very difficult to alter him, and it is one of the problems of present-day training that there are comparatively few good exercise riders available, but even if a horse has already been spoiled he can be greatly improved, sometimes cured, by being regularly ridden by a good horseman.

However, 'scatty' and unmanageable horses are not always rendered so only by bad riding: it is equally possible to bring them to this state by bad training, by failing to appreciate or understand their temperament, by always jumping them off, by never varying the form of exercise, and so on. I noticed when riding out with Fred Darling, one of the greatest flat-race trainers of the century, that when doing a preliminary canter before fast work, every lad was made to sit down in his saddle, ride with a long rein, and go no faster than a hack-canter. By this means the horses were taught to understand when they were supposed to go fast and when they were not, and until they felt a rider 'getting up their necks' they knew that they were not expected to do more than lob along, as a result of which they were all remarkably temperate and well-behaved.

The modern racehorse, whether he is a jumper or a flat racer, does not take much stirring up, and the more settled he is at home, the easier it is to train him, and the better is he likely to perform on a race-course. Once he has really become upset it is not an easy task to get him to settle down.

Excitable horses are often best trained by themselves, or by riding them as a hack. Easter Hero, one of the most brilliant 'chasers of all time, used to pull very hard when worked in the guise of a racehorse, but in a double bridle was as perfect a hack as could be wished for. Such horses sometimes benefit by being hacked out two lots a day and by being made to stand and watch the others work, their fitness being achieved by cantering them about on their own occasionally letting them finish up at a good striding gallop, but never jumping them off the mark.

Indolent horses, on the other hand, work best in company and are the better of being sharpened up over short distances, otherwise it is very difficult to get them fit at all. One horse I knew would not even do more than canter in company at home (he went all right on a course), and the only way he could be got fit was by putting a rug and hood on him and making him sweat.

A horse either stays or he does not, and although a great deal can be done in respect of helping milers to get the trip over hurdles or fences by getting them to settle down behind other horses, it is impossible to make a sprinter into a stayer by galloping him over long distances. In fact, continued galloping over long distances will only tend to take away a horse's speed, which is an even more important factor in a hurdler or a 'chaser than a long-distance flat racer, since a jumper without speed always tends to get into trouble during a race. This does not mean that jumpers should not be worked over the distances at which they will have to run, but that, once they are fit and clean inside, they can be kept so by short, sharp work.

If a horse does his long work during the early stages of his prepara-tion, so that he is only going fast for a comparatively short distance over the last few furlongs, his muscles will be put in order without his speed being impaired, and when he is fit enough to go a good gallop over a mile and a quarter on the flat, there is little danger of him not being able to do the same for two miles or more over fences or hurdles.

It is a great mistake to run a horse that is soft in condition, even if only to give him an easy race: the excitement of the environment will probably cause him to do more than is wanted of him and this effort will put a considerable strain upon him, which he will be in no condition to bear, and will only do him harm. It is one thing to give a horse a run when he is not quite cherry-ripe, but quite another to run him when he is out of condition altogether. It is possible to do more damage by running a horse over fences in such a condition, than is the case on the flat, since it may cause him to have a fall through becoming tired, thus shaking his confidence.

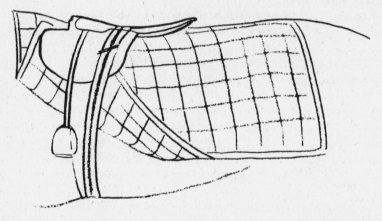

Sheet under saddle

Except in the case of entires, who never grow thick coats, as do mares and geldings, it is the custom to clip out jumpers in the winter. Some trainers clip horses out trace-high, leaving the legs and the upper part of the body, the head and the neck (except for the throat and a belt running down to the chest) untouched, others clip them out, legs and all. When a horse is in strong work it is generally admitted that it is preferable to clip him out entirely, except for his legs (which are trimmed with the leg-knife), and possibly his head—though it is rather unsightly to leave this unclipped—since, when clipped right out, a horse is more easily kept clean and dry, and is not so likely to catch a chill. Also an unclipped coat, particularly when heavy with sweat, represents a considerable addition to the weight a horse has to carry.

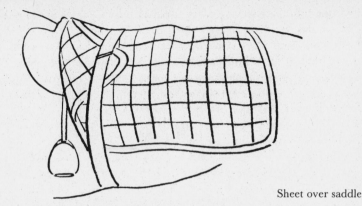

Sheet over saddle

The practice of clipping-out the inside of the ears—a favourite trick with horse-dealers to make a horse look sharper—serves no good purpose, as the hair in the ears is designed by nature to keep the cold, rain and any foreign bodies from getting into the ears, and to remove it is only to lay the horse open to ear-trouble.

Under the same category as clipping comes the trimming of manes and tails. Manes can be either hogged, plaited, or left long—in the latter case it is usual to pull them to a length of some six to eight inches. From the rider's point of view, a neatly-plaited mane is the best; an unplaited mane tends to get in the way when one picks a horse up preparatory to riding a finish, while a hogged mane, though it looks extremely neat on some horses, can be very painful if brought into contact with one's face, an accident which, it is true, should not occur but which, nevertheless, quite often does. A hogged mane needs regular attention, or it soon assumes an untidy appearance, though it is easier to keep clean than a plaited mane, which must be carefully brushed out every day and periodically washed.

Clothing is another subject of considerable debate in the training world. I have ridden for some trainers who send their horses out to exercise wearing two rugs and 'nightcaps', others who put no clothing on them at all, except in extreme cold or when a horse is doing no work. Horses get used to one system or the other, provided they do not feel the cold a great deal, and when all's said and done hunters come to no harm through being out all day without clothing, getting very hot and then hanging about for long periods on end.

If a racehorse is kept on the move after working he will be none the worse for going out without clothing, provided the weather is not too severe and he can stand the cold, but on the whole it is probably best to send them out with a sheet or rug, which can be removed when they do fast work, and put on again after they have pulled up. 'Nightcaps' are beneficial in wet weather in the case of horses that dislike the rain, but otherwise I have never been able to see much point in them.

The subject of bits has always been one that has caused great interest in all branches of riding. In the racing world some variation of the snaffle is almost universally used. Provided he has been properly broken and has not acquired the habit of getting his tongue over the bit, or is afflicted with a sore tooth or mouth, it should be possible to ride any ordinary horse in a plain snaffle, but there are a considerable number of horses who suffer from one-sided mouths, pull hard or get their tongue over the bit, and are difficult to ride in this bit. Before trying the many and various different bits which the saddlers' art has devised, it is always worth, where possible, starting from scratch again by putting the horse back on long

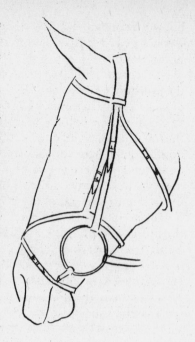

Cross-noseband

reins and re-mouthing him—that is to say if there is anyone on the premises capable of doing it—a course of long-rein driving often proving the answer to many ills such as obstinacy, jibbing and other forms of waywardness.

However, it often happens that there is no opportunity to do this—for example, if a horse arrives at a stable in the middle of the season—and by the process of trial and error, it is necessary to try and find a 'key' to his mouth.

If he is a hard puller, something like a chain snaffle—comprised of big, thick links—a 'Puckle' nose-band, or a cross-nose-band may do the trick—there is an American double-bit with a nose-band attached to it that is said to be effective, both with horses that pull and those that get their tongue over the bit, but I have only seen such a bit in use, so do not know its exact construction. Some favour a twisted snaffle, but because of its edges it sometimes makes a horse's mouth sore. Quite often horses start putting their tongue over the bit as a result of the bit being too low in the mouth, and without gagging the horse the bit should always be adjusted so that it is well up.

If a horse has a light mouth he is probably best suited by a rubber bit, this being particularly necessary when he is being schooled, as he will not be concentrating on jumping if a too-severe bit is distracting his attention.

It is sometimes debated whether or not a horse should be worked on the morning of his race. This is a matter about which it is impossible to make a rule. In the case of highly-strung, delicate animals, for them to be led out for half an hour will probably answer the purpose; with the majority, provided they are fit when they leave home, it will make no difference whether they are worked or not, but with some it will make all the difference in the world. I know of one particularly striking instance of this, which occurred in respect of a hunter-'chaser belonging to a friend of mine.

He had just worked the horse a good mile and a half half-speed on the morning of the race in which he was going to run, and as he was leaving the course he encountered a friend who was bringing his horse out to work and who remarked that it was a pity that he had not arrived earlier as the two horses could then have worked together. As my acquaintance did not think his horse had any chance he said that he did not mind working him again, so he sent him a good gallop for a second time. When he came to ride the horse in the afternoon he found to his considerable surprise that, far from the two morning gallops having an adverse effect, the horse ran better than he had ever known, from which accident he was able to reap considerable advantage, as the horse invariably ran about 7 to 10 lb. better after a strong gallop on the morning of the race, than when he was not worked at all, or given only steady work.

Such things can only be discovered by trial and error, and should a horse prove disappointing on a light preparation it is always worth experimenting with more drastic methods. But whereas one can always put more work into a horse whose performance suggests that he might previously have been under-trained, it is a very different matter getting a horse back to form after he has been over-done—sometimes he never does come back to his best—so that it is a better policy to try under-working a horse before resorting to the other extreme.

It is not an easy matter to find out how good a 'chaser or hurdler is at home. Jumping ability can turn flat-race form upside-down, and unless the characteristics of the horses in question are thoroughly understood, and the horse can confidently be expected to jump satisfactorily on a racecourse, a gallop on the flat at home can be very confusing with regard to a 'chaser or a hurdler, while few trainers have the amenities to enable them to send a horse two miles over fences or hurdles on the training ground. The best answer is probably to obtain pemission to gallop on a racecourse, which is sometimes possible, though not as easy as in pre-war days—probably because the increased number of runners cut up the track more than was the case before—when a Sunday morning at Lingfield or Hurst Park was sometimes like a miniature race-meeting, so numerous were the horses that were being schooled or galloped.

In those days training was a pleasant life and a profession in which it was not too difficult to make a fair living, though the lot of a jumping trainer was always a harder one than that of his counterpart on the flat. It is true that, since the war, stakes have risen greatly, thus giving a trainer (who usually gets 10 per cent of his patron's winnings) a chance of earning more, but against that, the costs of everything have gone up in a far greater proportion. Good fodder and skilled stable-men are scarce, the price of the former and the wages of the latter having soared, while training-fees have risen in a lesser proportion, with the result that, although the life is still enjoyable, the training of jumpers is a worrying affair, which can only be successfully conducted (barring the case of a few big stables) if it is supplemented by betting, coping, private means or some other source of income.

Success as a trainer therefore depends, not only upon knowledge and ability in the actual preparation of horses for their engagements, but upon the battle with bookmakers, which is liable to prove an uphill struggle, in which a first-rate stableman and horse-master can go under if he is not fortunate enough to be possessed of the mentality and ability to bring off an occasional coup.

Training is not an art that can be picked up over-night. It would, I reckon, take at least ten years to acquire the knowledge and experience upon which the career of a good trainer is based—I worked for nine years as a pupil in a racing-stable, at the end of which time I was only too conscious of how little I knew. I do not say that it would not be impossible to train winners on a less lengthy and exacting course of education—I succeeded in training an odd 'chase and hurdle race-winner of my own during my pupilship—for good horses will win in spite of the trainer, and a capable head-lad and a bit of luck will make up for a considerable degree of ignorance. But if a trainer is to make a success of it off his own bat, and be able to survive when he finds himself with bad horses and without a good head-lad, he must have a thorough knowledge of every branch of his calling, which can only be acquired from years of experience and a practical knowledge of every branch.

Nevertheless, those who have spent their whole life in the game are not always good trainers; perhaps it is that they lack imagination, that they are too set in their ways, or that they are not naturally possessed of horse sense, having entered the profession because, through circumstances and tradition, it never occurred to them to consider any other. Racing is by no means the only, or necessarily the most skilled, section of the horse world so far as stable-management and horsemanship is concerned—it always used to be said that driving men were the best horsemasters—and in these days when such aspects as the making and breaking of hunters are completely foreign to many trainers, some of whom are more at home in a car than on a horse, racing itself by no means always proves the source of the most successful trainers.

The possession of a suitable temperament is another necessary attribute to a good trainer. He must be prone neither to worry nor excitability; if inclined to the former, he will probably finish up in a strait-jacket which, in the second case is liable to be the fate of those who work under him, if they remain with him for any length of time—which is unlikely. And many who have every other qualification have fallen short of the success they might otherwise have achieved as a result of one or both of these traits.

Trainers differ greatly in method and habit. There is the 'carry on sergeant-major' type, who puts his head out of the bedroom window and gives instructions to the head-lad as to where to meet him on the training ground—thereby getting an extra half-hour in bed—and who skips through his horses at evening stables with an 'everything eaten up and all in order?' to the head-lad, and is half-way back to the warmth of his fire before the latter has had time to answer.

Then there is the martinet, who will be patrolling the yard when one arrives—he has probably been there since before the appearance of the first lad—and will not be slow in expressing his ire if anyone is a minute late. His stable will be run with relentless efficiency, and though he may be severer than most upon his lads, the chances are they will stay with him because they know exactly how they stand, get good presents and respect his experience and ability. He will ignore any attempts at conversation while out at exercise, but will descend like a ton of bricks on any breach of discipline such as going too fast in a gallop, getting in the way, or placing a horse in danger of being kicked.

He will stand no nonsense from his owners, but they will patronize him because he produces the results. Whether one rides a winner or a loser, his comments on the effort will be in accordance with the merit of one's performance, regardless of the result. 'Why did you come on the outside round the last bend?' was the only remark once made to me as I came in prepared for a laudatory reception after riding a winner.

Such trainers are always the best to ride for. They give credit where it is due, do not blame beaten jockeys when the cause of the defeat could not be attributed to their riding, and produce horses that are fit and know their job. One never feels quite at ease till work is over, experiencing something of the apprehension of the recruit on the barrack square, but to ride for them is to benefit greatly in knowledge and experience.

Less alarming is the rough-and-ready type. He will possibly combine some rather haphazard farming with training, and it is never quite clear where the stable ends or the farm begins, or to which department the various members of the establishment belong. The equipment will not be of a high order, nor will it be clean, there will be a tendency for bridles to be tied up with hay-strings, and the stirrups will invariably be rusty.

If the horses go out in sheets, no two will be of the same pattern or bear the same initials.

The horses will be well fed, but their manes and tails will probably be in need of a trim the former (unless the horse has just run, in which case it may have been trimmed) giving a very passable imitation of the coiffure generally associated with Roman chariot-horses, and the latter either trailing on the ground or cut rather too short and a bit crooked.

There will be no drama if one turns up a few minutes late—the horses have probably never gone out at exactly the same time two days in their lives—and such niceties as shaving or the wearing of clean boots and breeches will be quite wasted, the flannel-trouser-fishing-sweater type of garb being far more in keeping with the general environment.

The conduct of the work will be somewhat slapdash, and the geography of the gallops may be a trifle confusing—they may include such diversions as going through gateways or over a sleeper-bridge—but the whole affair will be fun, and there will not be a great deal of fuss if things do not go quite according to plan. After work, one is assured of a good breakfast, and the horses are usually fit and good jumpers—they have probably all been well hunted. When they win, there is often the added attraction of the starting price being in the region of 20 to 1.

It is often said in the training profession nowadays that it is not the horses that need training, but the owners, many of whom know nothing about horses, their capabilities and their peculiarities, expecting them to run with the consistency and regularity of machines. They are often equally ignorant of the recognized conduct and procedure of the Turf.

If a trainer is in a strong enough position to be independent of a particular owner's patronage, he is as well to ensure that the latter thoroughly understands the terms under which his horses are to be trained, otherwise a breach of the peace is certain to arise sooner or later. If he is not, he may have to use a good deal of diplomacy to cope with the situation.

So far as the trainer is concerned, his duty is to prepare the horses under his charge for the engagements mutually agreed upon by his patron and himself, to look after his patron's interests with regard to entries, forfeits (which can amount, unnecessarily, to a considerable sum if they are not carefully watched) and other expenses that may be incurred and to keep him informed as to the progess or otherwise of his horses.

If he has carried out these tasks conscientiously and efficiently, the trainer cannot be blamed if a horse does not win, for this regrettable, and unfortunately, common state of affairs will be due solely to the fact that the horse is not good enough, to bad luck, or to some inexplicable cause—a horse cannot tell the trainer he is not feeling his best—and owners who grumble at lack of success under these circumstances are better out of the stable. Time and again one hears an owner remark, 'I'm changing my trainer as I've done no good with him', when the rational (and cheaper) solution would be to change the horses.

On the other hand, if a trainer does not look after the interests of his patron—I once heard of an owner of former times paying full training fees for a horse that had been dead for a year—he cannot be surprised if the latter removes his horses.

19

Schooling

OF ALL THE different branches of training, that of schooling horses to jump is the most interesting. To start a horse off on his first lesson, and then see him gradually progressing through the various stages of his education until the day comes when he goes round Aintree, is a matter of absorbing interest and delight, and the making of a 'chaser as pleasant a hobby as anyone could wish for.

There are a great many theories concerning teaching horses to jump, but all are subject to the same general principles namely, the exercise of patience, starting over low obstacles, and instilling into the horse a blend of confidence and respect with regard to whatever he has to jump.

Horses are by no means all natural jumpers, nor do those who take to it quickest always turn out the best—Kellsboro' Jack, about the best horse round Aintree I ever saw, was slow to learn, having no idea what to do when first confronted with an obstacle—and if a horse appears bewildered and clumsy at first, it does not follow that he is necessarily a hopeless case, while those that are exceptionally bold and fluent from the beginning sometimes become over-confident, which means that there will be a day of reckoning sooner or later.

The earlier a horse begins to learn to jump, the better, since it is always easier for the young to learn than for the old, and provided they are kept to small obstacles and light riders, there is no harm in jumping two-year-olds.

The French start jumping their horses much sooner than we do, which is because they stage hurdle races and steeplechases for young horses at an earlier date than is the case in England, and many trainers in France school two-year-olds. The French are also great believers in jumping horses in a loose school, as are a few people in England and there is much to commend it, as it enables a horse to go through the motions without any weight on his back, gives him confidence and teaches him not to make mistakes, without risking injury to the rider.

But jumping in a loose school is only a means to an end; in practice, a horse will have to carry a man on his back, to which he must get used long before he can be considered anything like the finished article. A horse that is a fluent jumper loose is often quite at sea when he has to cope with the presence of a rider, and it is not a bad plan to jump him alternately loose and ridden, rather than accustom him to jump only without a man on his back, and then have to start from scratch with a rider.

The disadvantage of jumping a horse without anyone on his back is that he is more or less his own master, and can stop or whip round if he wishes, which, once he has discovered that he can do it, he may repeat in the future, whereas, with a good man on his back, he would not have been given the opportunity.

The first time a horse jumps, whether loose or ridden, it is imperative that he is not allowed to stop, run out or whip round, for if he succeeds in doing so, he will always have in the back of his mind the thought that he can do so again, and he may try it on at a most inconvenient and unexpected moment at a later stage. If there is not a good schooling-rider available, it is probably better to jump the horse loose or on a long rein, rather than entrust him to an incompetent one. Bad handling at this stage may destroy his confidence and spoil his style, causing him to jump straight up in the air and land on all fours, start off at a tearaway pace and get slower and slower as he nears the obstacle, finally lurching over it from a standstill, attempting to gallop straight through it, or running out.

It is advisable, the first time a horse jumps, to aim him at an obstacle which cannot hurt him if he jumps into it, on to it, or through it—a bundle of faggots or a few bushes heaped together are as good as anything—as he can then be ridden at it with confidence and will not become alarmed if he makes a mess of his first attempt, as might be the case if he put his foot through a hurdle, took a fall over a rail, or dropped his hind legs on a log. The obstacle should not be more than a couple of feet high, and it need be no more than two or three feet in breadth, its only purpose being to show him that he can get from one side to the other without injury or effort.

It is as well if he is given a lead the first time, as he will be keen to follow the horse in front of him, and after he has gone over a couple of times satisfactorily with a lead, he can be made to go on his own. The best results will be achieved if he is ridden as if he were a hunter, with a fairly long stirrup-leather and at a jog-trot or hack canter, as the rider will then have some control if the horse tries to stop or dodge out (which would not be the case if he were to ride too short), and the horse will learn to jump off his hocks, which he would not do if allowed to gallop straight over or through the obstacle.

A great many trainers consider this method a waste of time. They jam a novice between two old ones, put another in front of him, and gallop him at a low hurdle. He will get to the other side all right, for the simple reason that it is almost a physical impossibility for him to avoid it, but how he did so may be something of a mystery to him, and unless he has a certain amount of natural talent, he will probably find the whole experience rather bewildering and have learnt little or nothing about how to jump properly; with the result that he never makes a good jumper, or does so only after a season's experience on the racecourse.

However, this is a matter of opinion, and though the last-named method may work well enough in many cases as regards jumping hurdles, it is not, in the long run, the best way of introducing a jumper to the game, especially if he is eventually expected to run over fences.

To return to the less slapdash method; when a horse has got through the preliminary stage to the satisfaction of his trainer—that is to say, when he has jumped the bushes, or whatever constituted his first obstacle, properly—he can proceed to the next stage, this being to follow the lead-horse over a few flights of low hurdles at a steady canter. If he does this well, he can go upsides with his school-master, first on the offside, then on the near-side, and finally on his own.

The number of times he jumps at these two stages, and the days over which this part of his education is spread, must depend upon the speed with which he picks up the lessons; he may do it in half an hour, or he may take two or three days, but if he is a normal horse and is ridden with determination, sympathy and confidence, he should go through these two stages in the course of a morning's exercise.

If his first objective is hurdle racing, he can then be allowed to go over the small hurdles faster, working up to racing pace, but it is essential that his maximum speed is attained in the last few strides up to and including the take-off, as this will ensure that he jumps fast. A good schooling jockey will always be seen to squeeze a horse with his legs as he approaches the wings, keeping a firm, even hold of the horse's head to balance him properly and make him jump off his hocks, neither relaxing the pressure of the reins or of his legs until the horse has taken off.

The worst way of letting a novice jump is to let him tear away from the start and slow down as he nears the hurdle; this will cause him to jump slowly and to lose ground, and schooling jockeys who ride too short to use their legs and who start 'scrubbing' a horse with their hands (and consequently loosing his head), under the mistaken impression that they will make him go faster, cause a horse to lose

A successful early lesson

ground at his hurdles and to 'go on his front end' rather than jump off his hocks.

After this, he can go on to jumping full-size hurdles.

It is as well to let him jump with a lead the first time, although, if he has satisfied his trainer in the first stage of his schooling—and if he has not, he should not be jumping full-size hurdles at all—he should be capable of going upsides another horse, or even by himself, but the more confidence he can be given the better.

When sent upsides another horse he should go first on one side of him and then on the other, and if he does that satisfactorily he can be allowed to go on his own—in this respect, it is quite a good plan to set him off upsides another horse—or other horses—and then let him go on in front after jumping the first hurdle.

As far as pace is concerned, it is always best not to start off too fast, but to begin at a good swinging canter and increase as one reaches the wings; if one starts off at full speed the only change of pace that is possible is one of deceleration, which is the last thing that should be encouraged, since it means losing ground at the jump.

The final stage is to teach the horse to jump directly behind a horse in front of him, without seeing the hurdle till the last moment.

This is achieved by letting him follow two or three horses abreast, first six lengths behind, then three, then not more than a length. This teaches him to jump 'blind' and will prevent him starting to slow up, or being taken by surprise if he suddenly sees the horse in front of him take off, when he cannot see the obstacle himself, which is more than likely to occur during a race.

It does not follow that, because a horse has not been schooled on the lines suggested, he will not be a good ride the first time he runs—I have often ridden hurdlers who have done no more than jump a couple of small hurdles two or three times in company with another horse, before they ran in public, and had a first-rate ride—but if a horse is to be backed the first time out, the more skilled and confident a jumper he is under all circumstances, the less likely is it that the bookmaker will win. Because a horse jumps well at home with everything in his favour, it is no guarantee that he will do the same in a race with, perhaps, a wall of horses in front of him and the machine-gun-like rattle of hurdles being hit all round him, so that the more thorough his schooling, the better is his performance on a racecourse likely to be. If possible, it is a great help to be able to give him a final dress-rehearsal, in the shape of a gallop over hurdles on a racecourse in company with five or six other horses.

The English as a race are astonishingly casual, and trainers will often run, and bet on, horses who have only jumped a couple of hurdles in their lives, while others will send horses out for experience that have not even jumped properly at home, to which can be attributed not a few of the accidents that from time to time occur through horses swerving, trying to stop or run out, or jumping crooked, which means that they have not been thoroughly schooled.

A good rider will often make a bad or unwilling jumper jump straight and well, but a well-schooled horse should not have to rely on his rider for this guidance, and although a horse must be forgiven a jumping mistake—which even an experienced performer will make every now and then—consistently bad jumping is due, fundamentally, to insufficient or badly planned and conducted tuition on the training ground.

Horses tend to become careless through jumping the same obstacles, and one often notices that novices jump extremely well the first two or three times they are schooled, but do not bother to jump properly when they have got to know the obstacles too well. If they jump all right on a racecourse, this is only a warning to stop jumping them at home, and because a horse hits his hurdles he is by no means necessarily a bad jumper; in fact, a horse that knows how to hit a hurdle, so that it does not in any way interfere with his balance or progress, is usually a quicker jumper than one who always clears them, and he should not be encouraged to change his style. But the horse who makes mistakes that slow him up or threaten to put him down, must be corrected, or he will never become as good a hurdle racer as he is capable of being.

In the first lesson or so, a horse's characteristics in jumping will show themselves.

To start with, he will by nature be either a free horse or a lazy one. On top of that, he will be either a willing jumper or an unwilling one. If he is a free horse and a willing jumper, he will present no great problem, even if he has not many clues about how to jump—'I always like to see a novice that goes at his hurdles with a good heart, and I don't care if he flattens them', an eminent and highly successful trainer of jumpers once told me—for if he hits his hurdles without losing any ground or unbalancing himself, he is as well left alone, and if he hits them in such a way as to endanger his equilibrium and slow him down, he can be taught to pay them the necessary respect by lunging him over a hurdle with a stout pole fixed along the top, or by jumping him over some stiffer obstacle—some trainers cope with the situation by jumping such horses over small but stiff fences.

If he is lazy or over-careful, one can usually put him right by riding him over one or two low hurdles by himself, hacking him into them and peppering him with a series of quick, sharp cuts of the whip, from the time that he puts his nose in the wings until he has landed. As soon as he lands, he should be pulled back to a canter and the procedure repeated at the next hurdle, the whip being applied with the opposite hand. If he is allowed to tear away after the first application, the effect will be lost in the case of the second, the whole object of the operation being to teach him to increase his momentum in the last few strides he takes before he jumps. If he is particularly sticky by nature, it may be a help to put blinkers on him, since the element of surprise will then be greater, as he will not be able to see out of the corner of his eye when or whence the chastisement is coming. It is not necessary to hit him unmercifully, only hard enough to sting him, the effectiveness of the treatment lying in the speed and timing of the application. Some horses of this type react well to spurs.

If he is a free goer but an unwilling jumper, he will not be so easy to deal with, as he will want to tear off at a good gallop and, at the last moment, stop or run out. The former manœuvre is liable to prove unseating, while the latter is not always easy to prevent.

The first essential to coping with this kind of horse is that he should be ridden by someone who can control him, so that he can be made to go at the pace dictated by the rider and not by himself. This will have to be achieved, either by procuring the services of a good rider, or by finding a bit in which he can be managed. He should then be ridden over the small hurdles in the manner described above, on no account being allowed the slightest latitude and, if he stops, being made to jump from a standstill, which will be possible owing to the small size of the obstacle. If he whips round or runs out, he should always be pulled round in the opposite direction to that in which he went of his own accord, since every move he wins, however slight, will make him more difficult to cure, and he should be kept to small obstacles until he jumps them perfectly.

After that, he can be promoted to the full-size hurdles, but he should never be allowed to get out of his rider's control, nor be given the slightest chance to run out or stop, and until his jumping is perfect at home he should not be produced on a racecourse, as he will only constitute a possible danger to other runners.

If a horse has a fall in a race, it is advisable to give him a school at home before he runs again, in order to restore his confidence. If he starts to jump badly after he has had a race or two, he will have to be corrected according to his faults—one hurdler I had, for some unknown cause, started to catch his hind legs on his hurdles at the beginning of his second season. This made him lose a considerable amount of ground every time he jumped, but he was successfully cured by jumping him over a good-size tree-trunk at home, which made him keep his hind-legs out of the way after he had barked them on the tree once. In the heat and excitement of a race, a horse is often not aware of what he is doing, so that he does not always learn from experience on a racecourse, but when his attention is fixed on jumping, as it is when he is schooled quietly at home, he is more likely to realize what he is about and learn to amend his mistakes.

Once a horse has learnt his job and jumps consistently well in his races, the less he is jumped at home the better, as continued jumping will only tend to bore him and make him careless, will constitute an unnecessary risk and will place an added strain on his legs.

So much for the schooling and jumping of hurdlers.

The case of 'chasers is more complicated. Roughly speaking, there are two distinctive ways of introducing a horse to 'chasing. One is to hunt him first, then run him in a point-to-point or two and finally race him under N.H. rules; the other is to start him over hurdles and then put him straight over fences.

The first method is more common in Ireland than in England and may partly account for the fact that Irish 'chasers are usually better jumpers than ours, for hunting gives a horse confidence and enjoyment, and makes him clever and adaptable. A horse that has been well hunted in a good country, provided of course that he is the right type, almost always makes a good jumper of steeplechase fences, and the process of running him over the comparatively small and easy fences of the average point-to-point, makes an excellent stepping-stone to racing under N.H. conditions. The horse that has to go straight from running over hurdles to jumping fences has a more difficult task, particularly in England where the fences are a good deal bigger than in Ireland, and the contrast sometimes proves rather overwhelming in the case of horses that are not bold by nature. But circumstances are such that, in England, most 'chasers—unless they have been imported from Ireland or from France, where they have also been running over small fences—have to make the best of it. This is no particular problem if a trainer is well equipped with a series of good schooling fences of various sizes, but nowadays all that is available to a great many is a couple of plain fences and an open-ditch, the rest of a horse's tuition taking place on the racecourse.

While the essence of a good hurdler is fast jumping, a 'chaser must, besides being fast from take-off to landing, be imbued with a measure of respect for the obstacles, or he will soon find himself on the ground. And it is the attainment in his pupil of a perfect blend of regard for the fences, and confidence in his ability to jump them, that is the jumping-trainer's problem.

If a horse has been well hunted before he comes into training, all that should be necessary to produce him ready to run in a steeplechase (apart from the consideration of fitness) is to jump him over hurdles and over a set of good schooling fences, not quite as big as those found on the racecourse, but quite as stiff.

But the hurdler who is being put to 'chasing will not have anything like the experience of the horse that has been hunted. He may be a good, bold, natural jumper, but he will know little or nothing about putting himself right if he is meeting a fence out of his stride, and he will be unaware of the unbalancing effect of hitting a fence when he is going fast. Much, of course, will depend upon his individual characteristics. If he is an intelligent horse, he will probably sense from their appearance that fences are something very different from hurdles and will take no liberties with them; if he is a timid horse, he will probably start to shorten his stride and slow up as he approaches the obstacle, in order to make sure of getting over, but having no regard to the time he takes in doing so; if he is particularly bold—or stupid—he may try to take the fence on, having no thought of the likelihood of it bringing him down.

The first consideration must be the size, consistency, number and type of fences necessary to teaching a 'chaser his task. This will depend upon the ground available, and the amount of money the trainer is prepared to spend on putting up and maintaining the fences.

Since the average trainer cannot afford to throw money about, he will probably be content with two sets of three fences, consisting of two plain and one open-ditch, one set about 3 feet 9 inches in height, the other about 4 feet 3 inches, which should answer most purposes if they are well and properly made, though it is a help if the latter set could be extended to half a dozen, three along one stretch and the other three along a stretch at right angles, so that it is possible either to pull up after jumping the first three, or to swing left or right-handed as the case may be and go on and jump the other three. They should be sited so that the sun is not in the horses' eyes during schooling hours.

Schooling fences should not be big—they need not be as big as regulation fences—but they should be stiff, and I think they are the better for being slightly varied, in that some can be faced with gorse, others plain, while some can have a board at the foot of them as at Kempton. There is no need to dig out the open-ditch as on a racecourse, but the floor of the 'ditch' can be strewn with chalk if it is desired to give it a different appearance to the rest of the ground and it is not necessary to school horses over a water-jump, since, provided a horse goes into his fences with any impetus, whether he jumps the water or not is due almost entirely to the way he is ridden into it.

As a preliminary to jumping a horse over fences, some trainers like to put him over a well-gorsed hurdle driven vertically into the ground, which makes it about three feet six inches, instead of about three feet two inches, which would be the case if it were sloped as for hurdlers. The Wroughton stable used always to adopt this practice, and I think it is a good way of warming a horse up to the task, since it provides an obstacle that is not too alarming, but at the same time must be jumped if the horse wishes to avoid pricking himself on the gorse, while the fact that it is upright and not sloped teaches him to gauge his take-off.

The stiffness of the fences should be obtained by the tightness with which the birch is packed, not by placing a miniature telegraph-pole a few inches from the top of the fence on the landing side, as was the practice of a certain trainer—he succeeded in getting one lad knocked out and two horses on the ground on the only occasion upon which I was rash enough to ride schooling at his establishment—as this is too ruthless. Horses learn far more from a bad mistake which does not bring them down, than from a fall, since, in the first case they are frightened without being hurt, and in the latter are liable to be hurt without quite realizing how it came about. The consistency of the fences should therefore be designed with this aim in view.

With regard to their build, the first fence of each set should be a fairly easy one, with a reasonable slope from base to summit, but the others are the better for being almost upright, as they will teach a horse how to judge his take-off much better than a fence that is well sloped, and besides inviting him to make a mistake or two from which he will learn not to get too near his fences before taking off, it will stand him in good stead when he goes to Aintree, where the fences are more upright than elsewhere.

With regard to a horse's introduction to fences, the same procedure can be followed as for hurdles: he can be given a lead the first time, and after that be allowed to go upsides another horse, first on one side and then on the other, and finally being sent on ahead after jumping the first fence. This drill should take place first over the small fences, and later over the bigger ones, according to the horse's progress, to be followed, if practicable and necessary, by a school round a course.

If a horse falls or loses his confidence, he may have to be put back over hurdles; if he persistently clouts his fences, he will have to be taught a lesson by lunging him over a fixed pole or some other means; if he proves a sticky jumper, he can be sharpened up in the manner already described, it being advisable to use small fences or hurdles for the purpose.

The number of times a horse is schooled per week depends upon the stage of his schooling, his individual characteristics and his progress, but I would say that a novice needs jumping twice or three times a week and an experienced horse only a couple of times at the beginning of each season but this is a matter over which opinions differ a great deal, and I have ridden for trainers who were in the habit of jumping their old horses as frequently as their novices, and for others who followed the method first suggested.

An important aspect of schooling is the manner in which a horse should be protected against mishaps such as over-reaches. Such accidents are almost invariably caused by the shoe of one of the hind feet striking a fore-leg, so that one can either bandage the fore-legs or jump the horse without shoes behind. Provided the going is reasonably good, a horse can come to very little harm if he has no shoes behind—some trainers run their horses thus—and my personal inclination is, wherever practicable, to work a horse with no shoes behind.

Even if a horse is bandaged, he is not immune; a hind shoe has been known to cut straight through a bandage, and in any case, it is impossible to protect the coronet, and no shoes behind has always seemed the rational answer to me.

The less a horse carries on his legs the better, since any additions will only serve to collect mud and water and add to the weight on his legs, which, of course, applies even more so to racing than schooling.

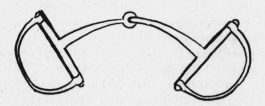

20
Crime and Punishment

HORSES, LIKE MEN, are by no means all perfect in behaviour. Many have developed bad ways through injudicious handling, after the manner of children who have been spoiled in their upbringing. Others seem imbued with a sense of indiscipline from birth, being quick to take any advantage of those in charge of them that opportunity may present.

In any undertaking that is to prove successful there cannot be two masters, and while a rider will benefit most from the natural talents with which a horse is gifted if he rides him with sympathy and understanding, the position in which it is the horse who dictates proceedings will probably sooner or later lead both his rider and himself into trouble. Every horse, therefore, should in reason be made to go where and when his rider wishes; if he moves only of his own volition, he is master of the situation and his rider will be little more than a passenger.

Whipping round, jibbing, running out and refusing to jump at home is the first step to doing so on a racecourse, and quite apart from the discomfort to the jockey and the fruitless expense incurred by the owner, they constitute a danger to other competitors. To allow a horse to get into bad ways at home is tantamount to producing a potential source of accident on the racecourse.

Some horses start refusing to jump for a specific reason, perhaps because they have developed a bad heart, or because their legs hurt them, or because they have lost their confidence as a result of a fall.

For the same reason, a horse may show a disinclination to go on to the gallop. One should therefore make quite sure, before setting out to punish a horse, that his misdemeanour is due to his character, and not to some physical disability. It should not be difficult to discriminate: much of a horse's character is revealed in his general appearance, behaviour and attitude, but rather than judge him unfairly, one should first make every endeavour to find out whether or not there is anything wrong with him.

While there is a good deal to be said for the Victorian precept, 'spare the rod, spoil the child', it is one which needs careful interpretation, since the misguided use of corporal punishment can be as damaging to the spirit and character of a horse as to that of a child. A horse should never be hit unless he is clear as to the reason for which he is being chastised, or for something which he cannot help—it serves no good purpose to hit him five minutes after he has whipped round and deposited one on the ground, or to chastise him for stumbling if his feet are too long—but if he has to be punished, the application of the rod should follow as quickly after the committing of the crime as is possible, half the effect being the suddenness with which it is delivered.

If a horse refuses to go away from the string, or sticks his toes in when he is being schooled, the advantage of the battle—and there will very probably be one—will lie with the horse if he is given time to realize what is coming to him. If he is to be hit at all, he should be hit hard—'don't keep a'tappin' of 'em, 'it 'em and 'old 'em,' was the principle upon which many old-timers worked, and there is a good deal to be said for it, since to hit a horse in such a way that he does not mind is only a waste of time, while to punish him by continual jobbing in the mouth and odd, half-hearted cuts, only serves to make him irritable and bad-tempered. He should either be dealt with properly or be left alone.

The principles of administering punishment are, first to administer it in the right way, and second to remain on the horse's back while doing so. A horse should be hit well round the quarters and he should not be allowed to run away during the procedure; if he is to be hit with the left hand, one should shorten the right rein so that his head is bent hard round to the right and he will then be bound to keep on the same spot, and though he runs round in a circle his quarters will keep meeting the rod.

Whatever the reason for his chastisement, the circumstance of being unable to escape the stick, through having his head pulled round and being therefore forced to keep presenting his quarters to it, will have almost as much effect in making him go where his rider wishes as the four or five cuts which should be all that is necessary to give him. If he still shows no inclination to obedience, the whip can be transferred to the other hand, his head be pulled round the opposite way, and the procedure be repeated, but the change-over must be quick, as he may succeed in plunging away if the rider starts fumbling about with his reins and whip.

It is no use attempting to beat a horse when riding with short stirrup-leathers, as one is almost certain to be put on the ground if he starts to buck or kick—it is easy enough to arrive there even when riding long—and one of the reasons for so many horses in racing stables being 'nappy' is that the average stable-lad rides too short to be able to cope with any form of rebellious action.

If a horse has already become confirmed in bad ways, and is therefore certain to try his tricks at the slightest opportunity, it is a help to send him out in blinkers, since their presence will be a help to the rider who has to chastise him, as the element of surprise will be greater.

In the case of a horse who has not previously shown any sign of nappiness and who for some reason or other suddenly decides to differ with his rider—perhaps because he may have been allowed to get a bit above himself—his disobedience should be nipped in the bud by a couple of quick, well-directed and heartily applied cuts, for if he is not corrected there and then, the seeds of a revolt which, in its later stages will be considerably more difficult to overcome, may begin to take root. When one sets out to put a horse in his place, it is no use riding him out with a sheet or rug on him, since the effect of hitting him will be nullified.

A horse that has been properly schooled from the beginning and has not been brought on too fast should give no trouble, and in nine cases out of ten, horses that refuse either do so as the result of bad horse-mastership, or for reasons mentioned earlier in the chapter, so that in the ordinary course of events these words will not be applicable, but should the occasion arise when a horse does give trouble in this way, it is as well to have some plan to cope with him.

As has been suggested earlier in the book, badly behaved horses can sometimes be reformed by putting them back in long reins and starting from scratch, but this does not always work, in which case time has been wasted on what might have been achieved in a morning. The secret of the matter is in diagnosing the cause of the trouble and prescribing the right treatment, which is a matter of insight and experience, and when in doubt, it is always best to seek the advice of wiser and more experienced men.

Unless one is confident of handling a punitive operation properly, it is better to hand the job over to someone capable of carrying it out the right way, or to admit defeat and continue as best one can, for to try and then fail is to render the last state worse than the first.

When a horse has had his lesson, he should be given a pat on the neck, his head should be loosed and he should be walked about quietly, so that he understands that it is all over and that no ill-will is borne.

As often as not, a horse that has been put in his place will become an entirely different character, a pleasanter servant and companion, taking an interest in his work instead of trying to think out ways of out-witting his rider, eating better and becoming generally more settled and sober in his ways.

Corporal punishment should always be looked upon as a last resort; it should be administered properly or not at all, and by the man on top and not one on the ground—the latter cannot be taken about like a kind of page-boy. To cause a horse unnecessary discomfort is the desire of no horse-lover, but there are times when it is necessary, and to hit a horse at home for doing wrong is in no way as cruel as hitting him on a racecourse when he is doing his best.

21

Owning

FROM A FINANCIAL point of view, it is difficult to imagine why any of us ever own a jumper. Compared to the flat, the stakes are paltry; betting is a hazardous affair—the safest jumper can always fall; the best racing takes place during the worst part of the year, and meetings are always being cancelled owing to the weather; the risk is greater—as a result, insurance premiums are higher—and there are no prospects of a horse bringing in huge stud-fees at the end of his career, or of a mare producing high-priced stock—at any rate, compared to what the progeny of a good flat race mare would command.

There is, however, something thrilling about being the owner of a 'chaser or hurdler. There is the delight of watching him jump; the races take longer to run; from an amateur's point of view, there is the added attraction of being able to ride him; horses are longer in training, so that one gets to know them better, and the whole affair is more fun and less commercial than owning a flat racer.

Unless the objective is to become an owner-trainer, the first move in ownership is to find a suitable trainer. Some owners are influenced by the district, in that they like to have their horses trained within reach of their home so that they can go to see them without difficulty, which is sometimes a mixed blessing as far as the trainer is concerned—'he practically lives with me' a trainer once remarked, with regard to one of his more troublesome patrons, the extent of whose interest was, as far as I remember, a half-share in a selling 'chaser.

In choosing a trainer one should take into consideration the lines upon which one is going to race. It may sound important to be able to claim to having a horse in a well-known stable, but from the owner's point of view there is much to be said for 'ruling in hell' rather than 'serving in heaven'. A trainer with a large string of good jumpers is not going to pay a great deal of attention to the one selling 'chaser or hurdler belonging to a humble and comparatively impecunious patron; it will make no difference to him whether the horse stays or goes, and the chances are that he will be used to do the 'donkey work' for the more pretentious members of the stable, so that, when it comes to racing, there may not be as much 'juice left in the orange' as there should be.

In the case of the small owner, therefore, it is usually better to seek out a trainer who has fewer horses, of a standard approximating to that of his own.

A trainer's all-round ability is best judged by the condition in which his horses consistently appear on a racecourse, by their jumping ability and by the number of fancied winners he turns out—the mere fact that he trains winners does not ensure that he is more than a good stableman, for it is not unknown, in such circumstances, for the horses that are backed to be beaten and those that are not to win, which can prove expensive. And to the owner who has to make his racing pay, a trainer's planning ability is almost as important as his horse-mastership. If an owner can afford to race irrespective of whether his horses pay their way or not, he will be best off with a trainer who is first a good stableman, as his horses will always look well, will keep running into a place, will win in their turn, and will earn enough in stake money to pay for some of their keep.

Some owners dislike the idea of trainers betting, but if the objective is to make money by betting, one can bet with considerably more confidence knowing that the trainer has supported the horse with his own money, than when he says, 'I think he will win,' but does not stand to lose.

Before finally deciding upon a trainer, one should come to a clear, mutual agreement as to the business side of the matter, otherwise a misunderstanding may arise in the future. In some stables, all the owners pool their resources as far as information about each other's horses is concerned. In others the affairs of each owner belong to a watertight compartment and are not divulged, and anyone who sends a horse to a stable run on the latter lines, under the impression that he is going to participate in the betting ventures of other patrons, is likely to receive a rude shock and will quite probably be asked to remove his horses, so that it is always advisable to know exactly the procedure of the stable in question, before sending a horse to be trained therein.

There is a certain type of owner who makes a point of having as small an interest in the greatest number of stables as possible, in the hope of getting stable information. Whether or not they succeed, depends upon the indulgence of the trainer, but those who own horses, or shares in horses, for this sole purpose deserve all they get if they find themselves 'put away', when one of the stables in which they are concerned has a winner.

It is advisable to have a clear understanding as to such affairs as presents to stable employees and to the jockey and trainer—I once came across an owner who was astonished when told that it was customary to give the trainer 10 per cent of the stake for winning a race—and it is as well to fall in with the usual custom of the stable with regard to such remunerations. A word of praise to the lad who looks after the horse (provided he does so properly), and to the jockey if he has ridden a good race even if he has not won, is a gesture that is appreciated, and there are occasions when a small present is not undeserved if a horse has consistently run well without being fortunate enough to win (in which case they would be automatically rewarded).

In the case of an owner who bets, it is only fair to gauge one's present to the jockey and trainer according to the amount won from the bookmaker, since the value of the race may be so small that the nominal 10 per cent is a meagre return for a good win. The present an owner gives his trainer and jockey naturally depends upon his resources, and they will prefer to be rewarded according to these, rather than to be given vague promises that are not fulfilled. Half the breaks that occur between owners and trainers are caused by no more than that they have never arrived, or attempted to arrive, at a clear business understanding from the beginning.

When an owner sends a horse to a trainer, he should tell him the general plan upon which he would like the latter to work—to prepare his horse or horses for a certain meeting, to put him by for a bet, to avoid entering at any particular racecourses, to run him regularly solely for the enjoyment of seeing him in action and to pick up anything in stake or place money that he can, or whatever his whims may be. But he should realize that the general plan must be subservient to the progress or otherwise of the horse, the responsibility in this matter being best left to the trainer. It is of no use expecting a trainer to have a horse ready for one's home meeting in December if he does not look like coming to hand until March, and it is always best to take the trainer's advice in everything concerning the physical aspect of a horse; if an owner has not sufficient confidence in a trainer to rely on his judgement in such matters, he should either train the horse himself or send him to a trainer he is prepared to trust—which he should have done in the first case. Training is a skilled profession. Sending a horse to a trainer is akin to entrusting a child to a doctor; one should either give him a free hand, or employ another, but never interfere with his work. Two people cannot train one horse, and if a trainer is to be given a fair chance he must not be chivvied by his owners as to whether he is giving such and such a horse too much or too little work, or otherwise be impeded in his task.

Owners that are always pestering their trainers about their horses seldom achieve much success. Successful trainers either will not tolerate them at all, or, knowing that there is certain to be a difference of opinion leading to the removal of the horses sooner or later, train the horses to their own advantage rather than in the owners' interests, and the latter will have to resort to trainers whose employment is dependent more upon their subservience to the will of their employers, than to their own ability.

Racing is a severe test of character. The pendulum of fortune swings violently between success and failure, and it is not everyone who can receive the former with modesty and grace, and the latter with cheerfulness and equanimity, there being a strong temptation to take good luck as a matter of course and to blame bad luck on the trainer or jockey. With regard to horses, more than any other commodity, a man's geese tend to be swans. He will bear with comparative calmness criticisms of his behaviour, his honesty, his clothes or his house—sometimes even of his wife—but suggest that one of his horses is not as good as he asserts, is a rogue, or a bad jumper, or has any defect of conformation, and one is on dangerous ground, the mildest of men being liable to fly into a rage, and the most tolerant to take affront.

'Keep yourself in the best company and your horses in the worst,' the famous Admiral Rous advised, and there is much to be said for it, since to over-rate horses can prove an expensive miscalculation, but is an easy frame of mind into which one can slip—I have often found my imagination carrying me away to such an extent that I have started to enter horses in valuable races at Kempton and Cheltenham, when the most unpretentious events at Plumpton or Warwick represented the true measure of their ability.

When an owner suffers a run of bad luck, he is very inclined to take the attitude that a change of trainer or jockey will put him back in a winning vein, but in nine cases out of ten it is not a change of trainer or rider that is called for, but a change of horses. Good horses make good trainers, good jockeys and contented owners, but bad horses do nobody any good, and the sooner the fact is faced that a horse is not worth keeping, the better it is for everyone concerned with him.

When one is fortunate enough to possess a good horse, there always arises the burning question of whether to sell him or keep him. For a rich man—unless he is a Midas by nature—there is no problem, for he can afford to keep him, but for a poor man it is different, and he will find in the long run that it is less costly to 'sell and regret' than to 'keep and regret'. In the case of someone who rides his own horses, the more different ones that pass through his hands, the greater the experience acquired and the more improved his riding, so that he will be as well to sell and buy again.

If a horse has proved a good servant over a period of years, he is owed a happy retirement or a good home. Many racehorses dislike being turned out in a field, being happier doing light work as hacks or in the capacity of leading young 'chasers in their early schooling lessons—like an old soldier, they miss the discipline and companionship of communal life—others are quite happy out at grass, but they should be looked over from time to time, so see if their feet require trimming, or if they need attention in any other way, and they should be brought in if the flies worry them in summer, or if they feel the cold in winter. If one cannot find a happy retirement of some kind for an old horse, it is far kinder to have him put down than to sell him regardless of his future fate, which may be anything between a livery stable or a Continental abattoir.

Having fixed upon a trainer, a newcomer's next move is to acquire a horse or some horses, according to his resources and inclinations. In this matter, it is always advisable to take the trainer's advice. Trainers never seem so well disposed towards horses which owners have bought on their own—there is sometimes a good reason for this, since, although there is a great deal of luck attached to the buying of horses, a novice in the game is open to many pitfalls and is more than likely to return with some dreadful animal quite incapable of winning a race of any sort, or even of standing training, which will therefore be no more asset to his trainer than to his owner who, however, having been responsible for buying it will be less willing to get rid of it than the trainer.

First, he will have to decide upon the type of horse he is going to buy, the selection of the individual he can leave to his trainer. If he wishes a quick return for his money, his best investment will be a horse that has already been schooled and has shown some form on a racecourse, or a horse off the flat likely to win a novices hurdle race.

To buy an unbroken prospective 'chaser means a long wait, and unless intending to have several horses in training, it is probably more satisfactory to buy the ready-made article. Many owners have bought horses out of France, where, before the war, they could be bought at a reasonable price; the same can be said of Ireland, but prices in both countries have soared during the last few years. When looking for a prospective 'chaser, Ireland is by far the best source to tap; there breeders specialize in the production of 'chasers and the type of horse produced is suitable for the job. In France, the average horse is too light of frame to stand up to English conditions, and though many good hurdlers come out of France, a top-class 'chaser for English conditions is more easily found in Ireland. Another reason for Irish horses being preferable to French horses as 'chasers is that they last longer, having been allowed to develop gradually, most French jumpers being raced at a much earlier age and being subjected to more severe use of the whip every time they run, that unless they are exceptionally tough, or have not had much racing, they often turn sour, so that, though their past form may be excellent they may be worthless with regard to the future.

It is not easy to buy a good hurdler out of an English flat-racing stable: either they are of unsuitable conformation and temperament, are unsound, or are pure sprinters or plodders—ideal types are too expensive or not for sale, and the poor man who cannot afford to go to France or Ireland can only look about him and hope for a chance bargain coming his way. On the whole, a horse in training from a jumping stable is probably the best type to choose, one, perhaps, which the owner wishes to sell in order to make room for younger horses. The trainer can be trusted to find out whether or not it is sound and honest, and its form will be available in any book of statistics.

Another type of poor man's horse that I have sometimes found to pay its way is an oldish horse off the flat that has shown some form at not too remote a date. He may be one that has become a bit tired of flat-racing but which, if carefully schooled, will take an interest in jumping, and, if one does not fly too high, can be placed to win selling hurdle races or small handicaps, without being over-exerted. Such horses should always be kept above themselves and should never be hit during a race, so that they have no reason to dislike their work. Two such horses that I bought cheaply before the war and who paid their way were Lucky Patch and Tramaway, who only cost about £200 each at the Newmarket Sales.

Every one has his own method of buying horses, but I think the first point to look at is a horse's head. If he has a mean, cunning head, he is unlikely to have the courage to make a jumper, no matter how good the rest of his conformation may be, while an honest, kind-looking head usually indicates a willingness to do his best, however moderate his ability. After that, it is as well to start at his feet and work upwards. If he is weak behind the saddle he will not have the power to jump; if short or straight in front, he is unlikely to be a good ride; if he is slackly put together he will probably be too slow and clumsy in his movements to jump well in a race; if he is too narrow he will be unlikely to survive jumping mistakes.

It is difficult to make any clear rules in such matters, and when the price must be modest, it is certain that at least one fault will have to be overlooked, and I think that perhaps the horse's general outlook and personality is more important than too critical an insistence on perfection of conformation—slightly bent hind-legs, or fore-legs that are a trifle straight, provided they are strong and sound, in a horse that appeals as a gay, active and resolute individual, is, I think, preferable to a more truly made individual who seems of a dull, melancholy-looking, or mean disposition.

Half the pleasure of owning a horse is in being able to admire and enjoy his appearance and conformation—an aspect which may be lost on some owners—and a nice horse, to anyone capable of appreciating him, has an aesthetic value which a less attractive but more lucrative one can never possess, though it is the exception rather than the rule for a badly made horse to be a good one, and a sound principle to place conformation before breeding.

A further aspect of buying a jumper is that of acquiring an unbroken or untried horse, with the idea of eventually selling it at a profit. In pre-war days, this type of horse could be found fairly cheaply in Ireland, but this is no longer the case, high prices being asked for all horses of any promise, regardless of whether they are tried or not. Undoubtedly there are a far greater number of prospective jumpers to be found in Ireland than anywhere else, but unless the stranger is particularly fortunate in having 'his card marked', he will not find it easy to buy anything cheaply.

Possibly the best way of achieving this particular objective is to look round the English bloodstock sales at Newmarket and elsewhere for a well-made, backward or unbroken two-year-old—I am always vaguely suspicious of horses that have been broken but are stated to be untried (unless one is well acquainted with the vendor), as it is not impossible that they have been found wrong of their wind, or have shown every sign of being useless as a racehorse.

Unbroken or backward two-year-olds are not everyone's meat, and can therefore sometimes be bought rather more cheaply than horses of other categories; they do not appeal to flat race trainers, who prefer yearlings, or to jumping trainers, who usually want a horse they can get on with straight away, and are therefore not often in great demand. If one chooses an individual that is strong and big enough to jump, but at the same time will not take too long to come to hand, there is a fair chance of getting a three-year-old hurdle race out of him, perhaps even a race on the flat, without having to wait more than six months or so, depending, of course, on his condition when bought and upon the date of his purchase. To buy a big, awkward, backward two-year-old may be a good enough policy in the case of anyone who is prepared to wait until he is four or five, but in the ordinary course of events it represents too long a gap between purchase and possible return.

For one who intends to ride his own horses it is, I think, important to choose a type suitable to one's own physical characteristics. For instance, a small, light man will be better suited to a neat, active stamp of horse, than to a big raking, 17-hand animal that needs a great deal of holding together, while a big, tall man will be out of place on a small, short-coupled horse but will ride a big one better than his opposite type. A top-class rider will be able to adapt himself to any build of horse, but in spite of this a horse is more likely to produce the best results with a rider suited to him by nature, than with one who is either so big that he is all over him, or so small that he cannot hold him together. This, I think may, have something to do with the fact that the best steeplechase-riders are usually big men and the best hurdle race riders men of a smaller mould, each type corresponding with the stamp of horse most frequently found in the two branches of N.H. racing.

When anyone becomes an owner he will find a surprising number of people desirous of making or renewing acquaintance with him, particularly on a day when he has a horse running which might have a winning chance. The telephone will ring from the most unexpected quarters bringing unwonted enquiries as to his well-being, the purport of which becomes evident in some such afterthought as, 'by the way, what about yours in the 3.30 today?' And people that are almost complete strangers will address him on the racecourse in terms of unlooked-for friendliness with, however, a carefully veiled probe as to his horse's chances hidden among the pleasantries.

Generally speaking there are two main sources of such approaches: laymen who take a casual interest in racing, who, but for some obscure reason, seem to think that they have a right to know all about their friends' horses, regardless of the fact that they contribute nothing towards their keep, and professionals who make their living out of betting and whose object it is to find out all they can about the runners in any race in which they propose to speculate.

If it is immaterial to an owner whether or not he makes his racing pay, this aspect presents no more than a minor irritation, but if he has to try and show a profit he cannot afford to broadcast the strength of his hand, or he will not get the best of the market, which means that he will not achieve his aim, for it is only by betting at a price that is proportionate to—or better than—the chance of his horse that it is possible for an owner to win in the long run. The stakes in N.H. racing are not sufficient to enable him to rely on a horse earning enough to keep himself, unless he is a particularly good one.

One often hears the remark, 'Oh, but my pound will make no difference,' and though the pound itself will not affect the price, the money invested by the numerous other people to whom the invest or imparts the information certainly will. And to expect that he will keep silent on the matter is to hold an Utopian view of human nature, for among casual racegoers there is always an instinctive desire to appear knowledgeable, and the temptation to show that they are the possessor of stable information often over-rides the first rules of 'security'.

The professional will probably keep the information to himself, but this speculation is likely to be of such a size as to give the bookmaker a clear intimation as to the situation, and it will not be long before the price shrinks noticeably in the market.

There are various ways of coping with such enquirers. One owner-trainer used to play on a slight deafness by replying to any pertinent question with regard to his horses' chances, 'Thanks, old boy, but I've just had one,' and it depends upon the individual what method he chooses.

The most effective is to mow the questioner down ruthlessly with some such remark as 'My horses are entirely my own business, and I don't go to the expense of keeping them in training for your benefit,' but this method cannot always be employed, for diplomatic reasons, and a more subtle procedure usually has to be adopted.

Some owners deal with the matter by pronouncing every runner they have as being sure to win, which has the desired effect in the end, as the recipients of the information will soon get tired of backing the considerable proportion that have no chance, and they will never know whether they are in possession of an 'operation order' or a 'cover-plan'. The disadvantage of this method is that it tends to create the impression that the employer of it is a man of considerable stupidity and unreliable judgment, an impression which, in respect of prospective fathers-in-law, wealthy uncles without heirs, and similar persons of importance, it is not always advisable to create.

On the whole the best form of counter-attack is a direct but delphic pronouncement, 'I have backed him for a little each way' was the formula attributed to one famous old-time trainer—or an observation delivered with such complicated verbosity that the questioner is left in a more confused state than before. 'I'd fancy him if he'd been jumping better at home and if the going was a shade firmer, but he is always a better horse on a left-handed track, so the course should suit him, though I wish I could have got Stopham to ride him, as he always goes

best for him. But I don't want to put you off and I think you should
have a bit each way on him in case he casts up, but don't blame me if
he doesn't win. Forgive me if I leave you now, I want to go and see
him saddled,' spoken with a cheerful and willing frankness, is the kind
of reply that forms a fairly effective cloak to one's activities, without
creating umbrage or resorting to rudeness, and which has the advantage of providing for any aftermath. 'I told you to have a bit on him' is
a truthful statement should one be reproached as a result of the horse
winning, while, 'I warned you not to have too much of him' suffices
equally well in the case of defeat.

But whatever the attitude to ownership, the first step is to acquire a
horse that can win a race. Good horses cost no more to keep than bad
ones, and if a horse turns out useless it is better to cut one's losses and
get rid of him than to keep on paying the expenses incurred, in the
hope that he will one day get them back.

22
Breeding of Jumpers

BECAUSE A HORSE is a successful sire of flat racers it does not follow that he will also be a good sire of jumpers. It is true of a flat race sire that none of the best offspring are usually put to jumping, but one or two invariably find themselves running under N.H. rules, and it soon becomes evident if there is any inherent ability to jump or not. In some cases horses sire winners both on the flat and over fences, but as a rule top-class sires of flat racers and jumpers divide into two distinct categories.

This is understandable, since the respective tasks of the jumper and flat racer are entirely different. The former races throughout the winter, often in deep going, has to carry big weights and to possess the strength and courage to jump; the latter races mostly in the spring and summer, seldom has more than 9 st. 7 lb. on his back, and in an ordinary season is usually running on good or firm going. Almost invariably, a good 'chaser has a line of purely jumping blood close up in his pedigree.

Two outstanding sires of 'chasers have been My Prince and Cottage; the former sired the 'National winners Gregalach, Royal Mail, Reynoldstown (who won it twice), and those brilliant and gallant 'National failures Easter Hero and Prince Regent, both of which won the Cheltenham Gold Cup, and were the best 'chasers of their era, while the latter got Workman, Lovely Cottage and Sheila's Cottage, all 'National winners, as well as Cottage Rake, one of the best 'chasers ever seen, who has won two Cheltenham Gold Cups to date.

The presence of the names of Cottage or My Prince in a pedigree is, therefore, a fairly reliable sign that a horse will make a jumper—far more reliable than, say, the presence of Gainsborough and Fairway, who were outstanding sires of flat racers, but never got a jumper of any note I can think of.

One of the difficulties of breeding jumpers is that, owing to the fact that a 'chaser seldom reaches his best before he is six, it often takes a long time to discover whether or not the offspring of a sire are going to be good jumpers, and in some cases a sire is long past his prime, or is even dead, by the time he has made his name. One such case was that of Mr. Toots, sire of Cool Customer (at his best only a few pounds behind Cottage Rake), Klaxton, Mr. Fitz and Secret Service, who had died by the time the merit of his stock had been discovered.

The foundation of English jumping blood is made up of the two sires Melbourne and Hermit. Melbourne, who was foaled in 1834 got the 'National winner, Emigrant, and is the ancestor of Marco, who sired a 'National winner in Sprig, and also got Marcovil, sire of My Prince and Hurry On, the latter getting another great sire of jumpers in Werwolf, sire of such as Airgead Sios, Bogskar, winner of the 'National and that fine hurdler, Free Fare. Melbourne is also the ancestor of Man o' War, sire of the 'National winner, Battleship, who became one of the leading sires of jumpers in the U.S. Any representatives of the Melbourne line can be relied upon as a good influence in a jumper, one example being Coronach (by Hurry On), maternal grandsire of National Spirit, the best hurdler of his day.

Hermit, winner of the Derby in 1867, besides becoming so strong an influence in the jumping world, was a great sire on the flat. Like Melbourne, he now comes a long way back in modern pedigrees and his direct line has now died out; while we owe him a great debt his name has no practical significance at the present time.

Another great flat race sire, who also exerted an influence on the breeding of jumpers was St. Simon, sire of St. Damien, who got Lutteur III, the only French horse ever to win a 'National. The 'National winners Master Robert, Tipperary Tim and Poethlyn also trace to St. Simon, as does Mieuxcé and a number of successful jumpers.

Cottage, who has been mentioned with My Prince as being one of the two best jumping sires of modern times, was by Tracery, a very high-class stayer on the flat, his dam being by Marco. The Tracery line has come to the fore in the jumping world again, through the Lincoln winner, Flamenco by Flamingo, by Flamboyant, by Tracery. Flamenco is the sire of such as Poor Flame, a really good 'chaser who went wrong. The Heron, and Prince of Denmark.

• Another successful sire of a few years back was Jackdaw, sire of the 'National winners Grackle and Kellsboro' Jack, and of that brilliant mare, West Indies, who began life as a flat racer, winning the Irish One Thousand Guineas, and then became one of the most spectacular 'chasers of her day, being unfortunately killed while schooling. Jackdaw blood often appears in a jumping pedigree nowadays, and is an asset in the breeding of any prospective jumper. Jackdaw was also the sire of the famous Brown Jack who, before he made a name for himself on the flat, was a top-class hurdler and a winner of the Champion Hurdle.

A jumper need not necessarily be jumping-bred on both sides of his pedigree; Victor Norman, who became a good 'chaser after he had done with hurdling, was by the flat-race sire, King Sol, but his dam, Tickets, was by Trespasser, perhaps the best hurdler of all time, though he was not a very good sire, even of jumpers. And the fact that a horse is entirely flat race bred on one side of his pedigree or the other is no reason for dismissing him as a prospective jumper, provided he has the appropriate blood on the other, but a purely flat race bred horse is usually one to avoid; to start with, if he is any good he will cost too much, and even if he has the right build and strength there is no guarantee that he will have the right temperament. An outstanding exception is the triple 'National winner Red Rum, by Quorum out of Mared, by Magic Red; he also won on the flat as a two year old.

It has been remarked earlier in the book that a measure of speed is an essential quality in any good jumper, and it is therefore as well to avoid, either in buying or in devising a mating, the combination of too much stamina without some promise of speed.

Prince Regent was out of an own-sister to that great sprinter, Diomedes, and Victor Norman's sire, King Sol, was a sprinter, too, and although it is always dangerous to attempt to make any rules in such matters I think one should always look for a line of speed, represented through either a 'class' horse (a horse of classic ability on the flat), or through one of intrinsic speed, such as Flamenco, winner of the St. James's Palace Stakes at Ascot, as well as the Lincoln, who did not get beyond a mile. On the whole it is preferable to introduce the speed through the dam, as in the case of Prince Regent, but there are a number of examples of the reverse procedure being successful, one that comes to mind—besides that of Victor Norman—being General Factotum, a very useful horse both over hurdles and fences who was by Figaro, winner of the Stewards' Cup.

In the breeding of jumpers, conformation, size and substance is a more important aspect than pedigree. A badly-made weed will sometimes win a good race on the flat, but it will never carry 12 stone over fences—or even hurdles—and it is a waste of time and money to try to produce good jumpers from anything except mares and sires of reasonably good bone and build.

Purity of blood does not seem to be essential, either, in a jumper. Easter Hero was not in the Stud Book—he traced to an Arab mare who performed in a circus—but in such cases there is usually a good tap-root in the tail female line, in the shape of a mare who was either a good producer or performer. Easter Hero's Arabian tap-root bred a large number of winners.

The eugenics of jumpers have never been so closely studied as those of flat racers, and it is therefore not easy to pass judgment on such matters as the relative merits of inbreeding and outcrossing in the production of jumpers, but bearing in mind the kind of work a jumper has to carry out, I would think that an outbred horse would be more likely to prove suitable than one that is closely inbred, and except for the French hurdler, Le Paillon, who finished second to National Spirit in the Champion Hurdle and was closely inbred to Phalaris, I cannot think of a good inbred jumper in recent years. In recent times Vulgan, Fortina and Menelek have proved highly successful sires of jumpers.

Throughout every aspect of jumping the practical is more important than the theoretical, and in breeding this precept should be no less carefully observed. Lines of blood are a useful guide, but they are not everything, and they should not be given precedence over soundness, conformation, performance, and good feeding and stud management, which are the basis of success.

23

Courses

CHELTENHAM IS A course for horses that can stay, jump and have
courage. The executive put up valuable prizes, it is extremely well
run and consequently produces the best level of competition of any
racecourse in the country.

The other jumping courses in England fall into three categories: the
Park meetings around London, those in other parts of the country
where flat-racing also takes place, and those which confine themselves
only to jumping, being less important and less well-equipped editions
of Cheltenham.

Of the London courses the best is Sandown—I do not offer biased
praise, for there is no course over which I have had more falls—particularly from the spectator's point of view. Like Cheltenham, the
course is built on a slope and it is possible to see the racing as well from
any part of the lawn as from the best place on the stands, but in this
respect it goes one better since the horses never go as far away as at
Cheltenham, every detail of running being easily followed—too easily
I have sometimes found after parting company with my horse under
rather ignominious circumstances, an occurrence which might be dis-
guised successfully on some courses, but never at Sandown.

Like Cheltenham, it is a severe course with an uphill finish, but is
right-handed instead of left-handed. In pre-war days its particular
feature was three fences which were met in quick succession at the
beginning of the back straight, and which were a source of innumerable falls. The first has now been removed, with the result that a horse
is given a better chance to recover from a mistake. Sandown is
another course over which front runners do not often win, this
tendency being most marked in heavy going, and though the fences
do not seem as stiff as they used to be—I draw my comparison from
1939 and 1949—they are no obstacles for a bad jumper.

When riding over fences one can usually take a chance and come up
on the inside, as the fences are 'open', having no rails running beside
them, but over hurdles it is seldom wise to try to get through on the

rails in the straight, as an opening will probably never appear, and it is best to make one's run through the middle of the field or on the outside. There is a certain dignity about Sandown that not every other course possesses: a wood rises gracefully at one corner, giving an almost French atmosphere as the horses walk past it on their way through the members' enclosure to the course, and the band, provided on important occasions such as the Grand Military meeting, adds a gaiety to the natural pleasantness of the surroundings. There is something rather heartening about setting out, even on the worst of jumpers, to the cheerful lilt of 'Take a Pair of Sparkling Eyes', or the rousing notes of 'The Soldiers' Chorus', which one sometimes experiences when going to the post early, before the appearance of the main body of runners causes the bandmaster to silence his musicians in the middle of a bar.

Of the other London courses Kempton is good. Like Sandown it is right-handed, but is much less severe, having no hills, and particularly suited to fast, active horses as opposed to out-and-out stayers. It always seems to me that the fences at Kempton are the best made of any Park course.

Lingfield is left-handed, and although there is a hill to climb on the far side, it is an easy course, for the finish is on the level and there is a long run downhill to the straight. Over fences one can usually rely upon finding an opening on the inside approaching the first fence in the straight, as there is a long gap where one crosses the flat and hurdle racecourse between leaving the last bend and coming into the fence in question. Horses are very inclined to swing wide at the bend, leaving an opening of which considerable advantage can often be taken. The going tends to become very deep after rain, and correspondingly firm when there has been a lack of it. When it is exceptionally deep it is sometimes worth sacrificing going the shortest way by pulling out where the ground is least cut up, the less tiring conditions of galloping more than outweighing the disadvantage of going the longer way—I remember 'Frenchie' Nicholson employing these tactics to good purpose on one occasion.

The fences have always been comparatively soft and, both over fences and hurdles, it is a pleasant course round which to ride.

Gatwick is no longer in use, being now an airport. It was a hard but good track, with a long run-in and big, stiff fences—perhaps a legacy of the days when the substitute National took place there—and, as at Lingfield, the going was liable to reach extremes.

Windsor is hardly a London meeting, but it is usually classed as such. No one could pretend that it is a good racecourse—half the racing goes on virtually out of sight—but it is a very enjoyable meeting and is well run. With regard to jumping it is open to every hazard a racecourse executive can be expected to face: it stands the usual risk of frost, and, in addition, the proximity of the river makes it particularly susceptible to fog and floods—the same can be said of Worcester—and it has not been unknown to arrive and find racing impossible, when under conditions a mile or two away it would have been feasible.

The track is laid out in the shape of a figure eight, the first bend of the two-mile course being left-handed, the last the reverse. This leaves a good deal of scope for manœuvre, since it is possible on the one hand to save a great deal of ground, and on the other to go miles out of one's way. With a fast horse one can start on the inside and then gradually work one's way across so as to arrive on the rails coming round the last bend, but on one lacking in acceleration there is a good chance of being cut off while attempting the second part of the manœuvre, so that one's tactics must be adjusted to the horse in question, a 'via media' policy often proving best in the case of a slow horse.

Except for one season when they were unusually strong, the Windsor fences have never been very formidable, but in spite of this there have always been a fair number of falls, particularly in heavy going. This, I think, is due to horses tiring and becoming unbalanced when they find themselves having to gallop on the opposite leg with the change of direction, and I have noticed that in seasons when the going has not been deep, falls have been less numerous.

As in pre-war days one of the best courses at which both jumping and flat racing are held is Newbury.

It is a wide, flat course, very well suited for the spectator and perfect for the rider. It has long straight, good bends, and if a horse is beaten there, in nine cases out of ten it is because he is not good enough. It is left-handed, and the going is good.

Newbury is a course on which one does not need to be in a hurry, particularly with a horse that has a turn of speed; there is plenty of time to work one's way into a challenging position, that is to say if the horse in question is good enough, and the long run-in gives one ample opportunity of getting a horse balanced before asking him for his final effort.

Of the other courses where both flat-racing and steeplechasing are held, the best are, Doncaster, Ascot, Newcastle and Nottingham.

It seems strange that the scene of a classic race should be that of steeplechasing also, but such is the case with Doncaster, where a steeplechase course was laid out after the last war. The bend by the stands is a little sharp, but the venture has been a great success and the executive deserve every credit for the valuable prizes they have put up for races such as the Great Yorkshire 'Chase.

Newcastle is a fine, galloping course which stages good racing.

Old timers would be staggered at the idea of jumping at Ascot where, however, top-class jumping is now staged. It is a good, fairly stiff course, but for the spectator the action is rather remote.

Nottingham is quite a good course: there is plenty of room, a long run-in and the fences are well spaced, and though I would not say it is as good as was Birmingham it is very adequate.

Wolverhampton, Leicester, Newcastle, Ayr and Catterick are other courses combining jumping and flat-racing with success.

Leicester is right-handed and undulating, the others left-handed and flat. To these can be added Carlisle, Catterick, Chepstow, Folkestone, Haydock Park, the last named a first-rate track, where some of the fences have drops on the landing side.

Of the remaining courses where only steeplechasing and hurdle racing are held, the best, I would say, are Wetherby, Worcester and then Wincanton. Wetherby is as good a course as one could wish for. Left-handed, it has good bends, a square approach to each fence, a good run-in, and well-built and fair fences.

There is a slight hill running downwards round the bend past the stands, but the rest of the course is flat, and the stands give a very good view of the racing. Worcester is flat and left handed.

Wincanton is a spacious, right-handed track, more or less flat, with a good run-in and easily-rounded turns. Its executive are one of the most progressive in the country and have raised the status of the course from one of comparatively obscurity to being one of the best of the minor tracks to be found.

Jockeys are very superstitious about courses and everyone has their lucky and unlucky tracks. Why, I do not know, but it is a fact that cannot be escaped. For this reason I have always disliked riding at Fontwell as much as I have enjoyed visiting it as a spectator, the reverse holding for Plumpton. There is little to choose between these two courses from the rider's point of view; Fontwell is a sharp, figure-eight course for steeplechases, and a straightforward left-handed course as regards hurdles, presenting no particular hazard to the rider—except the very occasional, but extremely alarming, occurrence of a loose horse in a steeplechase turning round and meeting the field head-on—and providing a first-rate view for the spectator.

Plumpton is a sharp left-handed course, with a hill down which horses approach the second fence and hurdle in a manner that would do credit to the Gaderene swine.

The many other little country jumping meetings scattered all over the country, ranging from Taunton to Kelso, are as numerous as they are entertaining. Newton Abbot sees the opening of the season and belongs to a group consisting also of Devon, Exeter and Taunton. Chepstow caters for Wales, Perth supports Ayr and Kelso in Scotland; Hereford and Ludlow comprise a group on their own, as do Stratford, Southwell, Market Rasen and Towcester; Bangor-on-Dee is a humble neighbour of Aintree; Hexham represents Northumberland, and Fakenham caters for Norfolk.

Centralized racing has been one of the chief points advocated by many who wish to bring about reforms in our courses. That reforms are needed is undisputed; the average accommodation on most racecourses is old-fashioned and inadequate, and must remain so until the arrival of better times, but that we should do away with our small jumping meetings is a mistake. They are the nurseries of horses and jockeys, and of trainers and owners also, and as such are an essential branch of N.H. racing. Moreover, they bring a great deal of enjoyment to a great many people, to some of whom the local meeting is the event of the year, and they are an integral part of our English country life.

Plans of Courses

THE PLANS AND descriptions of racecourses are reproduced from
RACEFORM UP-TO-DATE (Chaseform) by kind permission of
the joint proprietors and publishers, Sporting Chronicle Publications
Ltd and Raceform Ltd.

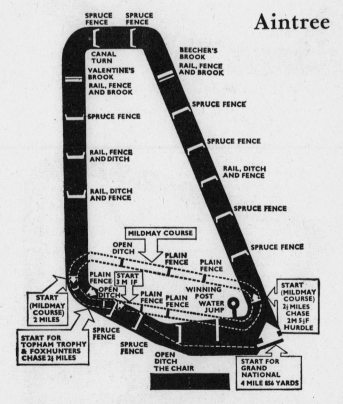

Two L.H. courses. A Triangular circuit of nearly 2¼ miles with a flat run-in 494
yards for the Grand National (30 unique fences) and the Mildmay Course,
approx. 1¼ m round with conventional fences.

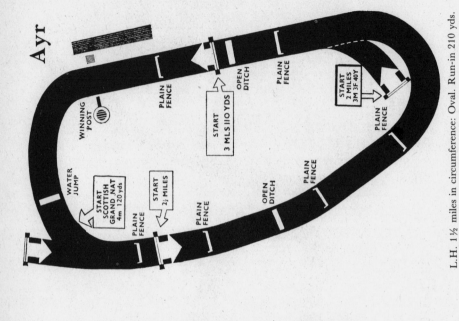

Ayr

WINNING POST

PLAIN FENCE

OPEN DITCH

PLAIN FENCE

START
3 MLS 110 YDS

START
2 MILES
3M 3F-40Y

PLAIN FENCE

PLAIN FENCE

WATER JUMP

START
SCOTTISH
GRAND NAT
4m 120 yds

START
2¼ MILES

PLAIN FENCE

PLAIN FENCE

OPEN DITCH

PLAIN FENCE

L.H. 1½ miles in circumference: Oval. Run-in 210 yds.

Ascot

START
2½ M

PLAIN FENCE

PLAIN FENCE

OPEN DITCH

PLAIN FENCE

START
3M 5F

WATER JUMP

OPEN DITCH

START
3M HURDLE

START
2 MILES

PLAIN FENCE

PLAIN FENCE

WINNING POST

PLAIN FENCE

START
3 MILE CHASE
3¼ MILE HURDLE

PLAIN FENCE

R.H. Circular course of 1¾ miles in circumference with an uphill finish. The course is laid out on the inside of the flat race track and was opened for N.H. racing in the 1965–66 Season.

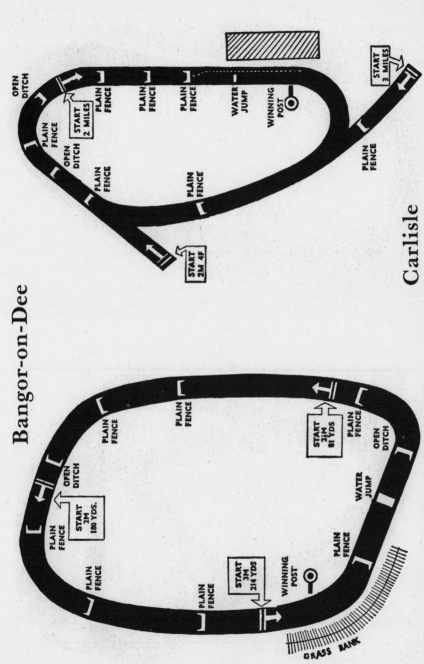

Bangor-on-Dee

Carlisle

R.H. 1 mile 5 furlongs circuit. Undulating. Run-in 250 yds.

L.H. 1¼ circuits for 2 miles. Perfectly flat and all grass. Run-in 325 yards. Course completely enclosed and rebuilt 1972; watering system installed 1973.

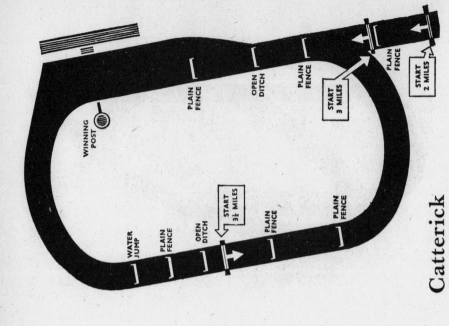

Catterick

L.H. Oval course, 1 mile 127 yds., almost flat. Run-in approx. 240 yds.

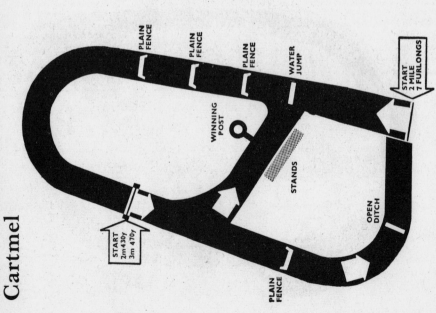

Cartmel

L.H. Oval course, about 1 mile, 1 furlong. Flat. Run-in about 4 furlongs.

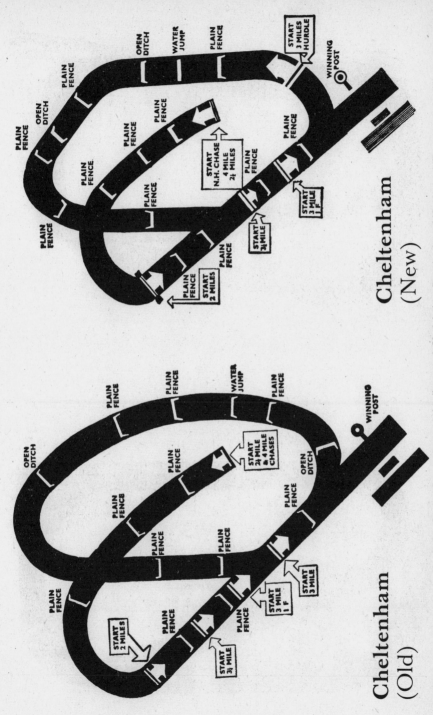

Cheltenham (New)

Cheltenham (Old)

L.H. Oval courses, approx. 1½ miles round. Undulating. Run-in about 237 yds., uphill. The National Hunt Course, 4 miles, for the National Hunt Steeplechase, 24 fences, is run over the old course, after starting from the 4 mile-chute start in the centre of the course.

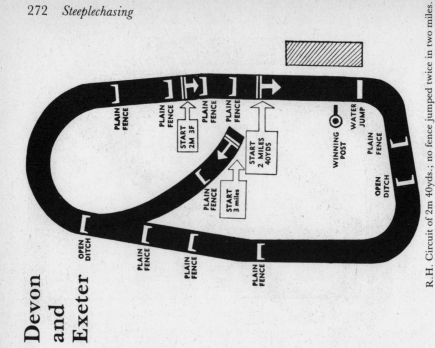

Devon and Exeter

PLAIN FENCE

PLAIN FENCE

START 2M 3F

PLAIN FENCE

PLAIN FENCE

START 2 MILES 40YDS

START 3 miles

PLAIN FENCE

WINNING POST

WATER JUMP

PLAIN FENCE

OPEN DITCH

OPEN DITCH

PLAIN FENCE

PLAIN FENCE

PLAIN FENCE

R.H. Circuit of 2m 40yds.; no fence jumped twice in two miles. Rather undulating. Run-in about 250 yards, last ½ mile straight.

Chepstow

START FOR WELSH NATIONAL 3 MILES 6 F.

WINNING POST

PLAIN FENCE

START 2 MILES

PLAIN FENCE

PLAIN FENCE

OPEN DITCH

PLAIN FENCE

START 2½ MILES

START 3m 3f

PLAIN FENCE

OPEN DITCH

PLAIN FENCE

WATER JUMP

START 3 MILES

PLAIN FENCE

PLAIN FENCE

L.H. Oval course. 2 mile circuit. Undulating but no steep gradients. Run-in 240 yds.

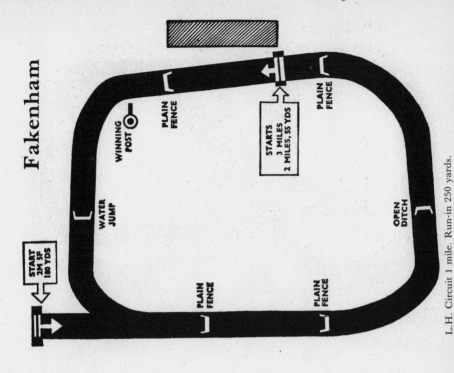

Fakenham

START 2M 5F 180 YDS

WATER JUMP

WINNING POST

PLAIN FENCE

STARTS 3 MILES 2 MILES, 55 YDS

PLAIN FENCE

PLAIN FENCE

PLAIN FENCE

OPEN DITCH

PLAIN FENCE

L.H. Circuit 1 mile. Run-in 250 yards.

Doncaster

PLAIN FENCE

PLAIN FENCE

PLAIN FENCE

PLAIN FENCE

OPEN DITCH

PLAIN FENCE

OPEN DITCH

WATER JUMP

START 3 miles 122yds

START ABOUT 3½M

START 2 miles 150yds

START ABOUT 2½M.

WINNING POST

PLAIN FENCE

PLAIN FENCE

PLAIN FENCE

PLAIN FENCE

PLAIN FENCE

PLAIN FENCE

L.H. About 2 miles in circumference, conical in shape, no steep gradients. Run-in 247 yds.

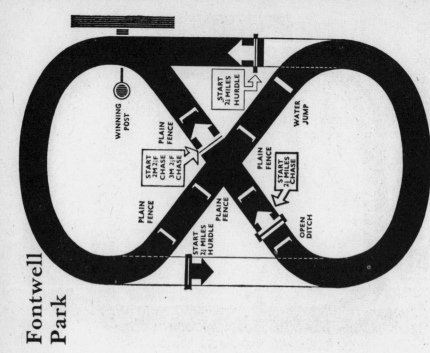

Fontwell Park

L.H. Course for hurdle racing approx. 1 mile round. Undulating, 9 hurdles per 2¼m. Run-in about 230 yards, Steeplechase course. Figure of eight. Run-in has slight left hand bend.

WINNING POST

START 2M 2½F CHASE / 3M 2½F CHASE

START 2½ MILES HURDLE

START 2¼ MILES CHASE

START 2½ MILES HURDLE

PLAIN FENCE

PLAIN FENCE

PLAIN FENCE

PLAIN FENCE

WATER JUMP

OPEN DITCH

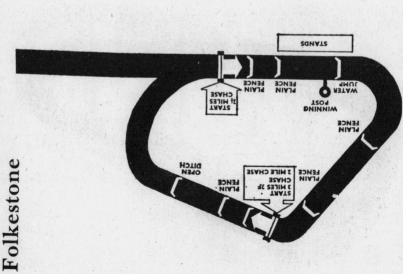

Folkestone

R.H. Circuit approx. 1m 3f. Undulating. Run-in 220 yds. Steeplechases, 250 yds. hurdles.

STANDS

START 2½ MILES CHASE

PLAIN FENCE

PLAIN FENCE

WATER JUMP

WINNING POST

PLAIN FENCE

OPEN DITCH

PLAIN FENCE

START 3 MILES 2F CHASE / 2 MILE CHASE

PLAIN FENCE

Hereford

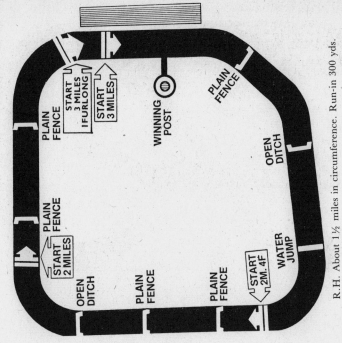

R.H. About 1½ miles in circumference. Run-in 300 yds.

Haydock Park

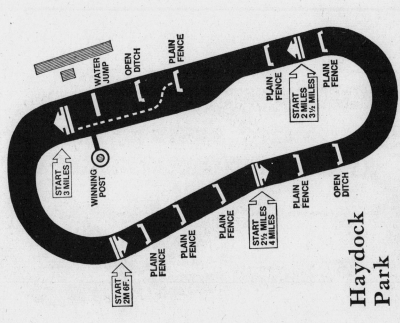

L.H. Undulating, 1 mile 5 furlongs circuit. Run-in 440 yds.

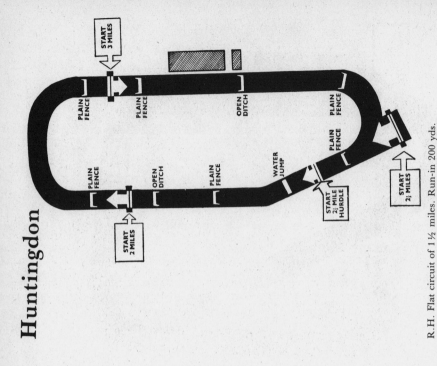

Hexham

START 2M 4F

PLAIN FENCE

PLAIN FENCE

OPEN DITCH

PLAIN FENCE

PLAIN FENCE

PLAIN FENCE

OPEN DITCH

START 3 MILES

WATER JUMP

START 2 MILES

OPEN DITCH

PLAIN FENCE

PLAIN FENCE

PLAIN FENCE

WINNING POST

L.H. Circuit approx. 1½ miles. Short hill just before straight. Run-in 250 yds. Full view from all enclosures.

Huntingdon

START 3 MILES

PLAIN FENCE

PLAIN FENCE

OPEN DITCH

PLAIN FENCE

PLAIN FENCE

PLAIN FENCE

OPEN DITCH

PLAIN FENCE

WATER JUMP

START 2 MILES

START 2¼ MILE HURDLE

START 2½ MILES

R.H. Flat circuit of 1½ miles. Run-in 200 yds.

Kempton

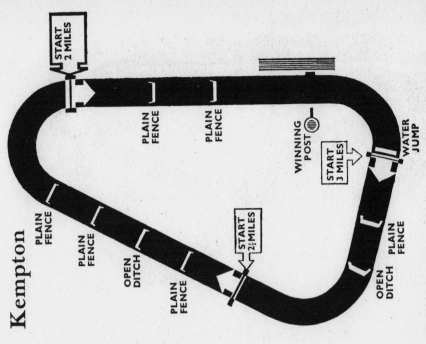

R.H. Triangular in shape, circuit of 1 mile 6 furlongs practically flat. Run-in 350 yds. approx.

Kelso

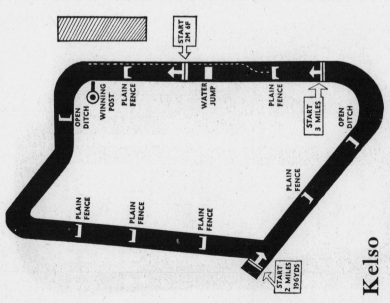

L.H. Circuit of Hurdle course is 1 mile 360 yds.; of the Steeple-chase course, 1 mile 600 yds. Run-in 440 yds.

Lingfield

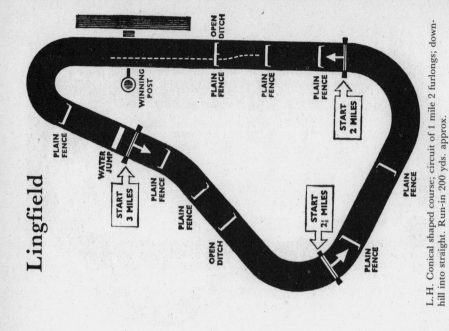

PLAIN FENCE

OPEN DITCH

PLAIN FENCE

PLAIN FENCE

PLAIN FENCE

WINNING POST

PLAIN FENCE

WATER JUMP

START 3 MILES

PLAIN FENCE

PLAIN FENCE

OPEN DITCH

START 2½ MILES

START 2 MILES

PLAIN FENCE

PLAIN FENCE

L.H. Conical shaped course; circuit of 1 mile 2 furlongs; downhill into straight. Run-in 200 yds. approx.

Leicester

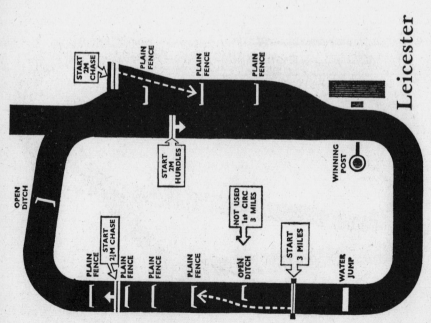

START 2M CHASE

PLAIN FENCE

PLAIN FENCE

PLAIN FENCE

START 2M HURDLES

OPEN DITCH

WINNING POST

PLAIN FENCE
START 2½M CHASE

PLAIN FENCE

PLAIN FENCE

PLAIN FENCE

NOT USED 1st CIRC 3 MILES

START 3 MILES

OPEN DITCH

WATER JUMP

R.H. Rectangular in shape. Undulating. Circuit of 1¾ miles. Run-in about 250 yds.

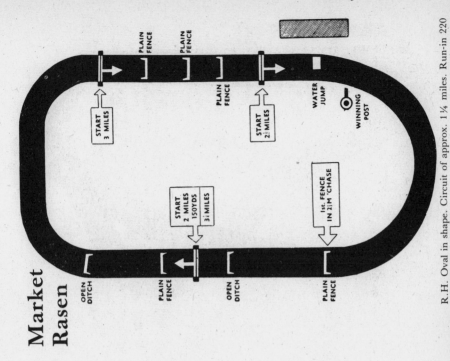

Market Rasen

PLAIN FENCE

PLAIN FENCE

PLAIN FENCE

START 3 MILES

START 2½ MILES

WATER JUMP

WINNING POST

START 2 MILES 150YDS

3¼ MILES

1st. FENCE IN 2½M 'CHASE

OPEN DITCH

PLAIN FENCE

OPEN DITCH

PLAIN FENCE

R.H. Oval in shape. Circuit of approx. 1¼ miles. Run-in 220 yds.

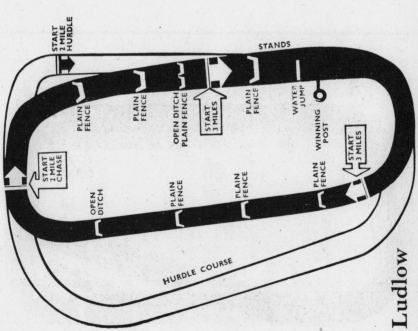

Ludlow

START 2 MILE HURDLE

STANDS

PLAIN FENCE

PLAIN FENCE

OPEN DITCH PLAIN FENCE

START 3 MILES

PLAIN FENCE

WATER JUMP

WINNING POST

START 3 MILES

START 2 MILE CHASE

OPEN DITCH

PLAIN FENCE

PLAIN FENCE

PLAIN FENCE

HURDLE COURSE

R.H. Oval course. Circuit of 1½ miles. Steeplechase course is perfectly flat. Hurdle course slightly undulating. Run-in 450 yds.

Newcastle

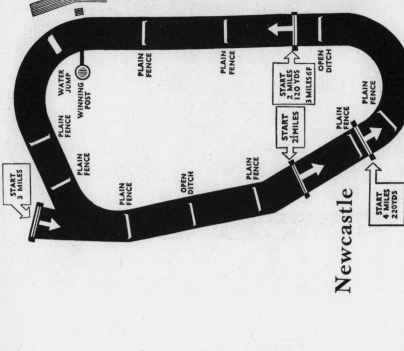

L.H. An oval Course 1¾ miles in circumference with a level straight finish at 4f, constructed inside the flat racecourses; run-in 220 yds.

Newbury

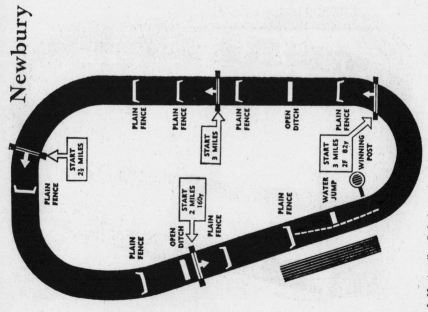

L.H. 1 mile, 7 furlongs in circumference. Oval and slightly undulating. Run-in 255 yds.

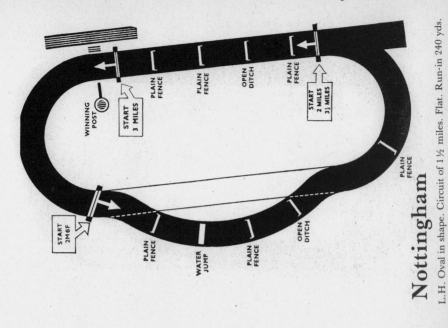

Nottingham

L.H. Oval in shape. Circuit of 1½ miles. Flat. Run-in 240 yds.

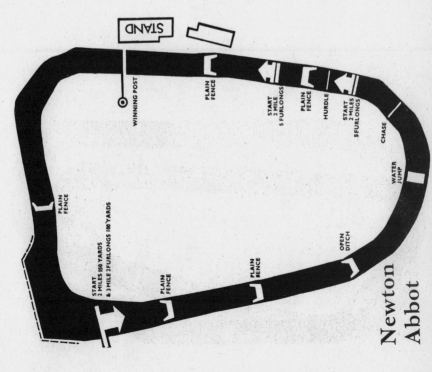

Newton Abbot

L.H. Oval in shape. Circuit of just over 1 mile. Run-in about 300 yds.

Plumpton

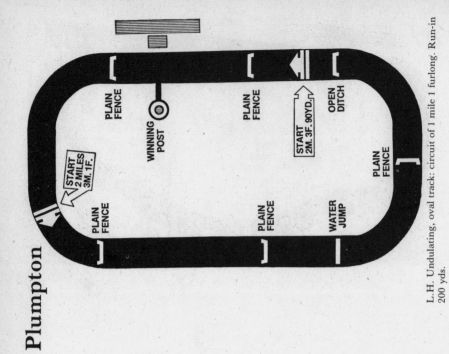

L. H. Undulating, oval track: circuit of 1 mile 1 furlong. Run-in 200 yds.

Perth

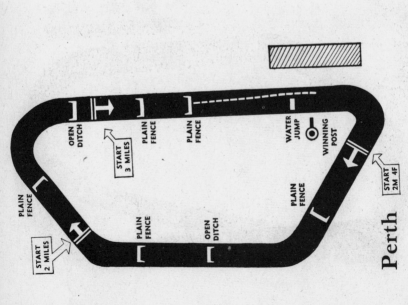

R. H. Circuit of about 1¼ miles.

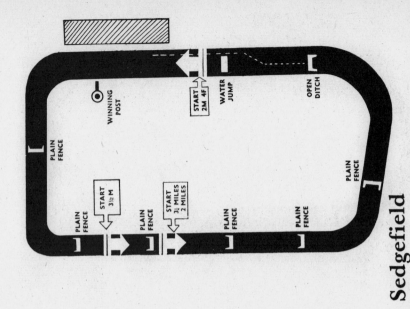

Sedgefield

L.H. Approx. 1¼ miles in circumference. Run-in: 'chases 500 yds, hurdles 200 yds.

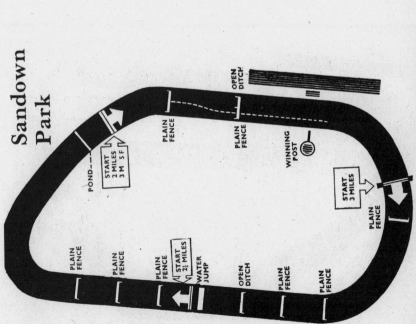

Sandown Park

R.H. Oval in shape. Circuit approx. 1m 5f. Uphill finish. 1st fence in 3 mile chase on down gradient. Run-in approx. 300 yds.

Stockton

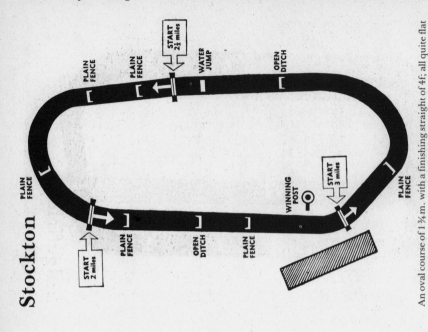

An oval course of 1¾ m. with a finishing straight of 4f; all quite flat with easy bends.

Southwell

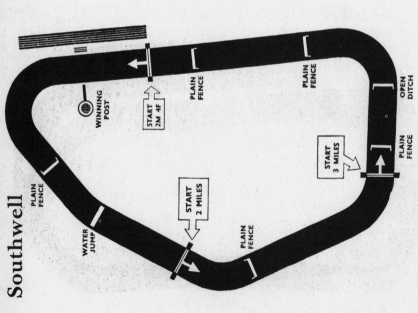

L.H. Triangular Course. Circuit approx. 1¼ miles. Run-in 250 yds.

Taunton

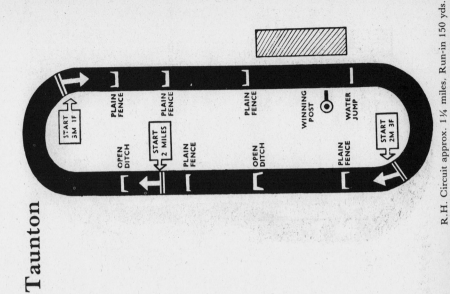

R.H. Circuit approx. 1¼ miles. Run-in 150 yds.

Stratford-on-Avon

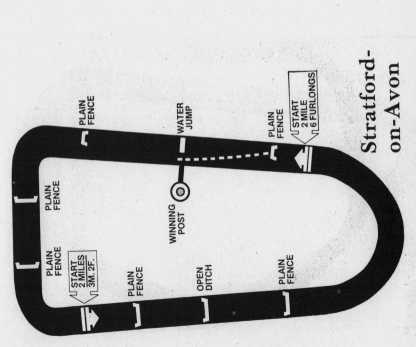

L.H. Circuit of 1 mile, 2 furlongs. Run-in 200 yds.

Uttoxeter

Towcester

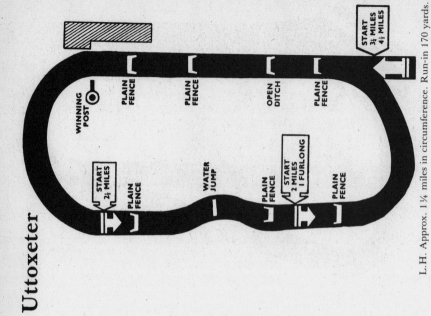

Uttoxeter

START 3¼ MILES 4¼ MILES

PLAIN FENCE
PLAIN FENCE
OPEN DITCH
PLAIN FENCE

WINNING POST

START 2½ MILES
PLAIN FENCE

WATER JUMP

PLAIN FENCE
START 2 MILES 1 FURLONG
PLAIN FENCE

L.H. Approx. 1¾ miles in circumference. Run-in 170 yards.

Towcester

START 2 MILES 50YDS

PLAIN FENCE
PLAIN FENCE
WINNING POST
PLAIN FENCE

OPEN DITCH
OPEN DITCH

PLAIN FENCE

START 3 MILES 190YDS
PLAIN FENCE

WATER JUMP

PLAIN FENCE
START 2M 5½F
PLAIN FENCE

R.H. Circuit about 1¾ miles. Undulating. Run-in about 140 yds.

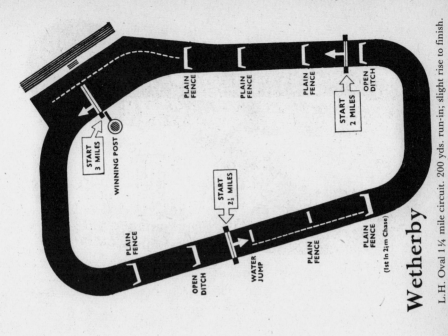

Wetherby

L.H. Oval 1¼ mile circuit. 200 yds. run-in; slight rise to finish.

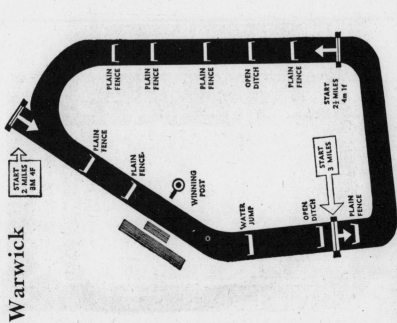

Warwick

L.H. 1¾ miles circuit nearly circular. Run-in 240 yds.

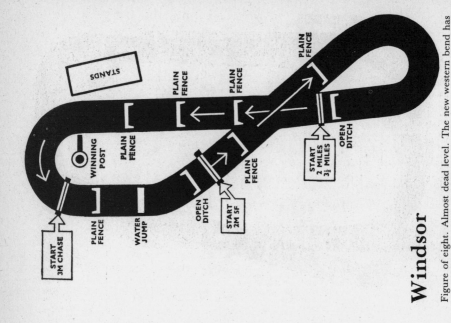

Windsor

Figure of eight. Almost dead level. The new western bend has cancelled out much of the sharpness. Circuit 1½ miles. Run-in 200 yards.

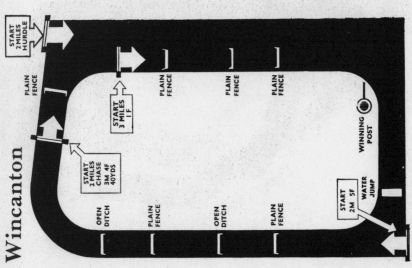

Wincanton

R.H. Good galloping course. Rectangular circuit approx. 1 mile 3 furlongs. Run-in 200 yds (approx.)

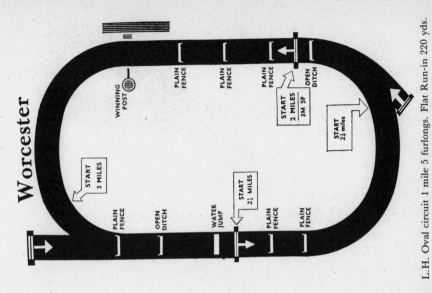

Worcester

WINNING POST

PLAIN FENCE

PLAIN FENCE

PLAIN FENCE

OPEN DITCH

START 2 MILES 3M 5F

START 2¼ miles

START 3 MILES

PLAIN FENCE

OPEN DITCH

WATER JUMP

START 2½ MILES

PLAIN FENCE

PLAIN FENCE

L.H. Oval circuit 1 mile 5 furlongs. Flat Run-in 220 yds.

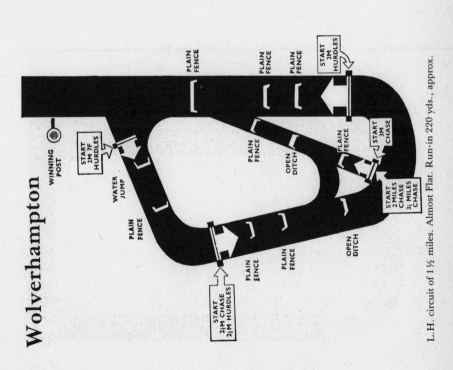

Wolverhampton

WINNING POST

PLAIN FENCE

PLAIN FENCE

PLAIN FENCE

PLAIN FENCE

START 2M HURDLES

START 2M 7F HURDLES

WATER JUMP

PLAIN FENCE

OPEN DITCH

START 3M CHASE

PLAIN FENCE

START 2 MILES CHASE 3½ MILES CHASE

PLAIN FENCE

START 2½M CHASE 2¼M HURDLES

PLAIN FENCE

PLAIN FENCE

OPEN DITCH

L.H. circuit of 1½ miles. Almost Flat. Run-in 220 yds., approx.

Index